D1327317

# TANKER OPERATIONS

*A Handbook for the Ship's Officer*

A multipoint offshore mooring. Oil cargoes are transferred between ship and shore via submarine pipelines. Ralph M. Parsons.

# TANKER OPERATIONS

*A Handbook for the Ship's Officer*

THIRD EDITION

BY

## G. S. MARTON

CORNELL MARITIME PRESS

*Centreville, Maryland*

Library of Congress Cataloging-in-Publication Data

Marton, G. S.,
       Tanker operations : a handbook for the ship's officer : by G. S. Marton.—3rd ed.
          p.    cm.
    Includes bibliographical references and index.
       ISBN 0-87033-432-8 :
       1. Tankers—Handbooks, manuals, etc.    I. Title.
    VM455.M33   1992
    623.88245′02′02—dc20                                                    92-8997
                                                                                CIP

Manufactured in the United States of America
First edition, 1978. Third edition, 1992; second printing, 1995

*In memory of Philip C. Marton*

# CONTENTS

**Preface**     *xi*

**1.**   **Types of Tankers**     **3**
     Crude and Product Carriers, 3
     Size, 6
     Changes in Tanker Design Since World War II, 6
     VLCCs and ULCCs, 10
     OBOs, 12
     LNG Carriers, 13
     The Next Generation of Tankers, 16

**2.**   **Petroleum and the Refining Process**     **20**
     Drilling, 20
     Processing, 22
     Crude Oils, 25
     Refining, 27
     Building Products, 31
     Blending, 33
     Petroleum Hazards, 34
     Grades of Petroleum Products, 35
     Sources of Information on Petroleum Products, 36

**3.**   **How Petroleum Cargoes Are Measured**     **39**
   **On Board Ship**
     Units of Measure, 39
     Gauging the Ship, 42
     Thieving, 45
     Determining Observed Volume of Cargo, 46
     Determining Standard Volume of Cargo, 49
     Determining Tonnage of Cargo, 53
     Loading and Discharging Rates, 55

**4.**   **Cargo Piping Systems**     **58**
     Learning the Cargo System, 58
     Types of Valves, 65
     Special Valves, 68

Valve Markings, 70
VLCC Piping Systems, 71
Inert Gas (IG) Systems, 71
Vent Systems, 73
Vapor Control Systems, 77

## 5.   Loading                                      78

Before Loading, 78
Start Cargo Slowly, 81
Removing the List, 81
Stress, 82
Loading the Centers, 82
Loading the Wings, 83
The Chief Mate's Loading Orders, 83
The Loading Watch, 87
Good Practices, 88
Offshore Moorings, 93
Line Displacements, 97
Loading to Final Draft, 99
Trimming the Ship, 100
After Loading, 101

## 6.   Discharging                                  102

Pretransfer Checkoff, 102
The Pumpman, 105
Types of Cargo Pumps, 105
Priming the Pumps, 112
Discharging Procedure, 113
Spills, 120
Line Displacements, 122

## 7.   Planning the Load                            123

The Voyage Orders, 123
Load Lines and Zone Limitations, 125
Important Terms, 128
Loading Plan and Calculations, 135
Computers and Loading Calculators, 140
Forms for Calculating Stress and Trim, 141
Loading to Final Draft, 143

## 8.   Ballasting                                   147

The Need for Ballast, 147
Planning the Ballast Load, 148
Choosing the Plan, 152

Clean Ballast versus Dirty Ballast, 152
Segregated Ballast Tanks (SBT), 154
Ballast-Handling Techniques, 155
Deballasting, 159

**9.    Tank Cleaning**                                          **160**
Why Clean Tanks? 162
Methods and Equipment, 163
Stripping and Disposing of Slops, 171
Crude Oil Washing (COW), 174
Line, Pump, and Bottom Flushes, 178
The Tank-Cleaning Team, 180
Dangers, 180
Explosion, 182
Static Electricity, 182
Inert Gas Systems, 185
Entering the Tanks, 186
Rescue, 192

**10.    Fire Fighting and Fire Prevention**                     **197**
What Is Fire? 197
The Elements of Fire, 198
Important Terms, 201
Theory of Fire Fighting, 203
Fire Prevention, 205
Extinguishing Agents and Equipment, 210
Fighting the Fire, 217
Prevention versus Cure, 226

**11.    Pollution Prevention**                                  **227**
Minimizing Routine Discharges, 227
Collisions and Groundings, 235
Preventing Spills, 240
What to Do If a Spill Occurs, 244
Laws Relating to Pollution, 245
Keep It in the Tanks, 246

**12.    The Tanker and the Law**                                **247**
International Conventions, 247
OPA-90, 249
Laws in Transition, 252

**13.    Inert Gas Systems**                                     **255**
A "Closed" System, 255
Basic IG System, 255

Purging, 256
Loading, 258
The Loaded Passage, 259
Discharging, 260
Tank Cleaning, 260
Gas-freeing, 261
IG System Components, 262
Controls, Indicators, and Alarms, 263
Automatic "Trips," 264
Other Major Components, 264
Specialized Systems, 270
Precautions and Reminders, 275
Know Your Ship, 278

14.    **Marine Vapor Control Systems**                         **279**
Vapor Control System Components, 280
Closed Gauging, 283
High/Low Vapor Pressure Protection, 286
Operations, 287
Conclusion, 289

**Appendix: Conversion Factors**                              **295**

**Bibliography**                                              **297**

**Index**                                                     **301**

**About the Author and Contributors**                        **314**

# PREFACE

WHEN I began writing the first edition of this book in 1976, I had no idea of the dramatic changes that would occur in the tanker industry in subsequent years. Much of the technology then thought of as "state of the art" or even "futuristic" has long since become obsolete.

*Tanker Operations* was last revised in 1983. Since that time, many important changes have occurred in the industry. This edition endeavors to address those changes. Much new material has been added—including 68 new illustrations and tables—and much has been deleted.

Over the years, the book has evolved considerably. It is still intended primarily as an introductory text for new or prospective officers. However, there is much in this new edition that will be of interest and, hopefully, of practical value to more experienced officers. Also, previous editions of the book have been used extensively as a reference by tanker charterers and owners; the present edition is expected to be even more useful to those individuals.

I feel very grateful indeed for the abundance of expert help and advice I have received while working on this edition. I am particularly indebted to my seafaring colleagues and others in the tanker industry who have taken the time to review the book and offer suggestions. In addition, three individuals—all recognized authorities in the industry—have taken time from their busy schedules to write new chapters for the book. Nick Blenkey, editor of *Marine Log* magazine, has contributed a chapter on tanker legislation, which includes a thought-provoking discussion of the Oil Pollution Act of 1990. Professor Mark Huber of the U.S. Merchant Marine Academy has written a chapter on marine vapor control systems. Professor Bob Stewart of the California Maritime Academy has contributed a chapter (which he and Professor Brian Law originally suggested in 1983) on petroleum and the refining process. The efforts of these three contributors have broadened and enhanced the book considerably.

Besides the contributions just described, many individuals and organizations have been most generous with their help. Some showed remarkable patience with my repeated phone calls, inquiries, and requests for illustrations. Without their help, this book could not have been written.

Special thanks to:

Ethel Ann Ackerman; Carlos E. Agnese; Alyeska Pipeline Service Company; American Bureau of Shipping and ABS Americas; American Cast Iron Pipe Company; American Institute of Marine Underwriters; American Institute of Merchant Shipping; American Petroleum Institute; American United Marine Corporation; Paul Anderson; Ansul Fire Protection Company; Apex Marine Corporation; Atlantic Richfield Company; the Scott Aviation Division of ATO, Inc.; Stephen R. Bayer; Gerry Bayless; Richard Beadon; Eric J. Beck; Ian-Conrad Bergan; Bethlehem Steel Corporation; Bingham-Willamette Company; Geoffrey B. Boulden; BP Pipelines (Alaska), Inc.; British Petroleum Company, Ltd.; Mel W. Brown; Henry Browne & Son, Ltd.; Butterworth Systems, Inc.; California Maritime Academy; Douglas B. Cameron; Vincent Cantwell; Chevron Corporation and Chevron Shipping Company; Bent Christiansen; Clement Engineering Services; Coastdesign, Inc.; College of Nautical Studies; Guy R. Colonna; Andreas A. Constantinou and the Consulate of Cyprus; Coppus Engineering Corporation; Kenneth M. Curtis; Cyprus Shipping Council; Judy Davidson; A. L. Diamond; Ed Doherty; Charles Dolan; Louis Dubrowski; Susan Duke; Elliott Manufacturing Company; Environmental Protection Agency; Exxon Corporation, Exxon Company (U.S.A.), and Exxon Shipping Company; Steve Faulkner; Thomas J. Felleisen; Bill Finhandler; Fire Equipment Manufacturers Association; Fisher Controls International, Inc.; FMC Corporation; Foster Wheeler Boiler Corporation; Gamlen Chemical Company; Gas Atmospheres; General Dynamics Corporation; General Fire Extinguisher Corporation; T. W. Gillette; R. W. Goldstraw; R. W. Gorman; John P. Goudreau; Al Griffin; Gulf Oil Corporation; Fred N. Hallett; Frank T. Hanas; Arthur Handt; Haywood Manufacturing Company; Karen Hecker; Chris Heizer; Hendy International Company; William Henry; Paula Hill; Robert A. Hogg; Bob Holecek; Deb Hollens; Peter Hollens; Howden Engineering, Ltd.; P. Howells; the Penco Division of the Hudson Engineering Company; Tom Hudson; John Hunter; Huntington Alloys, Inc.; Gems Sensors Division of IMO Industries, Inc.; International Association of Independent Tanker Owners (INTERTANKO); International Chamber of Shipping; International Maritime Organization; International Tanker Owners Pollution Federation; Sean M. Ireton; Diane Kalas; Mike Karr; Maureen A. Kenny; the Keystone Valve Division of Keystone International, Inc.; David Kitchell; Kockumation AB; Roger Kohn; Glen C. Kraatz; Makhan Lal; Joseph Langen; Brian Law; John J. Lee; Gene Legler; Ginny Lester; Judith Levis; Library of Congress Photo Duplication Service; Peter P. Lombard; Hugh Lowder; Scott Lubeck; Trevor

Lucey; the Harry Lundeberg School of Seamanship; Alex M. MacGillivray; Maine Maritime Academy; Jim Makris; *Marine Log;* the Maritime Institute of Technology and Graduate Studies; J. D. Maulsby; Maureen Marton; Thomas Marton; Beverly A. McLean; Bill McQuade; David H. Mead; Metritape, Inc.; Eleanor Miller; Mine Safety Appliances Company; C. Bradford Mitchell; MMC International Corporation; Edwin P. Moore; David Moss; National Academy Press and the National Academy of Sciences; National Audubon Society; National Fire Protection Association; National Foam System, Inc.; National Geographic Society; National Maritime Union of America; National Research Council; National Steel and Shipbuilding Company; Norfolk Shipbuilding Company; North Florida Shipyard, Inc.; Carl S. Novak; D. A. Nyberg; Claes Odman; Oil Companies International Marine Forum; Maureen Ott; M. J. Ott; Robert R. Owen; the Ralph M. Parsons Company; Paul-Munroe Hydraulics, Inc.; L. A. Pendexter; Penn-Attransco Corporation; Permea Maritime Protection; Shirley Peterson; Pia Philipp; Phillips Petroleum Company; Richard Plant; Dragos Rauta; Rotork Actuation; Saab Marine Electronics; Saab-Scania, Aerospace Division; Sailors Union of the Pacific; Salen & Wicander AB; Salwico, Inc.; San Francisco Maritime Museum; E. W. Saybolt & Company, Inc.; W. F. Schill; Seafarers International Union; Servomex (U.K.), Ltd.; Shell International Petroleum and Shell Oil Company (U.S.A.); Shipbuilders Council of America; Skarpenord Data AS; Bob Smith; Southern Oregon State College; Sperry Marine Systems; Star Enterprise; State University of New York Maritime College; Ole Arnt Strand; Sun Shipbuilding and Dry Dock Company; Bob Sutherland; John Tallent; Texaco, Inc.; Steven W. Tilghman; Transamerica Delaval, Inc.; TS Tanksystem SA; Underwriters Laboratories, Inc.; U.S. Coast Guard; U.S. Department of Transportation; U.S. Maritime Administration; U.S. Salvage Association; Valve Manufacturers Association; Viatran Corporation; Georg O. Viki; Vitronics, Inc.; Olympia Vouitsis; L. W. Waddell; Chris Warnett; Mike Welfare; West Coast Ship Chandlers, Inc.; L. A. Wilkes; Peter C. Will; Donna Williams; Robert C. Wilmott; Wilson Walton International; Worthington Pumps.

# TANKER OPERATIONS

*A Handbook for the Ship's Officer*

CHAPTER 1

# TYPES OF TANKERS

THE first oil tanker was launched slightly more than a century ago. In the relatively short time since then, tankers have evolved into efficient oil-moving machines—the largest mobile objects ever constructed.

Every tanker, whether a small coastwise vessel or a mammoth super-ship, is basically a hollow steel shell subdivided into tanks by longitudinal and transverse bulkheads (see figures 1-1 and 9-12). The engine room is located aft, as is the bridge on most ships.

A system of pipelines fitted along the bottom of the tank range carries oil to and from the tanks. Pumps are used for discharging; these are in-stalled in one or more pumprooms which in turn are connected to a main-deck manifold by additional piping. Oil is transferred from ship to shore and vice versa by means of flexible hoses and steel loading arms which bolt onto the ship's manifold.

Tankers come in all sizes and designs. They carry a variety of products, consisting mainly of crude oil and its derivatives: gasoline, diesel fuel, stove oil, bunker fuel, kerosene, jet fuel, and many others. In addition, a few specialized vessels carry exotic cargoes such as wine, vegetable oil, and molasses.

The type of cargo a tanker carries largely determines the complexity of her operation and, consequently, the amount of sweat and concentration required from her officers.


## CRUDE AND PRODUCT CARRIERS

Tankers can be divided into two broad categories: crude carriers and prod-uct carriers. Product carriers can be further subdivided into those carry-ing "clean" products, such as gasoline and diesel, and those carrying "black" products, such as asphalt and fuel oil. Although tankers tend to stay pretty much in a particular trade, there is no sharp dividing line between the types of tankers just mentioned. In fact, it is not uncommon for some tankers to carry crude, black-oil products and clean products at different points in their lifetimes.

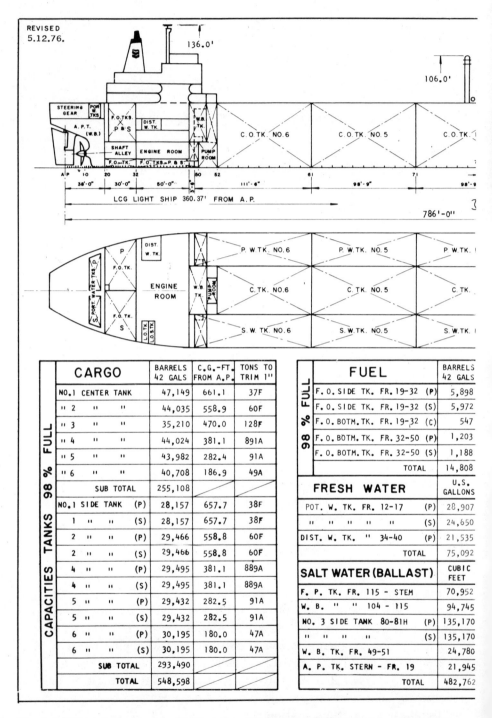

Fig. 1-1. General plan and particulars for a 70,000-dwt tanker. Chevron Shipping.

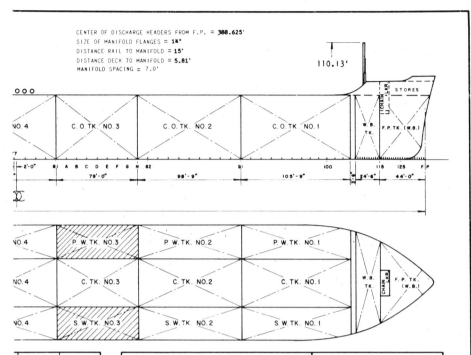

CENTER OF DISCHARGE HEADERS FROM F.P. = **388.625'**
SIZE OF MANIFOLD FLANGES = **14"**
DISTANCE RAIL TO MANIFOLD = **15'**
DISTANCE DECK TO MANIFOLD = **5.81'**
MANIFOLD SPACING = 7.0'

| C.G.-FT. FROM A.P. | TONS TO TRIM 1" |
|---|---|
| 54.0 | |
| 54.0 | 29A |
| 55.3 | 30A |
| 101.6 | 34A |
| 101.6 | 34A |
| | |

| C.G.-FT. FROM A.P. | TONS (2240LBS) |
|---|---|
| 29.1 | 107 |
| 29.1 | 92 |
| 82.5 | 80 |
| | 279 |

| C.G.-FT. FROM A.P. | TONS (2240LBS) |
|---|---|
| 757.4 | 2,028 |
| 729.1 | 2,707 |
| 470.0 | 3,862 |
| 470.0 | 3,862 |
| 126.1 | 708 |
| 22.27 | 627 |
| | 13,794 |

## MACHINERY

**ENGINE-** GENERAL ELECTRIC DOUBLE REDUCTION GEAR, CROSS COMPOUND STEAM TURBINE.
MAX: 20,000 SHP U.S.
@ 112 RPM

**BOILER-** TWO FOSTER WHEELER 2-DRUM, OIL FIRED WATER TUBE MARINE BOILERS.
600 PSIG - 905°F

## PARTICULARS

| | |
|---|---|
| LENGTH (O.A.) | 810.00' |
| LENGTH (B.P.) | 786.00' |
| BREADTH (MLD) | 105.00' |
| DEPTH (MLD) | 57.00' |
| GROSS TON | 35,588.74 |
| NET TON | 29,437 |
| PANAMA GROSS TON | 40,319 |
| PANAMA NET TON | 31,731.15 |

## INTERNATIONAL LOAD LINES   A B S

| | DRAFT | DISP'MT | DEAD'WT | FREE'BD |
|---|---|---|---|---|
| LIGHT SHIP | 3.88' FWD. 13.78' AFT | 14,877 | — | — |
| ASSIGNED SUMMER | 43.51' | 85,090 | 70,213 | 13.73' |
| TROPICAL | 44.41' | 87,060 | 72,183 | 12.83' |
| WINTER | 42.61' | 83,210 | 68,333 | 14.62' |
| FRESH WATER ALLOWANCE | 12.50' | — | — | — |

## S/S CHEVRON HAWAII

OWNER ...................... UNION BANK
OPERATOR ................. STANDARD OIL CO. OF CALIFORNIA
BUILDER .................... BETHLEHEM STEEL CORP. SPARROWS POINT, M.D.
DELIVERY ................. JUNE 28, 1973

OFFICIAL NO. 549197    HULL NO. 4638    CALL SIGN KNFD

Fig. 1-1. *(cont.)*

## SIZE

What marks a ship for a particular kind of service? Size is a vital factor. Given the wide range of sizes in today's tankers, it is convenient to classify them according to their carrying capacity, normally referred to as *dead-weight tonnage* (dwt). This is the amount of cargo, fuel, water, and stores a vessel can carry when fully loaded. It is expressed either in long tons (1 long ton = 2,240 pounds) or metric tons (1 metric ton = 1,000 kilograms = 2,204.6 pounds).

Table 1-1 separates tankers into four broad categories according to size. As the table indicates, product carriers are rarely designed to carry more than 35,000 tons deadweight. Crude carriers, on the other hand, are much bigger.

Table 1-1

FOUR BROAD CLASSIFICATIONS OF TANKERS ACCORDING TO SIZE

| Category | Tonnage Range | Type of Service |
|---|---|---|
| Handy or small-size tankers | 6,000 to 35,000 dwt | Mainly product carriers |
| Medium-size tankers | 35,000 to 160,000 dwt | Mainly crude |
| VLCCs (very large crude carriers) | 160,000 to 300,000 dwt | Crude exclusively |
| ULCCs (ultra large crude carriers) | 300,000 dwt and above | Crude exclusively |

Plans have been drawn for a crude carrier of *one million* deadweight tons, and it is generally agreed that such a vessel could be built. However, it now appears unlikely that such a ship will ever be constructed; the plans have been shelved, probably for good.

## CHANGES IN TANKER DESIGN SINCE WORD WAR II

World War II accelerated the tanker's development and in so doing precipitated important changes. Prior to the war the typical tanker was powered by a diesel or reciprocating steam engine; her speed was about 10 knots. She was tiny by today's standards. Her pumproom, located amidships, was fitted with steam driven reciprocating pumps. These were sturdy, but slow.

A new class of tanker, the T2, was developed and mass-produced during the war (fig. 1-6). It soon became the backbone of the American fleet. At 16,500 dwt, the T2 was considered a big ship in its day. The pumproom,

Fig. 1-2. Cutaway diagram of the *Gulfking*, a 30,000-dwt tanker built in 1956. A forward house, incorporating deck officers' quarters and bridge, typifies older construction. Gulf Oil.

Fig. 1-3. With 1.8 million barrels of Persian Gulf crude in her tanks, the 253,000-dwt VLCC *T. G. Shaughnessy* maneuvers alongside a dock in Nova Scotia. A smaller tanker loads refined products at an inner berth. Gulf Oil.

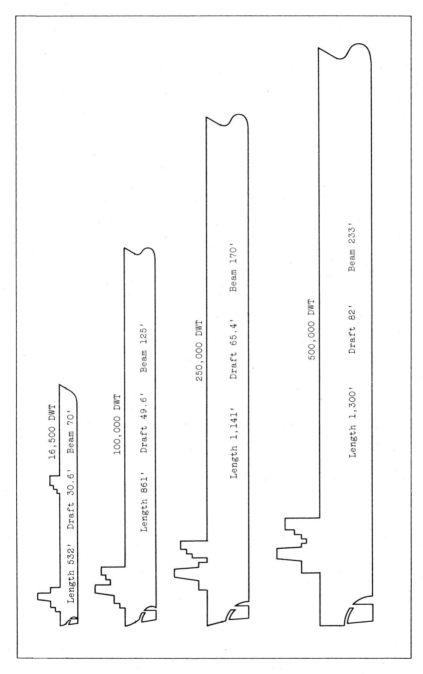

16,500 DWT
Length 532'    Draft 30.6'    Beam 70'

100,000 DWT
Length 861'    Draft 49.6'    Beam 125'

250,000 DWT
Length 1,141'    Draft 65.4'    Beam 170'

500,000 DWT
Length 1,300'    Draft 82'    Beam 233'

Fig. 1-4. This diagram shows the relative sizes of tankers. The size of tankers has increased dramatically since World War II. The first figure represents a T2. Exxon.

located aft, incorporated three centrifugal pumps and a direct pipeline system. These speeded up cargo handling significantly.

In the intervening years other changes have taken place. Tankers are bigger. The midship house, home of the deck officers and bridge for so many years, has disappeared. Virtually all new tankers are "sternwinders" fitted with a single house aft (fig. 1-7).

The reciprocating steam engine faded into the history books long ago. The improved design and fuel economy of diesel engines have made them the choice for most new construction. However, many large older tankers in the existing world fleet are still powered by geared turbines—a system in which a steam turbine is connected to the propeller shaft by reduction gears. These engines are largely a remnant of the years when bunker fuel was relatively cheap.

**Automation.** Most new tankers are at least partially automated. For example, cargo operations are often monitored and controlled from a console in the cargo control room. Automatic valves inside the tanks are opened and closed remotely.

Computers play an important role on most vessels and many are virtually computer-controlled; that is, cargo operations, navigation, and engine operation can be controlled automatically by computer. In addition, computers are often programmed to handle routine administrative chores, such as crew's wages. Or, in an emergency, a computer might offer an accurate medical diagnosis complete with suggested treatment for a sick crew member.

Automation is not the rule, however, on the many older—and usually smaller—tankers still in service throughout the world. Some are partially automated; many others are not automated at all.

## VLCCs AND ULCCs

Very large crude carriers, or VLCCs, are generally defined as tankers between 160,000 dwt and 300,000 dwt. Ultra large crude carriers, or ULCCs, are tankers of 300,000 dwt and over. VLCCs and ULCCs are the largest moving objects ever built by humans.

These ships roam the most solitary trade routes ever known to seafarers. They are so huge that few harbors can receive them. A typical voyage might begin at an isolated loading platform in the Persian Gulf. The ship loads quickly and begins her long voyage (perhaps a month or more) to the receiving terminal. This is usually a lonely dock or an offshore mooring far from civilization. Here the ship discharges her cargo

Fig. 1-5. The *K. R. Kingsbury,* 12,000 dwt, was launched in 1921. Bethlehem Ship-building Company Collection, San Francisco Maritime Museum.

Fig. 1-6. A T2 tanker, 16,500 dwt, makes her final voyage to lay-up. Designed and built during World War II, the T2s were considered big ships in their day. U.S. Maritime Administration.

Fig. 1-7. The *Sansinena II,* 70,000 dwt. Bethlehem Steel.

in a matter of hours and, after taking on saltwater ballast, starts the long voyage to the Gulf—an unending odyssey.

### OBOs

Ore/bulk/oil carriers, or OBOs, are specially built tankers capable of carrying bulk commodities such as ore and coal. Many are in the VLCC class.

Fig. 1-8. The *Chevron Washington,* 35,000 dwt, is powered by gas turbine/electric drive and has a double hull. The Oil Pollution Act of 1990 mandates double hulls for most new tankers. FMC.

On an ideal voyage an OBO carries oil in one direction, ore or coal in the other. Revenue is thus earned each way.

When tanker demand decreases, charter rates go down—often to unprofitable levels. In such situations the OBO demonstrates her most valuable attribute—versatility. She simply switches to ore or coal until freight rates for oil return to a profitable level. She thus continues to earn revenue while other tankers sit idle.

## LNG CARRIERS

Natural gas—composed mainly of methane—exists in abundance in most oil fields, either dissolved in the crude itself or wedged between it and the earth's surface. When an oil field is tapped, natural gas is released. In the

Fig. 1-9. Main engine room control console on board the 215,000-dwt VLCC *British Explorer.* British Petroleum.

past, this gas often had to be flared, or burned off, because no means was available for transporting it. In recent years, however, the situation has changed. The demand for efficient, clean-burning fuels eventually led to the development of a special class of ship, the LNG (liquefied natural gas) carrier (fig. 1-12). Such ships are designed to carry natural gas at extremely low temperatures—on the order of –260°F (–162°C)—thus keeping it liquefied.

It follows that LNG carriers must be carefully insulated. To accomplish this, a variety of designs are used. For example, one popular design incorporates spherical cargo tanks made from aluminum alloy; these are insulated with polyurethane. Because no refrigeration system is used on ships carrying LNG, a certain amount of cargo boils off each voyage and is lost. Most LNG carriers use at least part of this boil-off as fuel in their own boilers.

A closed system is used when loading and discharging LNG. Specially constructed flow booms are connected between ship and shore; these carry the liquid cargo. A *vapor boom* is also connected. This serves as a vent line

Fig. 1-10. The *Brooklyn*, a 255,000-dwt VLCC. U.S. Maritime Administration.

Fig. 1-11. The *Jag Leela,* 136,000-dwt ore/bulk/oil carrier. Kockumation.

between ship and shore. When loading, for example, vaporized natural gas is vented ashore. When discharging, the gas is vented from shore tanks to the ship. As a rule, a small amount of LNG is retained on board after discharging. This keeps the tanks cold for the next load.

## THE NEXT GENERATION OF TANKERS

In 1989 an event occurred that changed the international tanker industry permanently. Late on the night of March 24 of that year, the American tanker *Exxon Valdez* ran hard aground on Bligh Reef near Valdez, Alaska. The resulting spill—the worst in U.S. history—devastated the wildlife of Prince William Sound and made headlines throughout the world.

Following the grounding of the *Exxon Valdez,* there was an immediate demand for a "fail-safe" design to prevent future mishaps. In 1990, the U.S. Congress passed legislation mandating profound changes in tanker design and operation: the Oil Pollution Act of 1990 (OPA-90).

**Double-hulled tankers.** Among other things, OPA-90 requires that most new tankers be fitted with double hulls. And, in a further develop-

Fig. 1-12. A modern LNG carrier. Capacity: 125,000 cubic meters (64,000 dwt). General Dynamics.

ment, the National Academy of Sciences published in 1991 the results of a study which, among other things, endorses the idea of double hulls as a workable approach to safer tanker design (see Bibliography).

Figure 1-13 shows a cutaway diagram of a wing tank in a double-hulled tanker. For comparison, see figure 9-12, which illustrates the structure of a typical single-hulled tanker.

**Mid-deck tankers.** Another design, which may be accepted as an alternative to double hulls under pending regulations, is the mid-deck tanker. The design is based on a simple idea. In a traditional tanker design, when a tank is holed, oil tends to flow out because the hydrostatic pressure inside the hull is greater than that outside. A simpler way of putting it is that gravity forces oil out of the tank until the oil level inside the tank is approximately even with the surrounding water level.

In effect, the installation of a mid-deck cuts the cargo level inside the tanks in half. As a result, hydrostatic pressure outside the tank is greater than the pressure inside. When a tank is holed, oil cannot flow out—it is held inside the tank by the pressure of surrounding sea water. Extensive

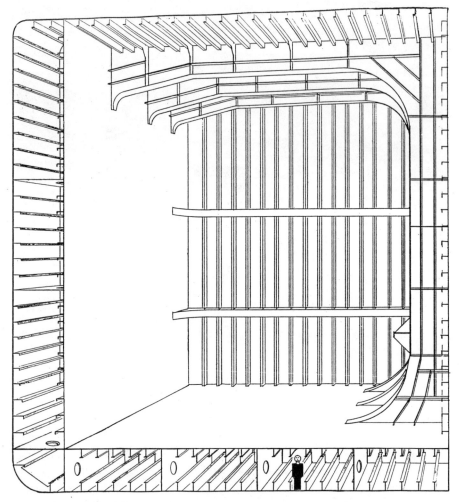

Fig. 1-13. Cutaway drawing of a typical double-hull tank arrangement (wing tank only is shown). Chevron Shipping.

tests, using models, have confirmed the viability of the mid-deck concept. (The diagram in figure 12-3 illustrates the theory behind the mid-deck design.)

Whether or not the new designs just described actually represent a "fail-safe" solution is debatable—and beyond the scope of this book. Tanker crews must work with the equipment they are given. It appears that the international tanker industry, and not just U.S. operators, will have to adopt designs similar to those just discussed. It therefore seems likely that an

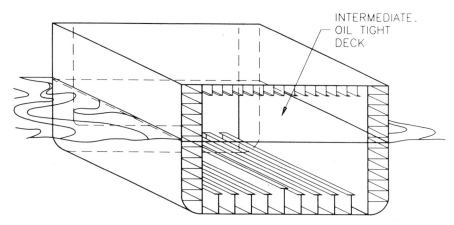

Fig. 1-14. The mid-deck tanker design is based on the idea of an intermediate oil-tight deck. Reprinted with permission from *Tanker Spills, Prevention by Design,* © 1991 by the National Academy of Sciences. Published by National Academy Press, Washington, DC.

increasing number of double-hulled and mid-deck tankers will enter the world fleet in coming years.

For a more detailed discussion of OPA-90 and resulting design changes, see chapter 12.

# CHAPTER 2

# PETROLEUM AND THE REFINING PROCESS

## BY ROBERT STEWART

Worldwide, we are seeing increasing industrialization and development. This increase in the standard of living usually increases the volume of petroleum resources being consumed in a society. Consequently, there is an increasing demand for these dwindling supplies of petroleum. Locating the oil reserves is just the beginning of a long trail that leads through the transportation industry and the refining process to the consumer.

A result of this continued demand for petroleum is that the developers of petroleum reserves have to search harder in order to find recoverable amounts of these reserves. The search for oil fields no longer occurs just onshore, rather the search now includes the oceans of the world. Searching the world's oceans for oil requires a completely different type of oil drilling equipment. Special platforms for drilling and then producing oil in this environment must also be developed.

## DRILLING

Crude oil found in the world today was formed millions of years ago, when dead plants and animals were buried in layers of rock. Oil formations are found under mountains, deserts, marshes, and seas. They are often found as much as two or three miles below the surface—or deeper. (Figure 2-1 illustrates some types of oil-bearing formations.) In order to reach these oil formations far beneath the earth's surface, a well must be drilled.

The drilling process, whether onshore or offshore, is essentially the same. A well is spudded, or started, and drilling advances downward with the well decreasing in diameter at intervals throughout its depth. Wells also may deviate from the vertical in order to reach more of the oil zone in a desired area. The well is dug by forcing a drill bit, usually rotating clockwise, into the rock or sediment at the bottom of the well. "Mud," a mixture that barely resembles the mud children make, is a mixture of clay, chemicals, and water. This mixture can be tailored to the specific needs of an individual well. The mud is pumped down the center of the drill string and

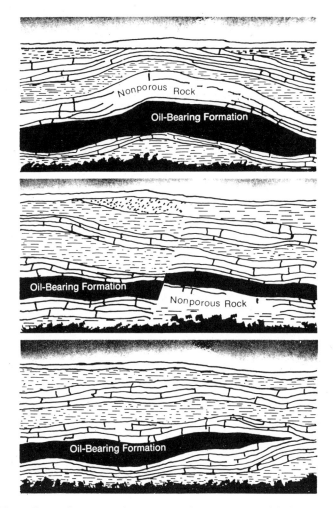

Fig. 2-1. *Top,* oil may be trapped in an *anticline,* or upward bulge of rock layers. Within the formation, the oil lies in tiny spaces between grains of porous rock. *Center,* oil may gather at a *fault,* a place where rock layers crack and slip past one another. Nonporous rock stops the oil flow from porous rock. *Bottom,* one of the hardest places to find oil is in a *stratigraphic trap.* Here, the porous layers bearing oil taper off under nonporous layers of rock. Shell Oil.

it exits through the mudports in the drill bit. The mud acts to cool the drill bit, clean away cuttings, and maintain hydrostatic pressure in the well. This hydrostatic pressure helps eliminate the possibility of having a well blowout. A blowout can cause a fire, explosion, or at the very least a waste of valuable reserves. Once the mud has completed its cycle down into the well and back up to the drilling deck, it can be sifted through a "shaker" to

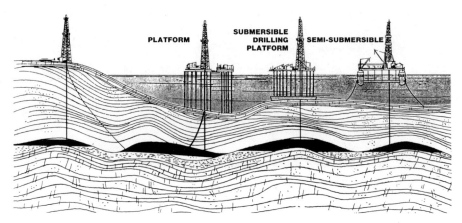

Fig. 2-2. Offshore drilling can be done by directional drilling from land or from both fixed and floating rigs and platforms. Shell Oil.

find any oil-bearing strata or debris that may cause problems in drilling. The field of oil well drilling and production continues to be a very technical and challenging field.

Once the well is drilled and lined with casing, oil can begin flowing. This is the end of the process for the oil well driller, but only the beginning of a long journey for the crude oil. Many wells have natural pressure in them that allows the oil to flow to the surface without the need for artificial lift. Other wells, and many older wells, require artificial lift to bring the oil to the surface. Pumps can be placed at the top of the well and suction taken to artificially lift the oil out of the well.

## PROCESSING

The first thing that happens to the oil after leaving the well is the primary processing. This usually consists of gas separation and dewatering. Many types of crude oils have large volumes of dissolved gases in solution. These gases can be removed by reducing the pressure of the crude oil after it leaves the wellhead. The gas and the oil can be separated and then sent on to further processing. The dewatering process simply separates the crude oil from water that may have intruded into the well strata. In many cases this is done simply by storing the crude and allowing the water to separate.

The oil, after initial processing, must travel from the oil field to the refinery for further processing. Onshore, this can be accomplished by underground pipeline. Offshore, crude oil can also be removed from the field by

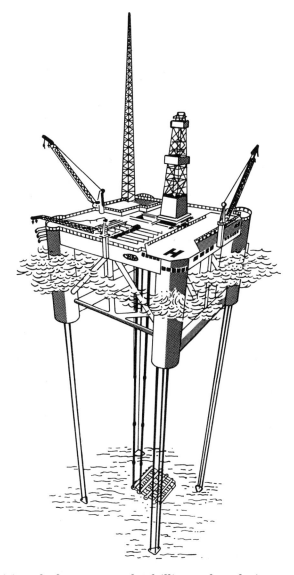

Fig. 2-3. A promising platform concept for drilling and producing operations in deep water is the tension leg platform (TLP). As a vertically moored floating structure, it is designed to move with the forces of wind, wave, and current rather than rigidly resist them like a fixed leg platform. Shell Oil.

pipeline, but these pipelines must be laid on the ocean bottom. Another method of removing oil from the field is by tanker. Tankers load their cargo from floating buoys or spread moorings, rather than directly from the drilling platform.

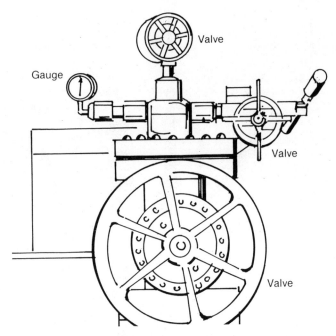

Gauge

Valve

Valve

Valve

Fig. 2-4. Wells flowing under their own pressure must be topped with a "Christmas tree"—consisting of gauges and valves—to control the flow of oil. Shell Oil.

Fig. 2-5. Many wells require artificial lift to bring the oil to the surface. Shell Oil.

Fig. 2-6. Platforms in the Gulf of Mexico. ARCO Photography Collection.

## CRUDE OILS

In many instances, the type and quality of the crude oil will determine into which products it can be refined. Crude oils vary from very sweet to sour in hydrogen sulfide, from heavy weight to light weight, and from yellow to black in color. These variables are not only a function of the field and depth where the crude originates, but also the type of crude oil.

Crude oils, generally, fall into three classifications: asphalt-base, paraffin-base, or mixed-base. Asphalt-based crudes contain little paraffin and are often high in sulphur, nitrogen, and oxygen. They are used for making gasolines and, of course, asphalt. Paraffin-based crudes are high in paraffin wax and can be refined into motor fuels, lube oils, and kerosene. Mixed-base crudes have some amounts of both paraffin wax and asphalt in them and can be refined into virtually all products, but, of course, in lesser amounts.

Due to the wide variety of sources of crude oils and the various qualities of the crudes, the American Petroleum Institute has devised a quality scale for petroleum products. This scale, known as the API scale, is based on the refined level of the cargo and its specific gravity. This is a value that can be calculated by a petroleum chemist. The scale runs from 0°–100° with most cargoes falling between 8°–70°. Many crude oils fall onto the scale in the 25°–35° range. They are not at the bottom of the scale even

Fig. 2-7. The Alaska Pipeline stretches from the North Slope, inside the Arctic Circle, to the port of Valdez. ARCO Photography Collection.

though crude oil is unrefined, due to the natural presence of light constituents such as gasoline.

Another variable in crude oil is its sweetness. This obviously is not sugar sweetness, but rather the presence or absence of hydrogen sulfide ($H_2S$). $H_2S$ has a rotten egg odor and can be toxic if breathed in large doses. Crude oil with a high content of $H_2S$ is considered sour crude, while low $H_2S$ crude is considered sweet crude.

## REFINING

Many of the longest and most heavily traveled sea routes are those over which crude oil flows to be refined. The economies of scale are such that ULCCs and VLCCs are very efficient in moving the crude from the drilling areas to the refineries.

Upon arrival at the refinery, the crude oil is removed from the vessel as quickly as possible and placed in storage. The vessel's cargo pumps lift the oil from the inerted cargo tanks and push it through the vessel's pipe-

Fig. 2-8. The search for petroleum has led to drilling in obscure areas of the world, including this remote spot in Alaska. ARCO Photography Collection.

lines and into the dockside hoses and pipelines. At some terminals, shore-side booster pumps assist the vessel in discharging the crude oil cargo. Shoreside and shipboard personnel work closely together helping to eliminate pollution and move the cargo quickly.

Once the cargo has left the tank vessel, it begins its journey through the maze of pipelines that make up a refinery. In the first step, crude oil may be stored for a period to allow water in the oil to separate out and be drawn off prior to refining. Even if this was done at the drilling platform, the process may still be repeated here to better clean the oil of water.

Many different methods are used in the refining of crude oil. Some of these are quite complicated and can vary as the type and quality of crude oil delivered changes. As new products are required, it may be necessary to create new refining methods to meet these needs. Refining consists of a number of different components, but basically the crude oil is broken down, then built back up into other products, and finally blended into the products we see in the marketplace. All of this requires a lot of chemistry and some very sophisticated equipment.

**Fractionation.** The initial process in refining crude oil is fractionation. This involves the breaking down of the crude oil into its component parts. Fractionation is completed by distilling the crude oil. By breaking down the crude oil into fractions, the products such as kerosene, gasoline, and asphalt are taken out of the mixture. The distillation unit is like a large boiler or a tea kettle. The crude is heated until the various fractions begin to "boil off." These fractions vaporize and then condense higher up the tower. Because different products have different boiling and condensing temperatures, this tower effectively separates out most of the components from the crude oil.

Part of the crude oil that does not vaporize in the distillation unit is called "residuum." This mixture can be used for fuel oil or further processed for other products. In some refineries, a second distillation tower may be present, in which the atmospheric pressure has been reduced to nearly a vacuum. In this tower, the residuum can be vaporized further, at a lower temperature, so that it will not chemically break down. Thus, more of the crude oil fractions can be drawn off through the vacuum distiller.

**Cracking.** A second component of the breaking down process of the crude oil is called "cracking." Cracking can be thermal cracking , which occurs in the distillation towers, or catalytic cracking, which uses a catalyst to assist in breaking down the crude oil mixture. A catalyst is a substance that

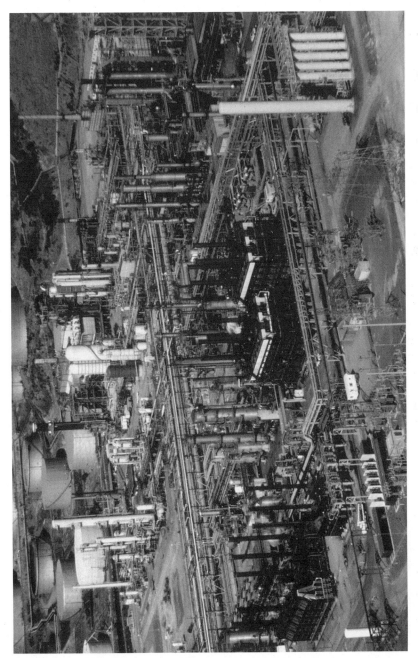

Fig. 2-9. Once the cargo has left the tank vessel, it begins its journey through the maze of pipelines that make up a refinery. Chevron Corporation.

Fig. 2-10. In the refining process, crude oil is first broken down, then "built back up" into different chemical compounds, and finally blended into the products we see in the marketplace. ARCO Photography Collection.

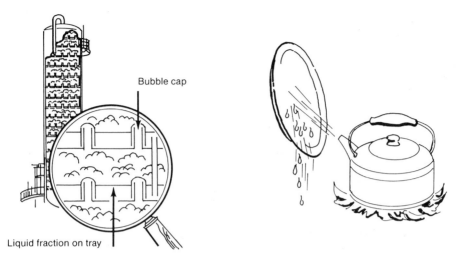

Bubble cap

Liquid fraction on tray

Fig. 2-11. The initial process in refining crude oil is called *fractionation*. The distillation unit is similar to a large tea kettle. The crude is heated until the various fractions begin to "boil off." Shell Oil.

assists in the breaking down of the crude oil residuum without itself experiencing any chemical changes. Catalysts may be fluid and pumped into a chamber to mix with the oil or they may be solid and have the oil passed over them. Following use, the catalyst is cleaned by burning. This removes the waste carbon from the surface of the catalyst and also helps heat the catalyst for further use.

There are cases where the residuum cannot be broken down by either the distillation tower or the catalytic cracker. In these cases, the residuum is sent on for further processing to the "coker." The coker unit processes the residuum into a cokelike product. This product can be either a liquid or a solid. The coke is created from the intense heating of the residuum in the coke furnace.

## BUILDING PRODUCTS

Once the crude oil and residuum are broken down into their component parts through the distillation towers or the cracking process, chemists begin building those products necessary to run an industrial society. The building of products occurs in many ways. These include reforming, alkylation, polymerization, and hydrogenation. Many refineries use a variety of these processes to build their products, while others depend on one or two of these processes to build theirs.

Fig. 2-12. A catalytic cracking unit, shown here, uses a catalyst to assist in breaking down the crude oil mixture. Shell Oil.

**Reforming** is the process of rearranging hydrocarbon compounds in the presence of heat and a catalyst without changing their chemical composition. The total number of hydrogen and carbon atoms in the molecule are not changed, but some bonds are broken and new bonds are formed. This process allows refineries to upgrade the octane of gasoline components, as well as building aromatic hydrocarbons. These aromatics are the basis for many plastics, explosives, and other hydrocarbon products.

**Alkylation** is the process of taking small hydrocarbon compounds and building them into larger ones. Different molecules can be combined to create products such as high octane gasoline or aviation fuel. The alkylation unit places the hydrocarbon and the alkylate catalyst in a furnace to allow them to mix together. The catalyst assists in the building of the complex hydrocarbon molecules desired.

**Polymerization** is very similar to alkylation except that the molecules built together are all of the same type. The process also involves taking smaller molecules and building larger ones. In both the polymerization and the alkylation process, both heat and a catalyst are used to speed up the process and make building conditions less severe.

**Hydrogenation** uses the free hydrogen molecules released when hydrocarbons are broken down and mixes these with unstable hydrocarbon compounds. In this way, the compounds that are being created can fill their necessary hydrogen bonds and become more stable. This allows the creation of complex hydrocarbon structures that will not decompose or break down as readily as the unstable hydrocarbons. Further blending of these compounds allows the creation of a variety of hydrocarbon-based products.

Although there are other methods of building, mixing, and rearranging hydrocarbons, the ones mentioned form the largest percentage of hydrocarbon treatments. In some cases, due to the $H_2S$ content of the crude oil, it must be "sweetened" before processing can begin. This process varies according to the amount of $H_2S$ and the desired sulphur end product.

## BLENDING

Once the chemistry of building the correct hydrocarbon compounds is complete, the components are ready to be assembled into the various products the refinery produces. These products vary by location, quality of crude oil, time of year, and market demands. A variety of products based on gasoline stocks can be created for different sectors of a market. Gasoline can be regular, high octane, no lead, summer or winter blend, or a combination of these with detergent added. Other products such as lube oils, greases, waxes, and a variety of solvents and other petroleum products are blended in the refinery to serve the needs of the marketplace.

Often the blending process creates products that are hazardous, flammable, toxic, or corrosive. These products must be contained in tanks or storage cylinders that allow for appropriate separation and reactivity precautions. In some cases, the products may react with the steel on the inside of a ship's tanks or the steel of a storage tank. In these cases, stainless steel or other lined tanks and pipelines are used to move these products.

Once blending and testing is complete, products may be moved away from the refinery in a variety of ways including tankers, pipelines, tank rail cars, or tank trucks. All modes of transport require special attention to the hazards and dangers of moving petroleum products. Such hazards involve not only the obvious environmental hazards, but many other dangers as well.

## PETROLEUM HAZARDS

As has been mentioned, the journey the crude oil makes from the well-head to the refinery and the products beyond is an interesting one. One thread that binds all of these products together is the hazard of petroleum cargoes. These cargoes are not simply a pollution hazard. They are also a health hazard as well as a fire and explosion hazard. This last point was made very clear by the 1989 fire and explosion aboard the tanker *Mega Borg* in the Gulf of Mexico.

**Fire and explosion.** In addressing fire or explosion hazards from petroleum products, it must be realized that the flammable component of the product is not the liquid, but rather the vapors. All petroleum products give off vapors. Many times these vapors cannot be seen or smelled, but they are present. As the temperature rises, at some point the concentration of these vapors will become heavy enough so that the air/vapor mixture becomes flammable. The temperature at which this occurs is called the flash point temperature. As discussed later in this chapter, petroleum cargos are classified according to their flash point and Reid Vapor Pressure (a measurement of vapor given off in a closed container heated to 100°F).

If the temperature continues to rise, a spark added to the air/vapor mixture may not only flash, but it may continue to burn. This temperature is known as the fire point temperature. If the temperature is elevated even further, the cargo may spontaneously combust. This temperature is known as the ignition temperature.

**Health hazards** are also a function of the petroleum vapors by virtue of their smell as well as their flammability. Most cargoes have a natural smell, or they will have an odor added in refining if they do not. Yet, because different people are sensitive to different odors, petroleum product smells must be measured in an objective manner. The system used is parts per million (ppm). Thus, the odor threshold of a product is the level in ppm at which it may be smelled by most people. A similar value to odor threshold is the threshold limit value (TLV). This value, measured in ppm, indicates the amount of a cargo it is safe to work around for 8 hours per day, 40 hours per week, 52 weeks per year. Obviously, some cargoes are safer than others, and there are cases where cargoes have been endured in high concentrations, well above the TLV, for short periods without damage to the individual.

Other hazards from petroleum products include *contamination* and *reactivity*. Ship's crew should, at all times, avoid ingesting petroleum products. Many of these products are poisonous. Even simple skin or eye contact with many products can cause health risks.

## GRADES OF PETROLEUM PRODUCTS

A wide variety of petroleum products are shipped by sea, and nearly all are flammable. Some, like gasoline, are extremely flammable while others, like lubricating oil, are relatively safe. The more flammable substances require special precautions and, for that reason, petroleum products are graded according to their volatility (table 2-1). They are divided into two main groups:

**Flammable liquids** are those that give off flammable vapors at or below 80°F (26.7°C). These are further subdivided into grades A, B, and C on the basis of their Reid Vapor Pressure.

**Combustible liquids** are those that give off flammable vapors at temperatures above 80°F.

Table 2-1

GRADES OF PETROLEUM PRODUCTS

| Grade | Flash Point | Reid Vapor Pressure | Examples |
|-------|-------------|---------------------|----------|
| A (flammable) | 80°F or below | 14 psi or above | Natural gasoline, very light naphthas |
| B (flammable) | 80°F or below | More than 8½ psi but less than 14 psi | Most commercial gasolines |
| C (flammable) | 80°F or below | 8½ psi or below | Most crude oils, creosote, aviation gas grade 115/145, JP-4 jet fuel |
| D (combustible) | above 80°F but below 150°F | ____ | Kerosene, some heavy crudes, commercial jet fuels |
| E (combustible) | 150° or above | ____ | Heavy fuel oils, lubricating oils, asphalt |

## SOURCES OF INFORMATION ON PETROLEUM PRODUCTS

A number of government agencies and private companies publish references that address the hazards of carrying bulk liquid petroleum products. These texts are designed to assist those parties carrying the products in moving them safely. The texts generally deal with three or four different types of hazards in addition to general information. These include fire and explosion, health, reactivity, and environmental hazards. Each area is addressed separately for the individual products.

The fire and explosion area addresses flammability, flash point, vapor pressure, and extinguishing agents. The health hazards area addresses odor threshold, TLV, contamination, and ingestion. The reactivity area addresses contamination, ingestion, and compatibility of the cargoes. The environmental area addresses spill clean-up procedures and hazards to water life.

**CG-388.** There are two texts used extensively in the maritime industry when dealing with hazardous liquids in bulk. The first of these is published by the U.S. Coast Guard and is called CG-388, *Chemical Data Guide for Bulk Shipment by Water*. The text is divided into a number of areas to assist the reader in its use. In the first section, terms used in the text are defined and explanations are given for health hazard numbers listed. The second section of the text consists of the product pages. Each product has a single page on which all included information is listed. The first page of the section acts as the example. Thereafter, all products are listed alphabetically by their most common name. Obviously, because the same products are manufactured by a variety of companies, many of these products have a number of synonyms. In the text, the third section consists of the synonym index. By using this index, regardless of the name you know a cargo by, you can find it or a synonym listed in the text. The alphabetical product index concludes the text.

**Chemical Hazards Response Information System (CHRIS).** A similar text to CG-388 is CHRIS, the Chemical Hazards Response Information System. This text is also a publication of the U.S. Coast Guard. The complete text consists of four different manuals. Manual number one is titled *A Condensed Guide to Chemical Hazards*. This manual can be used for response to fire, exposure, or pollution from one of the 1000 compounds listed. Manual number two, *Hazardous Chemical Data*, lists specific chemical, biological, and physical data for the 1000 compounds in-

GASOLINE, MOTOR

Synonyms— Petrol

Formula—$C_5H_{12}$ to $C_9H_{20}$

Appearance-Odor —Colorless to straw-white liquid; sweet, pleasant odor

Specific Gravity— 0.72 - 0.76

Chemical Family— Hydrocarbons

Applicable Bulk Regulations 46 CFR Subchapter ___D___

United Nations Number .......... 1203
CHRIS Code ................... GAT

| | 60 to | | 140 to | |
|---|---|---|---|---|
| Boiling Point ......... | 199 | °C | 390 | °F |
| Freezing Point ...... Unavailable | | °C | | °F |

Vapor Pressure 20°C(68°F) (mmHg) ___190___
Reid Vapor Pressure (psia) ....... ___7.4___
Vapor Pressure 46°C (115°F) (psia). ___12.5___
Vapor Density (Air = 1.0) ........ ___3.4___
Solubility in Water....... Negligible

## FIRE & EXPLOSION HAZARD DATA

Grade— C: Flammable liquid
Electrical Group— D

General— Dangerous fire and explosion hazard in presence of heat or flame.

Flash Point (°F)........... —40
Flammable Limits ......... 1.4 - 7.6%
Autoignition Temp. (°F) ..... 495
Extinguishing Agents ....... $CO_2$, dry chemical, foam, water fog
Special Fire Procedures ...... Tanks exposed to fire should be kept cool with a water spray.

## HEALTH HAZARD DATA

| Health Hazard Ratings | Odor Threshold (ppm) | TLV (ppm) |
|---|---|---|
| 1, 1, 2 | 0.25 | 500-1000* |

General— Liquid irritating to skin and eyes on contact. Vapor inhalation leads to intoxication.

Symptoms— Inhalation: Marked vertigo, inability to walk a straight line, hilarity, incoordination, intense burning in throat and lungs, possibly bronchopneumonia, nausea, vomiting.

Short Exposure Tolerance— 0.5 to 1.6% vapor concentration was fatal to a man after 5 minutes exposure; 500 to 30,000 ppm was fatal to a youth.

Exposure Procedures— Inhalation: Immediately remove victim from contaminated atmosphere. If breathing is interrupted, artificial respiration should be applied immediately. A physician should be called.

## REACTIVITY DATA

Stability— Chemically stable.

Compatibility— Material: Almost any usual material of construction is suitable. Natural rubber is softened and will deteriorate rapidly.

Cargo: Group 33 of compatibility chart.

## SPILL OR LEAK PROCEDURE

Wear polyethylene gloves, face shield, protective clothing. Have all-purpose canister mask available. Secure ignition sources. Small spills may be flushed away with water.

If a spill occurs, call the National Response Center 800-424-8802.

Remarks: *Proposed change of TLV to 300.

Fig. 2-13. Sample page from *CG-388, Chemical Data Guide for Bulk Shipment by Water.* U.S. Coast Guard.

cluded in manual number one. Manual number three, *Hazard Assessment Handbook,* discusses how to estimate spill concentrations, fire, and toxicity after a spill has occurred. Manual number four, *Response Methods Handbook,* is written specifically for Coast Guard personnel and is intended to be used in training or at a spill site.

Mariners aboard tank vessels are usually involved only with the first two of the four manuals. This allows them to make all necessary decisions concerning the safety, compatibility, and hazards of a particular product. Thus, the manuals can be consulted either prior to the loading of cargo or in the case of an emergency concerning the cargo. In this way, all of the provisions of the manual can be met with at some point in the transit.

In some cases, individual companies publish product information sheets concerning their specific product. These are obviously product specific sheets, but in some cases the sheets are also location specific. Thus, the hazard response can be based on the ability of a specific terminal to respond.

It is apparent that there are a variety of hazards involved with the transporting and refining of petroleum cargoes. These hazards include not only personal health and safety hazards, but also fire, explosion, and environmental hazards. Texts and reference materials are available from a number of sources. These should always be consulted prior to the handling of any petroleum products.

CHAPTER 3

# HOW PETROLEUM CARGOES ARE
# MEASURED ON BOARD SHIP

C ARGO gauging—ullaging—is one of the first things a new officer must learn. The techniques used are simple, but they must be mastered thoroughly and performed meticulously. It is wise to gain an understanding of these techniques before setting foot on board a tanker.

The first step in the ullaging process is to take the ullages themselves; we will discuss how this is done shortly. When the ullages are known, the following information can be determined: 1) observed ("gross") volume of cargo, 2) standard ("net") volume of cargo, 3) tonnage of cargo, and 4) loading/discharging rate.

A tanker is ullaged each time she arrives in port; this is also done just before sailing. The ullages are recorded on forms (fig. 3-1), which are then distributed to ship, terminal, and main office of the vessel's owner or charterer. Ullages are also taken at intervals during the loading or discharging operation as a means of determining the amount of cargo on board at a given time.

In a situation where custody of the cargo is being transferred, an independent inspector often takes the ullages. If custody of the cargo is remaining within the company, which is not uncommon since many oil companies operate their own tanker fleets, then the final ullages are generally taken by one of the ship's officers.

Regardless of who is doing the final gauging, it is imperative for ship's officers to understand the process thoroughly. The authoritative source of measurement information for tank vessels is chapter 17 of the American Petroleum Institute's *Manual of Petroleum Measurement Standards*. Every officer would be wise to read it carefully.

## UNITS OF MEASURE

The following units of measure are commonly used on tankers:

1 barrel = 42 gallons (U.S.)
1 cubic meter = 6.2898 barrels
1 ton (metric) = 1,000 kilograms

# Ullage Report

| Dock | | Incoming cargo | Ship | |
|---|---|---|---|---|
| Port | | Outgoing cargo | Voyage number | |
| | | | Date | Time |

| Tank No. | Grade | Ullage Feet | Inches | Trim adjustment | Adjust ullage Feet | Inches | Gross bbls. | Temp. | Net 60° bbls. | Water Inches | Bbls |
|---|---|---|---|---|---|---|---|---|---|---|---|
| **Port** | | | | | | | | | | | |
| 1 | | | | | | | | | | | |
| 2 | | | | | | | | | | | |
| 3 | | | | | | | | | | | |
| 4 | | | | | | | | | | | |
| 5 | | | | | | | | | | | |
| 6 | | | | | | | | | | | |
| 7 | | | | | | | | | | | |
| 8 | | | | | | | | | | | |
| 9 | | | | | | | | | | | |
| 10 | | | | | | | | | | | |
| 11 | | | | | | | | | | | |
| **Starboard** | | | | | | | | | | | |
| 1 | | | | | | | | | | | |
| 2 | | | | | | | | | | | |
| 3 | | | | | | | | | | | |
| 4 | | | | | | | | | | | |
| 5 | | | | | | | | | | | |

(Tank numbers go up to eleven)

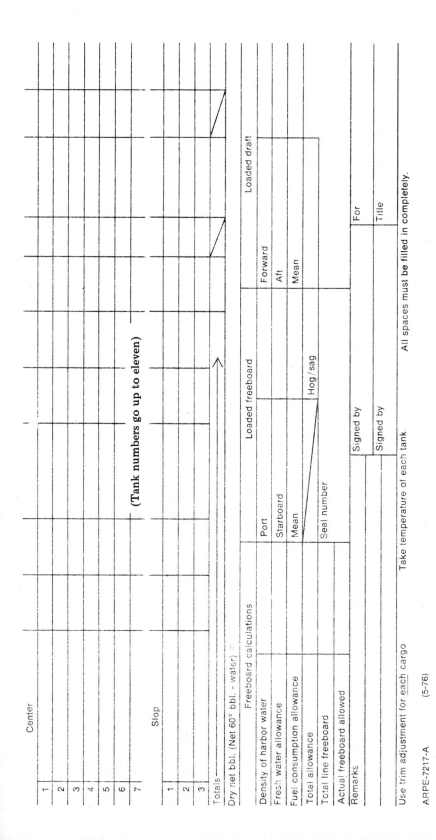

Fig. 3-1. Ullage report form. ARCO.

1 ton (long) = 2,240 pounds
1 standard ("net") barrel = 42 gallons (adjusted to standard temperature)
1 observed ("gross") barrel = 42 gallons (at observed temperature)

The above units are used with the following formulas:

standard volume = observed volume × volume correction factor

tonnage = standard volume × stowage factor

The volume correction factor and stowage factor are found in the Petroleum Tables, which are based on chapter 11.1 of API's *Manual of Petroleum Measurement Standards* (see tables 3-4 and 3-5). Note that the stowage factor used in a given situation reflects the type of units being used to measure volume. Typical examples are long tons per barrel and metric tons per barrel.

The U.S. petroleum barrel (42 gallons) is still widely used on ships of U.S. registry, and it is an important unit of measure in the international petroleum industry. The long ton also continues to be used on American ships; the metric ton is used by virtually all other nations.

Tanks are often calibrated in cubic meters or barrels. However, it is not uncommon to encounter ships that have been calibrated in cubic feet or other units. Such differences may make the gauging process seem confusing, but in actual fact the differences are superficial. Regardless of the units employed, the same basic techniques are used to ullage tankers throughout the world. An officer who masters these techniques will have little difficulty making the transition between ships of different registry.

The appendix at the end of chapter 14 lists a complete table of conversion factors for the various units of measure commonly employed on tankers in the world today.

## GAUGING THE SHIP

When a tanker is new, each tank is calibrated and a set of tables is prepared; these tables indicate cargo volume at various ullages (see table 3-1). *Ullage* is the distance from an above-deck datum (usually the top of the ullage hole) to the surface of the liquid in the tank (fig. 3-2). This distance is most often measured in meters and decimal parts of a meter— except on American tankers, where it is usually measured in feet and inches or feet and decimal parts of a foot.

In the not-too-distant past, ullage covers were left open during loading and discharging so that cargo could be gauged manually with a hand tape

Table 3-1

EXTRACT FROM CARGO TANK CALIBRATION TABLE
San Clemente Class Tanker
No. 1 Wing Tanks

| Ullage | Barrels | Cubic feet |
|--------|---------|------------|
| 5′ 00″ | 28,312 | 158,972 |
| 1″ | 28,269 | 158,730 |
| 2″ | 28,225 | 158,483 |
| 3″ | 28,181 | 158,236 |
| 4″ | 28,137 | 157,989 |
| 5″ | 28,093 | 157,742 |
| 6″ | 28,049 | 157,495 |
| 7″ | 28,005 | 157,248 |
| 8″ | 27,961 | 157,001 |
| 9″ | 27,918 | 156,760 |
| 10″ | 27,874 | 156,513 |
| 11″ | 27,830 | 156,265 |
| 6′ 00″ | 27,786 | 156,018 |

and plumb bob. Hand taping is still an accurate and reliable way of gauging cargo, and it is generally preferred by independent cargo inspectors. However, with the widespread use of inert gas systems came the need for "closed" ullaging methods. Furthermore, many ports now prohibit vapor emissions from tankers. The old method of opening ullage covers during the cargo operation has, therefore, given way to the use of closed systems.

Several types of closed ullaging systems are now in widespread use: float (figs. 3-5 and 3-6), radar echo (figs. 3-7 and 3-8), and submerged sensor (figs. 3-10 and 3-11). All three provide the same information—tank ullages—at the cargo control console (and/or locally at each tank).

As noted earlier, independent inspectors still prefer hand taping as an accurate and reliable gauging method. They also need to take cargo samples, temperatures, and water "cuts" (described in the next section). These tasks can all be accomplished, without leaking vapor, by using a vapor control valve, such as the one shown in figure 3-4, which is permanently fitted in the tank top. Ullages are taken by inserting a specially designed tape (fig. 3-3) through the valve. Typically, the same unit can also be used to take temperatures and locate the oil/water interface in the tank.

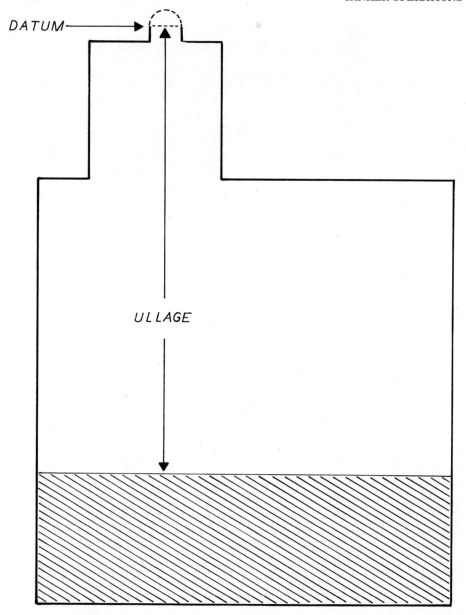

Fig. 3-2. Ullages are measured from an above-deck datum, usually the top of the ullage hole.

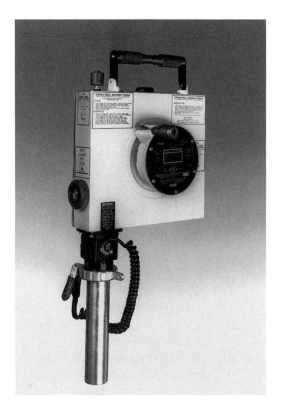

Fig. 3-3. Ullages can be taken, without leaking vapor, by means of a specially designed gauging tape. The tape is inserted through a vapor control valve such as the one shown in figure 3-4. Besides measuring ullage, the device shown here can also measure cargo temperature and oil/water interface location. MMC.

## THIEVING

Small amounts of water are frequently found in loaded cargo tanks. In the case of crude oil, such water is often present when the crude is pumped from the ground. Water also accumulates at the tank bottoms in the form of leftover ballast, tank washings, and condensation. This water is sometimes allowed for when ullaging. A process called *thieving* (also called *water cutting*) is employed for this purpose. A graduated metal rod is smeared with litmus paste, which changes color when contacted by water but isn't affected by oil. The rod is lowered until it touches bottom, then is retrieved. The amount of water at the bottom of the tank is determined by noting the place on the graduated rod where the paste changes color.

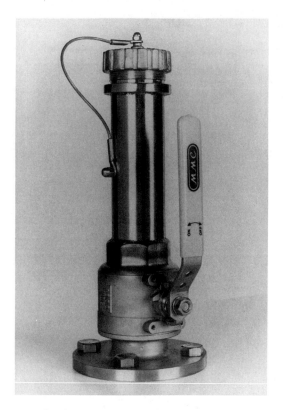

Fig. 3-4. A vapor control valve permits introduction of a specially designed gauging tape. MMC.

### DETERMINING OBSERVED VOLUME OF CARGO

After each tank has been ullaged, the calibration tables are entered to determine cargo volume. For the purpose of illustration, we will use the barrel as the unit of volume in the following paragraphs. Note that in everyday use on board ship, the term *gross barrel* (a term that has been used for many years on tankers) is more apt to be used than *observed barrel*. Similarly, the traditional term *net barrel* is still preferred to *standard barrel*. Although the older terms are incorrect in the strictest, most technical sense, they are used here in order to accustom the reader to the reality of shipboard practice.

After recording the ullages, one more step must be taken before entering the calibration tables; the ullages must be corrected for trim. As a rule, this correction must be made if the ship is trimmed a foot or more by the

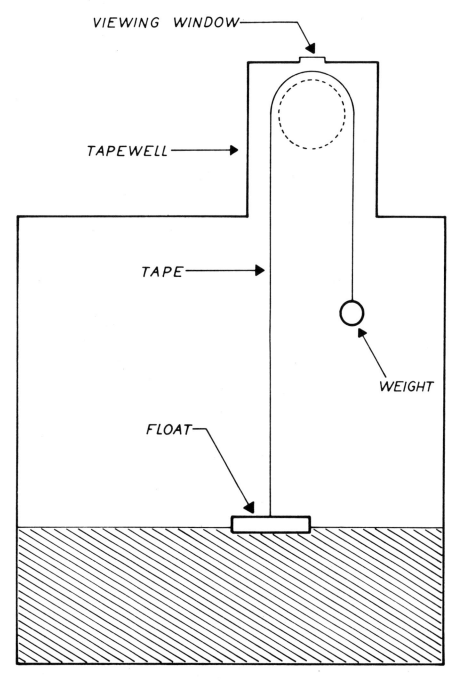

Fig. 3-5. An "automatic" tape of older design.

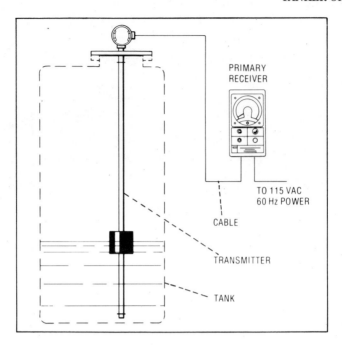

PRIMARY
RECEIVER

TO 115 VAC
60 Hz POWER

CABLE

TRANSMITTER

TANK

Fig. 3-6. The introduction of "closed" tank systems using inert gas has greatly changed methods of ullaging. Many tankers are now fitted with remote-indicating ullage systems, such as the one shown here. In this case a float moves up and down with the cargo level while transmitting a signal to the cargo control room. Sensors Division of Transamerica Delaval.

head or stern. Trim corrections are most often found on a separate page of the calibration tables (see table 3-2). Corrections are given in inches or fractions of an inch for various conditions of trim. These corrections must be added to, or subtracted from, the observed ullages—the sign of the correction indicates how it is to be applied. (On some tankers, trim corrections are made simply by dialing the trim into the cargo control console; see figure 3-9. On other ships, the correction is made automatically and integrated into the system on an instantaneous basis by the ship's computer.)

After correcting each reading, the main part of the calibration tables is entered and the number of gross barrels corresponding to each ullage is noted. These values are listed for given intervals of ullage (every inch, for example). Depending on desired accuracy, some interpolation may be necessary; this can be done by inspection. The sum of these figures yields the total number of gross barrels on board.

Table 3-2

SS *ATLANTIC ROVER*

Trim Corrections (in inches)

trim by the stern

| Tank | 1′ | 2′ | 3′ | 4′ | 5′ | 6′ | 7′ | 8′ | 9′ |
|------|-----|-----|-----|-----|------|------|------|------|------|
| 1C | +½ | +½ | +1 | +1 | +1½ | +1½ | +1½ | +2 | +2 |
| 2C | — | — | +½ | +½ | +1 | +1 | +1 | +1½ | +1½ |
| 3C | — | +½ | +½ | +1 | +1 | +1½ | +1½ | +2 | +2 |
| 4C | — | — | −½ | −½ | −1 | −1 | −1½ | −1½ | −2 |
| 5C | — | +½ | +½ | +½ | +1 | +1 | +1½ | +1½ | +1½ |
| 6C | — | +½ | +½ | +½ | +1 | +1 | +1½ | +1½ | +1½ |
| 1P | +½ | +½ | +1 | +1 | +1½ | +1½ | +1½ | +2 | +2 |
| 1S | +½ | +½ | +1 | +1 | +1½ | +1½ | +1½ | +2 | +2 |
| 2P | — | — | +½ | +½ | +1 | +1 | +1 | +1½ | +1½ |
| 2S | — | — | +½ | +½ | +1 | +1 | +1 | +1½ | +1½ |
| 3P | — | +½ | +½ | +1 | +1 | +1½ | +1½ | +2 | +2 |
| 3S | — | +½ | +½ | +1 | +1 | +1½ | +1½ | +2 | +2 |
| 4P | — | — | −½ | −1 | −1 | −1½ | −1½ | −2 | −2 |
| 4S | — | — | −½ | −½ | −1 | −1 | −1½ | −1½ | −2 |
| 5P | — | +½ | +½ | +½ | +1 | +1 | +1½ | +1½ | +1½ |
| 5S | — | +½ | +½ | +½ | +1 | +1 | +1½ | +1½ | +1½ |
| 6P | — | +½ | +½ | +1 | +1 | +1½ | +1½ | +2 | +2 |
| 6S | — | +½ | +½ | +1 | +1 | +1½ | +1½ | +2 | +2 |

Apply corrections to observed ullages.

## DETERMINING STANDARD VOLUME OF CARGO

All petroleum products have an important characteristic in common—they expand when heated, contract when cooled. For that reason, petroleum engineers have established a standard temperature from which to calculate the standard volume of oil in a tank. In the United States, the American Petroleum Institute has set the standard temperature at 60°F (15.6°C). In nations using the metric system, the standard temperature is 15°C (59°F).

Determining net barrels of cargo is a simple matter of multiplying gross barrels by a volume correction factor obtained from the Petroleum Tables (see table 3-4).

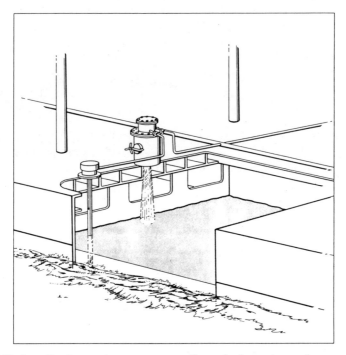

Fig. 3-7. Radar ullaging systems measure ullages by bouncing radar waves off the surface of the liquid in a tank. Such systems are intrinsically safe and extremely accurate (+/– 5 mm). Saab Marine Electronics.

**Cargo temperature** is normally ascertained by one of the following methods: 1) by automatic readout in the cargo control room, 2) by checking temperatures as cargo passes through the manifold and figuring an average (many ships are equipped with built-in thermometers at the manifold for that purpose), and 3) by direct immersion of a thermometer in the tank.

**API gravity** is nothing more than a convenient way of expressing the specific gravity of a product. An arbitrary gravity of 10.0° is assigned to fresh water. Numbers above 10.0° indicate products lighter than fresh water; those below, heavier. Light products such as gasoline have API values considerably greater than 10.0°, while a few products such as heavy fuel oil have values less than 10.0°.

A glance at table 3-3 shows that API gravity is easily converted to specific gravity and vice versa. This conversion is helpful, because ships of some nations (British ships, for example) use specific gravity instead of API.

Although it is possible to measure API and specific gravities on board ship, the preferred practice is often to use a figure provided by shoreside

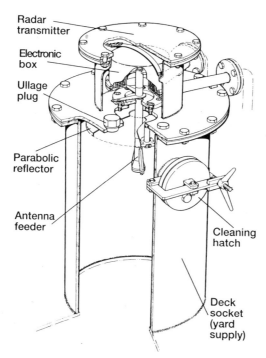

Radar transmitter

Electronic box

Ullage plug

Parabolic reflector

Antenna feeder

Cleaning hatch

Deck socket (yard supply)

Fig. 3-8. Transmitter unit for the Saab TankRadar. The radar transmitter measures the tank ullage; with specific data stored in a permanent memory, the computer can calculate the tank volume. This system also monitors cargo temperature and inert gas pressure, which, along with the tank ullage, are available as a direct readout at the control console or terminal. Saab Marine Electronics.

personnel. Shoreside measurements are generally more precise than those obtained by the ship, and the use of a single figure prevents discrepancies between shipboard and shoreside calculations.

On the other hand, in some shipboard installations, temperature and API are computed automatically by ship's equipment and obtained by direct readout on the monitoring and control terminal (often located on the bridge). Cargo volume and tonnage are also calculated automatically and appear as readouts on the terminal.

However, assuming that a direct readout for net barrels is not available, it is necessary to make a quick calculation. When API gravity and cargo temperature are both known, it is a simple matter to extract the volume correction factor from the Petroleum Tables (see table 3-4). The appropriate factor, when multiplied by gross barrels, gives the desired figure for net barrels.

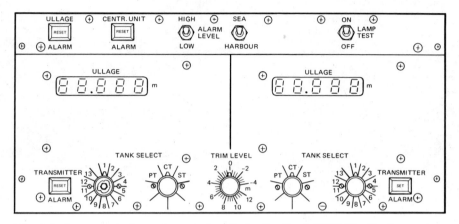

Fig. 3-9. Cargo control panel, central unit, for the Saab SUM-21 ullaging system. Two tanks can be ullaged simultaneously by using the tank select dials. Trim is corrected automatically by entering on the center dial. The SUM-21 was the prototype for radar ullaging systems. Although later superseded by the TankRadar, many of these units are still in use on tankers throughout the world. Salwico.

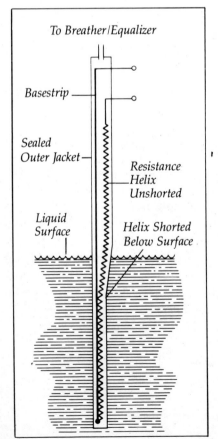

Fig. 3-10. The Metritape level sensor is an "electric tape measure" that hangs from top to bottom of a tank. Two wires out of the sensor top carry an electric resistance signal that is directly proportional to the tank ullage. When the sensor is submerged in a liquid, the weight of the liquid compresses the sensor and causes a short circuit in the submerged portion of the helix windings, thus changing the electrical resistance. A change in ullage of 1 meter causes a corresponding change of 1 meter in the length of unshorted resistance helix and an electric resistance change of 100 ohms. An ullage readout is displayed locally at the tank top and remotely in the cargo control room. Metritape.

Table 3-3

SAMPLE API AND SPECIFIC GRAVITIES

| Product | API | Specific Gravity |
|---------|-----|------------------|
| Motor gasoline | 61.0 | .7351 |
| Kerosene | 49.0 | .7839 |
| Gas oil | 39.0 | .8299 |
| Benzene | 29.0 | .8816 |
| Bunker fuel | 15.0 | .9659 |
| Heavy fuel oil | 9.5 | 1.0035 |

Table 3-4

EXTRACT FROM THE PETROLEUM TABLES
Volume Correction Factors for Generalized Products
(from API Table 6B)

API Gravity

| | 30 | 31 | 32 | 33 |
|---|----|----|----|----|
| Temperature | Factor for Correcting Volume to 60°F | | | |
| 75 | 0.9933 | 0.9933 | 0.9932 | 0.9932 |
| 76 | 0.9929 | 0.9928 | 0.9928 | 0.9927 |
| 77 | 0.9924 | 0.9924 | 0.9923 | 0.9922 |
| 78 | 0.9920 | 0.9919 | 0.9919 | 0.9918 |
| 79 | 0.9915 | 0.9915 | 0.9914 | 0.9913 |
| 80 | 0.9911 | 0.9910 | 0.9909 | 0.9909 |

## DETERMINING TONNAGE OF CARGO

The ship's officers—especially the chief mate—must frequently compute cargo tonnage. Tonnage is particularly important when figuring draft, trim, displacement, and stress.

To determine the tonnage of a given product, enter the appropriate section of the Petroleum Tables (see table 3-5). Pick out the stowage factor corresponding to the API gravity of the product. The tonnage is equal to net barrels multiplied by the stowage factor.

Let's illustrate with an example.

A parcel of gasoline is loaded, and the following information is known:

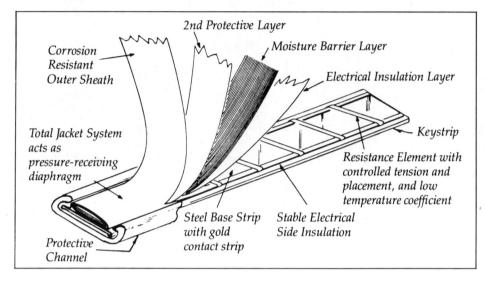

Fig. 3-11. Detail of Metritape sensor.

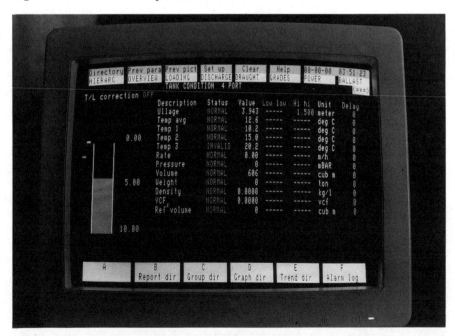

Fig. 3-12. In some shipboard installations, temperature and API/specific gravity are computed automatically by ship's equipment and obtained by direct readout on the monitoring and control terminal (often located on the bridge). Cargo volume, as well as tonnage, are also calculated automatically and appear as readouts on the terminal. Saab Marine Electronics.

gross barrels = 128,397
temperature = 72°F
API gravity = 59.0°

How many net barrels, and how many tons, of gasoline were loaded?
The first step in the solution is to enter the Petroleum Tables, from which the following information is taken:

volume correction factor = 0.9918
stowage factor = 0.11594 tons per barrel

Armed with the foregoing information, we are now able to make the necessary calculations:

0.9918 × 128,397 = 127,344 net barrels
127,344 × 0.11594 = 14,764 tons

Table 3-5

EXTRACT FROM THE PETROLEUM TABLES
(from API Table 11)

| API Gravity | Long Tons Per Barrel |
|:---:|:---:|
| 15.0 | 0.15082 |
| 15.1 | 0.15072 |
| 15.2 | 0.15061 |
| 15.3 | 0.15051 |
| 15.4 | 0.15041 |
| 15.5 | 0.15031 |
| 15.6 | 0.15020 |
| 15.7 | 0.15010 |

## LOADING AND DISCHARGING RATES

Loading and discharging rates vary considerably for different ships, different terminals, and different cargoes. For example, a ULCC might load 120,000 barrels per hour (16,000 tons per hour) at a terminal in the Persian Gulf, while a small product carrier might load less than 1,000 barrels per hour at a refinery.

Some of the factors that influence rates are size and number of pumps, size of shore lines, temperature and viscosity of cargo, number of tanks open, vapor control and inert gas system operation (for example, Can the IG system keep up with the pumps during discharge?), and the distance from shore tanks to ship.

## S.S. SHASTA VALLEY
### Loading Rates

Total gross barrels: 447,000

Start @ 0400

| | 0600 | 0800 | 1000 | 1200 | 1400 | 1600 |
|---|---|---|---|---|---|---|
| 1C | 5422 | 10,598 | 10,598 | 10,598 | 10,598 | |
| 2C | 7526 | 15,105 | 23,987 | 34,299 | 43,290 | |
| 3C | MT | MT | MT | MT | MT | MT |
| 4C | 8312 | 16,678 | 26,390 | 36,793 | 43,278 | |
| 5C | 9746 | 19,471 | 30,517 | 43,236 | 43,236 | |
| 6C | 10,224 | 20,550 | 32,130 | 39,987 | 39,987 | |
| 1P | | | | | 2681 | |
| S | | | | | 2681 | |
| 2P | | | | | 3191 | |
| S | | | | | 3240 | |
| 4P | | | | | 3235 | |
| S | | | | | 3235 | |
| 6P | | | | | 3786 | |
| S | | | | | 3742 | |
| Aboard: | 41,230 | 82,402 | 123,622 | 164,913 | 206,180 | |
| To Go: | 405,770 | 364,598 | 323,378 | 282,087 | 240,820 | |
| Rate: | 20,615 | 20,586 | 20,610 | 20,646 | 20,634 | |
| Est. Finish: | 0145 | 0145 | 0145 | 0145 | 0145 | |

Fig. 3-13. A typical form for computing loading rates.

In order to gain some idea of when the cargo will finish, the officer on watch must figure the loading or discharging rate at periodic intervals, typically every one or two hours. This procedure is a routine part of each cargo watch; it is therefore important to understand it thoroughly.

Rates are typically measured in barrels per hour, tons per hour, or cubic meters per hour, depending on vessel nationality and ownership. The process is simple, as explained in the following paragraphs.

First, gauge the ship at periodic intervals; determine the total cargo on board; find the difference between this figure and the last total; divide this difference by the number of hours elapsed between the measurements. The result is the loading or discharging rate per hour.

To determine estimated time of finish, divide the amount to go by the rate; this will give hours to go. Figure 3-13 shows a typical form for computing loading rates. A similar form is used when discharging.

CHAPTER 4

# CARGO PIPING SYSTEMS

M OST modern tankers are fitted with a direct pipeline system for handling cargo. Simply stated, the tanks are divided into groups, or systems, with a different pump and line for each system.

Figure 4-2 diagrams a direct pipeline arrangement for an 18-tank ship. The system incorporates three main cargo pumps, each handling two tanks across (that is, two center tanks and four wing tanks). Figure 4-3 illustrates another possible arrangement for the same ship. This time only two pumps are fitted—one for centers, one for wings.

In both cases a separate line runs from each pump along the bottom of the tank range to the tanks in its system. Shorter sections of pipe branch off from the main lines to each individual tank.

These pipelines vary in diameter from 10 to 12 inches (25 to 30 centimeters) on handy-size tankers to 36 inches (91 centimeters) on VLCCs.

## LEARNING THE CARGO SYSTEM

A new officer should make every effort to learn these systems quickly. In addition, it is important to know the location and purpose of the following:

**Tank valves.** The main pipeline carries oil along the bottom of the tank range. Along the way it connects to branch lines, one per tank. At the end of each branch line the piping spreads into a *bell-mouth,* an arrangement that resembles a large vacuum cleaner (see figure 6-11). This allows suction to be taken close to the bottom of the tank.

In addition, a tank valve is fitted near the end of the branch line. This valve is operated in one of two ways: 1) automatically, from the cargo control room or 2) manually, from the deck above.

While an increasing number of ships have been fitted with automatic valves, many still use manual control. And here a question arises: How do you operate a valve that lies deep within a cargo tank—perhaps 20 meters below the main deck—and is frequently submerged in oil?

To make tank valve operation possible, a metal reach rod connects each valve stem to a handwheel on the main deck (fig. 4-5). One turn of the handwheel produces a corresponding turn of the valve inside the tank.

Fig. 4-1. Sailors connect a loading arm to the manifold of a 215,000-dwt VLCC at Europort, the Netherlands. British Petroleum.

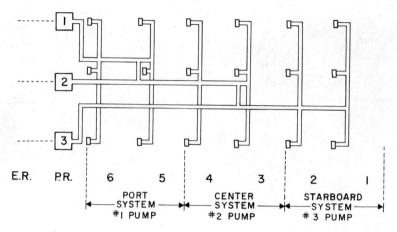

Fig. 4-2. Direct pipeline system incorporating three lines and three pumps. Cross-overs are provided between systems (no valves are shown). Bill Finhandler.

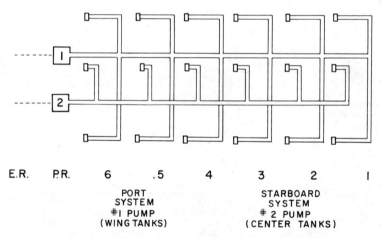

Fig. 4-3. Direct pipeline system incorporating two lines and two pumps. Center tanks are on one system, wing tanks on the other. Bill Finhandler.

The handwheel is fitted with a threaded indicator, called a *telltale*, which travels from "open" to "closed" as the valve is turned (see figure 5-8). One caution: Telltales sometimes stick, jam, or become stripped, thus causing an incorrect reading.

**Drops.** Cargo is loaded through filling lines called drops. These are located on each line in the pumproom and at various locations on the main deck. Each drop is equipped with a valve; this must be open when loading

Fig. 4-4. Loading arms are secured with bolted flanges or special hydraulic fittings. Exxon.

through that line. While discharging, drop valves are kept closed to prevent cargo from recirculating to the tanks.

*Line drops* route cargo into the underdeck piping system; therefore, individual tank valves must still be opened before cargo can enter the tanks.

A *tank drop,* on the other hand, serves a single tank; oil bypasses the main piping system and flows directly into the tank. Tank drops are more apt to be found on ships carrying refined cargoes, where the need for separation makes it desirable to bypass the main system.

**Crossovers.** The various systems are connected by sections of pipe known as crossovers. Each crossover is fitted with a valve, or valves, thus making it possible to isolate the systems or link them together, as desired.

When loading the same product in all tanks, as on a crude carrier, crossovers are generally opened to allow cargo to flow freely through all systems. In the case of differing products, as on a product carrier, crossovers must be closed to prevent mixing.

**Master valves.** At each place where the bottom piping passes through a bulkhead and enters the next tank, a valve is fitted in the line. This is a

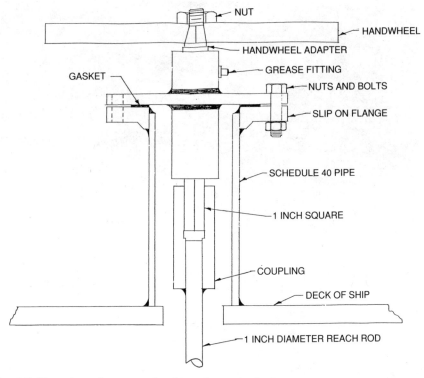

NUT

HANDWHEEL

HANDWHEEL ADAPTER

GREASE FITTING

GASKET

NUTS AND BOLTS

SLIP ON FLANGE

SCHEDULE 40 PIPE

1 INCH SQUARE

COUPLING

DECK OF SHIP

1 INCH DIAMETER REACH ROD

Fig. 4-5. To make valve operation from the main deck possible, a metal reach rod connects each valve stem to a handwheel. In the installation shown here, the coupling joining the reach rod to the handwheel assembly is formed by a square female fitting, which slides over a spindle, also square. Note the gasket, which provides a vapor-tight seal—especially important in complying with requirements for vapor control. (For comparison with a slightly different installation, see figure 5-8.) Elliott Manufacturing.

master valve. Master valves provide separation between tanks on the same line and make it possible to isolate a single tank completely.

**Manifold.** Cargo flows from ship to shore, and vice versa, through flexible hoses or hinged loading arms that bolt to the ship's manifold (fig. 4-6). By means of various valves built into the manifold, cargo can be routed to line drops along the main deck or to the pumproom—or to both simultaneously. The manifold may also be equipped with pressure gauges and thermometers for each line.

When learning the cargo systems, you should memorize which systems tie into each manifold line (that is, which tanks and pumps are commonly

Fig. 4-6. A tanker's manifold. Pipelines are blanked off when not in use. A fixed drip pan catches leaks from flanged couplings. Exxon.

tied into a given manifold outlet). Note the location of crossovers between manifold lines and observe how these are used to route cargo between systems.

**Pumproom.** The pumproom is the Grand Central Station of an oil tanker; all pipelines meet and interconnect in a relatively small area, usually located aft of the cargo tanks.

You should study the pumproom carefully. Learn the systems each pump is connected to, plus the designation for each pump (such as, number 1 main cargo pump, starboard stripper, etc.). Learn the location and purpose of every valve, including crossover, drop, pump suction, pump discharge, sea suction, and block valves to each main and stripping line. Locate all vent cocks and line drains. (You might try going over the entire piping system each night as you lie in bed. Try to visualize each valve, especially the important ones like crossovers and drops. This learning method works very well for many people.)

The pumproom diagram—usually posted in the chief mate's office— is a valuable tool. However, there is no substitute for climbing through the pumproom and seeing each valve. Ask yourself questions while doing this: *With this valve open and this one closed, which path will the oil follow?*

Follow and observe the pumpman when he changes the lineup. Ask him to explain what he's doing. Then, when you are confident you know the system, line it up yourself. Have the chief mate or pumpman check your work.

While exploring the pumproom, you will notice that drops are fitted into each line. As we have already learned, these make it possible to load through the pumproom. However, it is often preferable to isolate the pumproom while loading, and to bypass it by routing cargo through line drops on the main deck. To accomplish this, you must close the upper and lower master and block valves at the pumproom bulkhead, thus sealing it off from the rest of the cargo system. This practice is common when loading heavy crudes and fuel oils that might clog the intricate piping system of the pumproom.

While discussing the pumproom, we should note that some tankers don't have one. A number of product carriers are fitted with deepwell pumps, one per tank; thus no pumproom is needed. (See chapter 6 for a discussion of deepwell pumps.)

**Stripping system.** Many ships use a separate stripping system to pump out the last few barrels from each tank. Such systems often employ reciprocating or rotary pumps, or eductors—all of which are well suited to the task of draining tanks. (Eductors have proved themselves especially useful for this purpose.) Because they handle a relatively small amount of cargo, stripping lines, valves, and pumps are considerably smaller than those used on the main systems.

As a rule, main and stripping systems are kept separate, but crossovers make it possible to connect them if desired. Stripping pumps can therefore discharge or take suction through the main lines whenever necessary. (Some vessels use no stripping system whatsoever, except a small valve and a short branch line running from the main line in each tank. On these ships all stripping is done through the main line.)

**Cargo control room.** On many tankers, cargo operations are directed from the cargo control room (fig. 4-7). From this room, the officer in charge can monitor cargo ullages, pressures, and temperatures. Also, it is often possible to operate cargo system valves and pumps from the control room. A typical cargo control room contains the following:

1. ullage indicators;
2. tank temperature indicators;
3. cargo system pressure indicators;
4. stress, draft, and trim indicators;
5. controls for valves and pumps;
6. inert gas system controls, indicators, and alarms;
7. tank high and low level alarms;
8. computer terminal and loading calculator;
9. communication equipment, such as telephones and radios.

Traditionally, cargo control rooms have been equipped with a mechanical console fitted with manual switches and push buttons. However, the use of microcomputer technology for cargo monitoring and control has been refined to such a degree that cargo control rooms may someday become a thing of the past. On a number of tankers, cargo operations are now controlled from the bridge, where officers monitor ullages, take temperatures, monitor the inert gas system, start and stop pumps, open and close valves, and even control the ship's engine—all from a single terminal (see figure 5-6).

## TYPES OF VALVES

The cargo piping system of a typical tanker incorporates valves of various designs. These include the following:

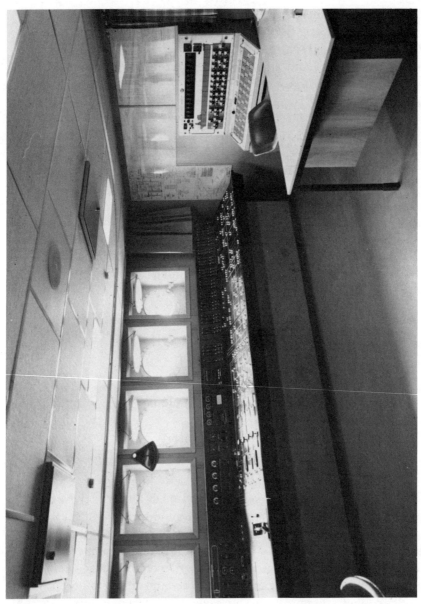

Fig. 4-7. Cargo control room of an older tanker. Traditionally, automated tankers have been equipped with a mechanical console fitted with manual switches and push buttons. (For comparison with a newer alternative, see figure 5-6.) Kockumation.

**Gate valves.** As the name implies, this type of valve employs a metal gate, fitted in grooves, which slides across the valve opening (fig. 4-8). The gate is fitted with a threaded spindle which connects to the valve stem. When turned by means of a handwheel, the spindle edges the gate slowly

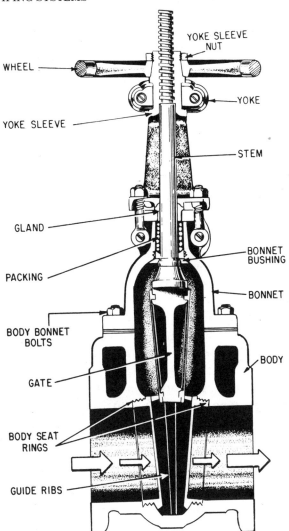

Fig. 4-8. Gate valve. U.S. Coast Guard.

upward or downward. It is necessary to turn the handwheel many times—perhaps 30 or more—to move the gate from fully open to fully closed. Gate valves are therefore too slow and cumbersome to be easily adapted to automatic control.

But they have advantages. They are dependable and durable. When fully open, the gate retracts into the valve body and offers no resistance to the flow of oil—a definite advantage over valves with swinging gates.

**Butterfly valves** are fitted with a swinging gate (fig. 4-9), which remains in contact with cargo even when the valve is fully open. Butterfly valves offer several advantages:

1. They operate easily and quickly ($\frac{1}{4}$ turn swings the gate from fully open to fully closed).
2. They adapt readily to automatic control.
3. They are more compact and less expensive than gate valves.

They also have several disadvantages:

1. It is generally more difficult to adjust cargo flow precisely with a butterfly valve than with a gate valve.
2. The valve gate remains in the center of flow, even when fully open, thus offering resistance and slowing the rate.
3. Butterfly valves tend to develop leaks more readily and need more frequent maintenance than gate valves.

**Globe valves** are not as common in cargo systems as gate and butterfly valves, but they are favored on some vessels. They operate as follows: A round disc is fitted on the end of a threaded stem and as the stem is turned with the handwheel, the disc wedges into the valve aperture, directly against the flow of oil. This action is a little like stopping a bottle with a cork. Globe valves tend to be difficult to operate in large sizes and at high pressures, and because oil must change direction as it flows through the valve, an undesirable pressure drop may occur on the outlet side. Nevertheless, globe valves are valuable whenever a precise throttling, or control of pressure, is desired.

**Angle valves** are basically globe valves in which the inlet and outlet flanges are turned at a 90-degree angle to each other, forming an elbow (fig. 4-10). Angle valves produce less resistance to flow than a globe-valve/elbow combination; they are therefore the economical choice when a valve is needed at a bend in a pipeline. Like globe valves, angle valves provide excellent throttling control in the partially open position.

### SPECIAL VALVES

Certain valves perform special functions in the cargo system:

**Check valves.** To prevent oil from backflowing into the tanks, a check valve is normally installed on the discharge side of each centrifugal pump.

Fig. 4-9 Butterfly valve. Valve Manufacturers Association.

Each valve contains a weighted or spring-loaded gate that swings up under pressure, allowing oil to flow out the discharge line. When the pump stops and pressure ceases, the gate swings shut against the valve seat, preventing oil from running back into the tanks.

Because check valves operate automatically, many officers tend to forget them or take them for granted. They are foolish to do so because check valves sometimes stick, causing spills when least expected.

You should never assume a check valve is working properly. Whenever the pumps are stopped, even temporarily, close the block valves at the manifold for sure protection against cargo backflow.

**Relief valves.** Each cargo pump is equipped with a relief valve and a short recirculating line. Whenever the pressure becomes excessive on the

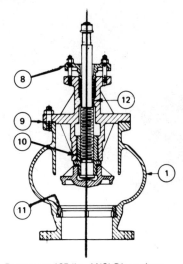

Flanges are 125 lbs. ANSI Dimensions.

| REF. NO. | NO. PCS. | PART |
|---|---|---|
| 1 | 1 | BODY |
| 2 | 1 | BONNETT |
| 3 | 1 | STEM |
| 4 | 1 | BONNET BUSHING |
| 5 | 1 | LOCK NUT |
| 6 | 1 | LOCK WASHER |
| 7 | 1 | DISC |
| 8 | 1 | GLAND |
| 9 | 1 | GASKET |
| 10 | 1 | LOCK PIN |
| 11 | 1 | SEAT RING |
| 12 | 1 | GUIDE BUSHING |
| 13 | 1 | HANDWHEEL (NOT SHOWN) |

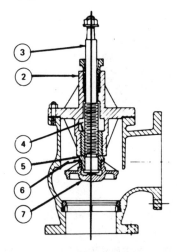

Fig. 4-10. Angle valve. Hayward Manufacturing.

discharge side of the pump, the relief valve opens and allows oil to recirculate to the suction side, thereby relieving the pressure.

## VALVE MARKINGS

On most tankers a system of one sort or another is used for marking valves and main-deck handwheels that operate valves inside the tanks. This practice reduces confusion and diminishes the risk of serious mistakes.

Pumproom valves are often numbered; numbers are stencilled on each valve and are also indicated on a plan kept in the ship's office. Manifold valves are sometimes marked to indicate which pumping system each line normally ties into (for example, No 1 pump—1, 2, 3, 4, across).

The marking of handwheels on the main deck is especially helpful because they operate valves remotely (a situation where crew members are most likely to become confused). Tank suction handwheels are commonly painted a characteristic color, such as bright green. In addition, the tank number may be stencilled on deck next to the handwheel (1C, 3P, 5S, etc.).

In the same manner, crossovers and master valves are distinguished by the color of their handwheels (for example, masters painted yellow; crossovers, red and white). Stripping valves may also be color coded.

## VLCC PIPING SYSTEMS

VLCC piping systems often resemble those used on smaller tankers. Pipelines, valves, pumps, and the tanks themselves are bigger, however, and the systems are more likely to be automated.

Some systems are unique to VLCCs. For example, a number of these big ships are fitted with a single pipeline, common to all tanks, that runs the length of the tank range. All of the pumps take suction through this line. Such an arrangement is possible because cargo separation is not a critical factor on crude carriers.

**Free flow systems.** On some VLCCs the main cargo piping can be bypassed. These ships make use of free flow systems, consisting of sliding gates at each tank bulkhead.

When these gates are opened, the usual stern trim of the ship causes oil to flow aft by gravity. Since the cargo pumps are located at the after end of the tank range, this arrangement allows efficient draining of the tanks with little or no need for stripping.

## INERT GAS (IG) SYSTEMS

Explosion is an ever-present risk on tankers. This is particularly true on tankers employing high-velocity, high-volume tank washing systems, and on those using crude oil washing (COW). For this reason most tankers over 20,000 dwt are now fitted with inert gas systems. These systems are designed to lower oxygen levels inside cargo tanks, thus inerting the atmosphere and making explosion impossible.

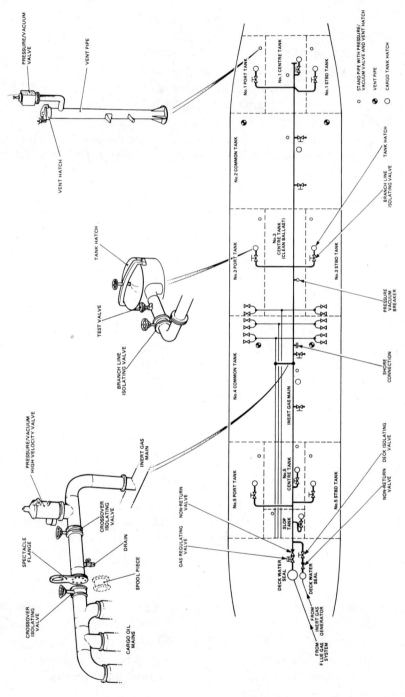

Fig. 4-11. Deck layout of inert gas and vent piping. Note that the ship shown here is fitted with an IG generator as well as a flue gas system. Permea Maritime Protection.

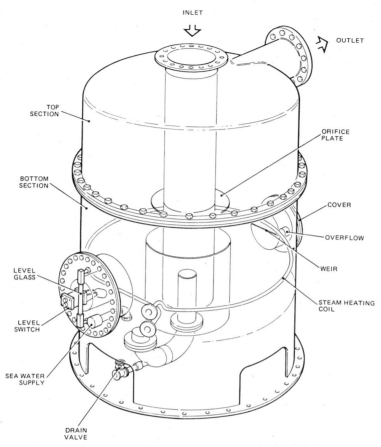

Fig. 4-12. Deck water seal. On ships with inert gas systems, the deck water seal prevents the backflow of hydrocarbon gas to the engine room. Permea Maritime Protection.

Flue gases from the ship's boilers (or in some cases from a special inert gas generator) are used for this purpose. These gases—mainly nitrogen and carbon dioxide—are cooled and filtered, then blown into the tanks with special fans. When properly inerted, the oxygen content of cargo tanks remains under 8 percent—well below the amount needed to fuel an explosion. See chapter 13 for a detailed discussion of inert gas systems.

## VENT SYSTEMS

When oil is loaded into an empty tank it displaces the air inside, causing a buildup of pressure. Similarly, when a full tank is discharged, oil leaving

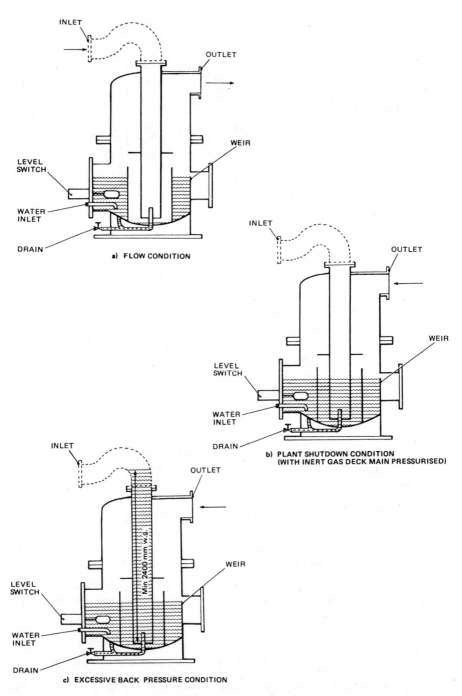

a) FLOW CONDITION

b) PLANT SHUTDOWN CONDITION
(WITH INERT GAS DECK MAIN PRESSURISED)

c) EXCESSIVE BACK PRESSURE CONDITION

Fig. 4-13. Deck water seal operation. Permea Maritime Protection.

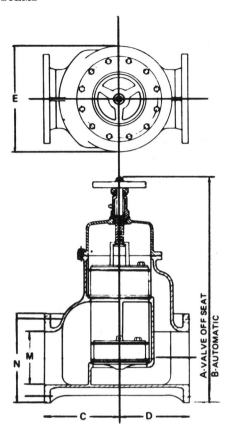

Fig. 4-14. Pressure-vacuum relief valve. Hayward Manufacturing.

the tank pulls a vacuum behind it. In order to equalize these pressure differences, a vent line is needed.

On a typical handy-size tanker, vent lines run from each tank to a single, larger line. This line carries the vapors to a mast riser, where they are vented well above the main deck. On ships with inert gas systems, the inert gas delivery line often serves a double purpose—it also acts as the vent line (see figure 13-13).

Vent lines are equipped with special valves called pressure-vacuum (PV) relief valves (fig. 4-14). In the *open* position, PV valves allow the free passage of air and vapors between tank and atmosphere. In the *closed* position, PV valves are designed to lift at a preset pressure or vacuum. Therefore, when a PV valve is closed, it effectively seals the tank (or tanks) on that line—unless a dangerous pressure or vacuum develops.

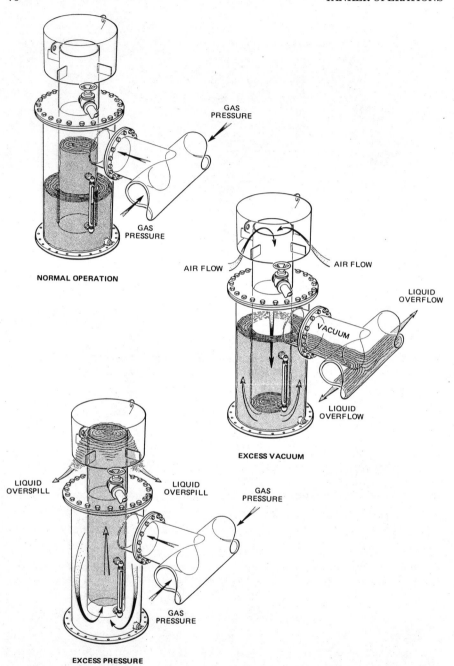

NORMAL OPERATION

EXCESS VACUUM

EXCESS PRESSURE

Fig. 4-15. Ships with inert gas systems are fitted with a liquid-filled PV breaker to protect the system from dangerous pressure or vacuum conditions. Permea Maritime Protection.

By sealing vapors inside the tanks, PV valves prevent the loss of cargo by evaporation. They also prevent the loss of inert gas and keep the IG system pressurized. (On ships with IG systems, the liquid-filled PV breaker provides an important backup to the mechanical PV valves—see figure 4-15.)

On some ships a single PV valve serves several tanks. On others, each tank is fitted with its own PV valve and, in some cases, its own high-velocity vent line allowing each tank to vent individually to atmosphere.

## VAPOR CONTROL SYSTEMS

Many ports in the world now prohibit the venting of hydrocarbon vapors from tankers. As a result, tankers calling at such ports must not only be fitted with a "closed" tank system; they must also be equipped with a means of dealing with vapors displaced by loaded cargo and ballast. Figure 5-3 shows how a typical vapor control system works. Such systems generally make use of the ship's inert gas system piping to route displaced vapors ashore through a special vapor line.

For a more thorough discussion of vapor control systems, see chapter 14.

# CHAPTER 5

# LOADING

MOST tanker spills occur while loading; therefore, the loading operation should command extra diligence from the ship's officers. Nearly all spills are preventable. Most are caused by human errors, with carelessness, impatience, and simple negligence leading the list.

## BEFORE LOADING

The prevention of spills starts before the first barrel of oil enters the tanks. In fact, before any cargo operation, loading or discharging, the ship's officers perform a series of inspections which greatly reduce the chance of cargo contamination, spills, explosions, and fires.

Some companies use a checkoff list for this purpose. This is an excellent practice, especially since the accidental omission of even one item could cause a disaster. A new officer would be wise to make a list and use it religiously, even if his fellow officers do not.

Such a list should include the following items, each to be checked carefully before starting any cargo operation:

**1. Scupper plugs.** Make sure all deck scuppers have been plugged.

**2. Sea suctions.** While checking the pumproom, make sure the sea valves have been lashed in the closed position. They should never be secured with locks.

**3. Hose connections** should be checked for tightness, making sure a drip pan is in place under each.

**4. "Bravo" flag and red light** must be displayed prominently.

**5. Cargo system lineup.** At least two officers should check the lineup, paying particular attention to crossovers and drops. The appropriate drops must be open and, if loading two or more products, the crossovers separating these systems must be closed.

Fig. 5-1. Loading at an offshore terminal. Many terminals use single-point moorings (SPMs) like the one shown here. Gulf Oil.

**6. Cargo tanks and tank valves.** Check that all tanks to be loaded are empty. Make sure each tank valve is closed, and remove the handwheel lashings from the tanks to be loaded. Tanks already containing cargo should be lashed closed in order to prevent accidental opening. In addition, it is a good idea to check void spaces, such as peak tanks and cofferdams, to make sure they are empty.

**7. PV valves** should be checked carefully. Whether PV valves should be open or closed depends upon the ship and the circumstances. For example, in ports where vapor emissions are prohibited, all PV valves must be closed. On the other hand, on a noninerted tanker loading in a port with no venting restrictions, they would be open.

**8. Pretransfer conference.** Find out the following from the terminal: In what sequence will the various products load? What loading rate can be expected? How many shore pumps will be used? How much notice does the terminal need before the cargo finishes? What signal should be used for shutting down? Will there be a line displacement?

**9. Mark hoses with chalk.** It is a good idea to mark each hose with the name of the product being loaded (some officers even draw an arrow indicating direction of flow). In the event of a spill or broken hose, it would be disastrous to shut down the wrong product (it has happened!). The simple precaution of marking each hose can save you from this kind of blunder.

**10. Mark cargo status board.** This is most often a chalkboard with a plan of the cargo tanks superimposed on it (fig. 5-2). Display this board in a prominent place, so that each watch stander can maintain a clear mental picture of all cargo activity. Mark the status of each tank with appropriate symbols indicating *open, closed, full,* or *empty.*

**11. Inert gas system.** Before loading begins, the inert gas system is normally secured. If loading in a port where venting of IG and hydrocarbon vapors is permitted, the mast riser bypass valve will be opened—thus allowing the inert gas to vent freely to the atmosphere as it is displaced by incoming cargo. (For a further discussion of inert gas systems and vapor control systems, see chapters 13 and 14, respectively.)

**12. Declaration of Inspection.** This form lists certain inspections that the law requires tanker crews to perform prior to transfer of cargo (fig. 5-4). It must be signed by each watch officer.

Make sure a copy of this form is posted in a prominent place in the ship's office; it is often the first thing Coast Guard officials look for during periodic inspections.

**13. Vapor control system.** In ports where the venting of petroleum vapors is prohibited, all PV valves and mast riser bypass valves must be closed. As vapors in the tanks are displaced by incoming cargo, they must be piped ashore to the vapor recovery unit—usually via the inert gas lines and a special vapor hose (see figure 5-3). It is important to make sure this system is lined up properly before loading commences. Also, vapor control procedures should be discussed thoroughly with the terminal ahead of time. See chapter 14 for a more detailed discussion of vapor control systems.

Fig. 5-2. The status of each tank is marked on a chalkboard. Chevron Shipping.

When all inspections have been completed, the ship is ready to load. Open the block valve at the manifold, plus the tank valve for each tank to be loaded. Note these on the status board and give the dock the "go ahead" to start loading.

### START CARGO SLOWLY

Begin the transfer slowly, making sure there are no leaks at the manifold. Confirm that cargo is actually entering the tanks by checking the control console ullage reading.

### REMOVING THE LIST

Some ships have a natural list, and this may cause problems when loading the wing tanks. Oil tends to gravitate toward the low side, causing a further tendency to list, which in turn causes more oil to gravitate, etc. Therefore, one of the first steps when loading should be to remove the list. This is done by loading cargo in a wing tank on the high side of the ship until the list has been removed.

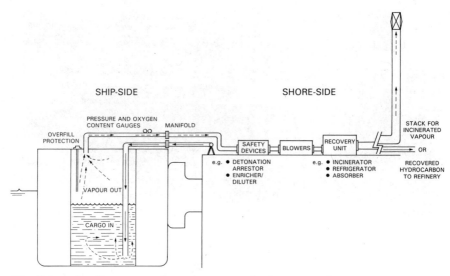

Fig. 5-3. As loading occurs, incoming cargo displaces petroleum vapors and inert gas already in the tanks. If operating in a port where vapor emissions are prohibited, vapors must be sent back ashore via the vapor control system. A schematic of a typical system is shown here. The inert gas system piping is used, with additional valving and connections, to route the displaced vapors to the ship's manifold, and then ashore, for collection and/or disposal. Oil Companies International Marine Forum.

## STRESS

Stress is a vital consideration on tankers, even alongside the dock. Virtually all tankers tend to hog when empty, so it is important to avoid loading cargo in the extreme ends without placing some weight in the middle. The best procedure is to spread the load more or less uniformly through the tank range, thus equalizing stress and preventing a dangerous hog or sag condition during the loading operation.

On large ships stress must be checked at regular intervals—even hourly—while loading. This is most often done with a loading calculator or computer (see chapter 7).

## LOADING THE CENTERS

There are many methods of loading a tanker—almost as many methods as there are tankermen. So it is difficult to generalize or offer a single procedure to fit all circumstances. However, one generality holds true: all loading methods strive to fill the tanks without spilling oil. If your method accomplishes this, it is probably a good one.

Some tanker mates prefer to load the center tanks first, but this is not an immutable rule. A tanker can be loaded quite successfully by the opposite method—wing tanks first, then the centers. In most cases the exact method used is dictated by the chief mate.

Center tanks are considerably larger than wing tanks, and the cargo level rises more slowly. It follows that centers offer a greater margin of safety when topping off. During the final phase of loading, this margin of safety can be valuable, especially when the terminal is slow shutting down. It is therefore advisable to save at least one center tank (preferably a slack tank) for last.

## LOADING THE WINGS

Wing tanks are small, relatively speaking. Depending on the ship, a wing tank may hold only one-third to one-half as much as a center tank. Wing tanks therefore tend to fill up more quickly than center tanks.

Some crude carriers are fitted with sluice gates between each wing tank and its adjacent center tank. In such cases it is possible to load center and wings simultaneously through a single tank valve in the center tank. As the center tank fills, cargo gravitates through the gates to the wing tanks, thus filling all three tanks as a unit.

## THE CHIEF MATE'S LOADING ORDERS

For the guidance of watch officers, the chief mate normally fills out a cargo plan with the following information: 1) products to be loaded in each tank, 2) final ullage for each tank, 3) gravity and approximate temperature for each product, 4) total barrels or cubic meters of each product, and 5) final draft and trim.

The mate posts this plan in a prominent place in the ship's office or cargo control room. In addition, he makes out a set of loading orders outlining the way in which he wants the cargo loaded (fig. 5-5) Here he specifies loading sequence and any special instructions he may have, such as important valves to be opened, closed, or lashed. He also notes which tank or tanks should be loaded last.

Each officer is expected to study these orders carefully before taking charge of the deck. Should any doubt arise about the loading orders, it is always best to call the chief mate and ask him to clarify the situation.

## Declaration of Inspection—Ship/Shore Safety Checklist Prior to Bulk Cargo Transfer

This is No Carbon Required paper.

| Vessel | | | |
|---|---|---|---|
| Transfer facility | | | |
| Port of | Date | | |
| Location | | | |

The following list refers to requirements set forth in 33CFR 156.120, 156.130, 156.150, 156.160 and 46CFR 35.35-30, U.S. Coast Guard and Atlantic Richfield Company's Terminal Regulations (see reverse side). The spaces adjacent to items on the list are provided to indicate that the detailed requirements have been met:

| | | Deliverer | Receiver |
|---|---|---|---|
| 1. Communication system/language fluency | (156.120 (q) (v)) | | |
| 2. Warning signs and red warning signals | (35.35-30) | | |
| 3. Vessels moorings | (156.120 (a)) | | |
| 4. Transfer system alignment | (156.120 (d)) | | |
| 5. Transfer system: unused components | (156.120 (e)(f)) | | |
| 6. Transfer system: fixed piping | (156.120 (g)) | | |
| 7. Overboard discharges/sea suction valves | (156.120 (h)) | | |
| 8. Hoses or loading arms condition | (156.120 (i)) (156.170) | | |
| 9. Hoses: length and support/equipment | (156.120 (b)(c)(j)) | | |
| 10. Connections | (156.130) | | |
| 11. Discharge containment system | (156.120 (m)(n)) | | |
| 12. Scuppers or drains | (156.120 (o)) | | |
| 13. Emergency shutdown | (156.120 (r)) | | |
| 14. Repair work authorization | (35.35-30) | | |
| 15. Boiler and galley fires safety | (35.35-30) | | |
| 16. Fires or open flames | (35.35-30) | | |
| 17. Lighting (sunset to sunrise) | (156.120 (y)(z)) | | |
| 18. Safe smoking spaces | (35.35-30) | | |
| 19. Spill and emergency shutdown procedures | (156.120 (w)) | | |

| | (156.120(s)(t)(u)) |
| --- | --- |
| 20. Sufficient personnel/designated person-in-charge at site | |
| 21. Transfer conference | (156.120(w)) |
| 22. Inert gas system in operation. (Indicate N/A if vessel/barge not equipped.) | |
| 23. Fire fighting equipment is properly laid out and readily available. | |
| 24. Emergency towing wires rigged, fore and aft. (Indicate N/A if barge). | |
| 25. Doors and ports are properly opened or closed (Indicate N/A if barge). | |
| 26. All flame screens properly fitted and in good condition. | |
| 27. Ventilators suitably trimmed with regard to prevailing wind condition. | |
| 28. Main transmitting aerials switched off. (Indicate N/A if barge). | |
| 29. Electric cables to portable equipment are disconnected from power. | |
| 30. Window type air conditioning units are disconnected. | |
| 31. No unauthorized craft alongside. | |
| 32. Pumproom bilges are dry and gas free. (Indicate N/A if there are no pumprooms.) | |
| 33. Agreement to begin transfer | (156.120(x)) |

I do certify that I have personally inspected this facility or vessel with reference to the requirements set forth in Section 35.35-30 and Atlantic Richfield Company's Terminal Regulations and that opposite each of them I have indicated that the regulations have been complied with.

| Person in charge of Receiving Unit | Title | Time and date |
| --- | --- | --- |
| | | |
| | | |
| | | |
| | | |

| Person in charge of Delivery Unit | Title | Time and date |
| --- | --- | --- |
| | | |
| | | |
| | | |
| | | |

Time completed

AMI—1540-C (8-90)     Front                                    Distribution: White–Terminal; Canary–Vessel

Fig. 5-4. Declaration of Inspection. A form similar to this one must be signed by each officer before taking charge of the deck. ARCO.

S.S. Shasta Valley          LOADING ORDERS          Voyage = _21_

| Product | API | T° | Gross | m | Net | BPT | Tons |
|---|---|---|---|---|---|---|---|
| Low Sulphur Fuel Oil | 21.5 | 145 | 444,824 | .9668 | 430,056 | 6.925 | 62,102 |
|  |  |  |  |  |  |  |  |
|  |  |  |  |  |  |  |  |
|  |  |  |  |  |  |  | Total 62,102 |

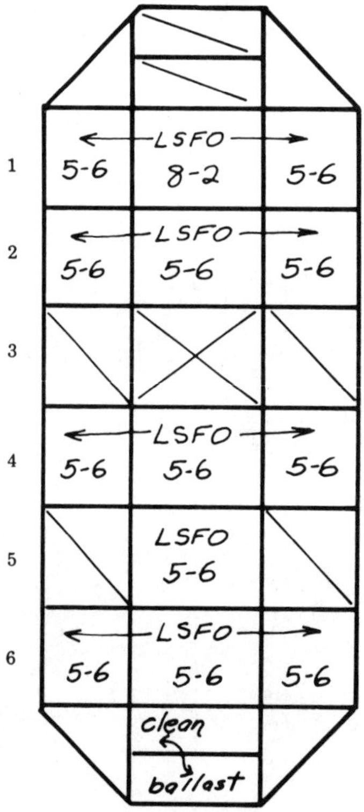

Draft:
  F: 39-09
  A: 42-07
  M: 41-02

① Load to outages shown; #1 Center is final tank.

② Take gauges every 2 hours & figure rates. Also dial tonnages into loading calculator every 2 hours & watch the stress.

③ Take temp. of cargo at the riser every hour & note on blackboard.

④ There will be a 3000 barrel line displacement at the end of loading; inform the shore when #1 Center reaches an outage of _11'9"_ so they can shift tanks.

⑤ Shore will be using 2 pumps. Have them take one off the line if the pressure gets too high.

⑥ For any questions or problems, call me. Otherwise call me about one hr. before cargo finishes.

J. Thomas C/M

Fig. 5-5. The chief mate's loading orders. Note that the term *outage*—as used here—is synonymous with *ullage*.

## THE LOADING WATCH

Therefore, the first step before taking over the loading watch is to study the chief mate's loading plan and orders. At this time you should also sign the Declaration of Inspection, if you have not already done so.

At the start of a loading watch, a good practice is to check every tank valve to make sure each is in the position indicated on the status board. Likewise, you should check the ullage of every tank, not just the ones being loaded. This simple precaution has prevented many spills.

Oil moving into or out of a "closed" tank could indicate several potentially serious problems: 1) a valve which has been opened by mistake, 2) a broken reach rod, 3) a jammed valve, and 4) a break in the below-deck piping. If this happens, shut down until the source of the problem has been found and corrected.

Fig. 5-6. Depending on the ship, the loading watch may be stood on deck, in the cargo control room, or—as shown here—on the bridge. The installation shown here enables the officer on watch to monitor cargo tank ullages, temperatures, stress, draft, trim, and inert gas pressure on a single screen. Cargo system valves can be operated by touching a light pen to the screen. Saab Marine Electronics.

**When in doubt, shut down.** Possibly the single most important thing for a new tankerman to learn is: *Never hesitate to shut down cargo operations.* Whenever in doubt, the first step should be to shut down. Do this *first;* then straighten out the problem. It is far better to lose a few minutes than risk a spill.

Shut down without hesitation in the following situations:

1. The pressure rises suddenly for no apparent reason.
2. You see oil in the water adjacent to the ship.
3. The hose fouls between ship and dock or begins to leak.
4. A tank valve jams.
5. You spot a fire on the dock or on another ship nearby.
6. The ship begins to drift away from the dock or the mooring lines become excessively slack.
7. A mooring line parts.
8. You smell smoke.
9. Another vessel approaches too closely.
10. Any other situation develops that could prove a hazard.

Anybody who wants to be a successful tankerman should engrave these words in his mind: *When in doubt, shut down.* Learn this, and you will keep the oil where it belongs—in the tanks.

### GOOD PRACTICES

As mentioned previously, it is difficult to cover all possible situations when giving advice on loading. However, certain precautions and practices are common to all loading watches. Here are a few:

**Watch the pressure.** Pressure on the cargo system is usually low at the start of loading; in fact, it may not register on the pressure gauges at all. As tanks fill up, pressure tends to rise slightly. This should be kept within established limits for the vessel.

Cargo pressure while loading is proportional to the number of open tank valves. Close a valve, the pressure rises; open one, it falls. It is thus possible to decrease the flow of oil to a full or nearly full tank by opening one or more empty tanks.

This technique is particularly helpful when topping off, since it slows the loading rate to a safe limit. In fact, it is often possible to stop the flow completely and gravitate cargo from a full tank to an empty one while still loading.

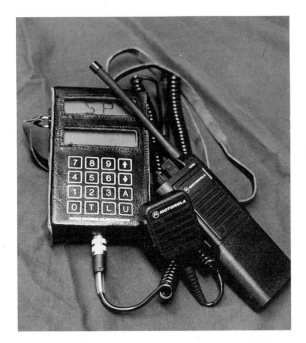

Fig. 5-7. This portable unit, used in conjunction with the Saab TankRadar ullaging system, allows the officer on watch to monitor tank ullages from any point on the ship within radio range. (It also displays temperature and inert gas pressure and indicates high and low level alarms.) The unit is connected to a walkie-talkie which, besides relaying the tank data to the unit, can be used for voice communication. Saab Marine Electronics.

**Never close off against shore pressure.** Keep at least one tank open at all times or you will run the risk of a broken hose and a bad spill.

**Watch the mooring lines.** As a ship fills with cargo, she sinks lower in the water. At most docks this causes the mooring lines to become slack. In conjunction with a falling tide, this tendency may cause the ship to drift rapidly away from the dock, with resultant risk of broken hoses and loading arms. For this reason, always keep a careful eye on mooring lines and tides. Don't hesitate to shut down, if necessary, while the sailors are tending lines.

**Two crew members on deck.** Practices vary, but it is generally a good idea to keep at least two people on deck, besides yourself, while loading. Most sailors are cooperative about this, as they should be—their job is to be on deck, not inside drinking coffee.

**Closing valves.** Make sure you and your watch use the proper method of closing manual tank valves. After closing, open one or two turns to flush the sediment from the valve seat; then close firmly, taking care not to jam. After closing any tank valve, manual or automatic, keep a careful eye on the ullage reading to make sure the flow of cargo has, indeed, stopped.

**Two-valve separation.** On ships carrying refined products it is extremely important to keep the various systems separated, so that incompatible products cannot mix: Considering the time, effort, and expense involved in the refining process, it is not surprising that tanker companies want to avoid contamination. Therefore, it is best to keep two closed valves between different cargoes whenever possible. This is an especially valuable procedure on old ships, where a single valve would be most liable to leak.

**Pumproom.** It is possible to load through the pumproom, if necessary, but the practice is generally avoided. If it is necessary for some reason to load through the pumproom, check frequently during the loading operation for leaks. It is rather embarrassing, not to mention dangerous, to fill the pumproom with cargo, and it has happened. Also, incompatible cargoes have been known to mix via open pumproom crossovers—check crossovers carefully before loading.

A more common practice is to bypass the pumproom by loading through drops on the main deck. In such instances, the pumproom is isolated by closing upper and lower block valves, thus protecting the pumproom from excessive pressures and possible leaks during loading.

**Ullages.** Remember that ullages are measured from an above-deck datum. A full tank may show an ullage of several feet.

**Finish cargo in a slack tank.** The practice of finishing in a slack tank is an excellent insurance policy against spills. If for some reason—such as communication failure, a jammed valve, failure of pump controls, or human error—the cargo flow is not stopped when the ship gives the "shut down" order, the extra room in a slack tank can prove to be a valuable asset.

**Hoses and loading arms.** Check for proper alignment and support. Remember that hoses and loading arms form a fragile bond between ship and shore. They are easily broken.

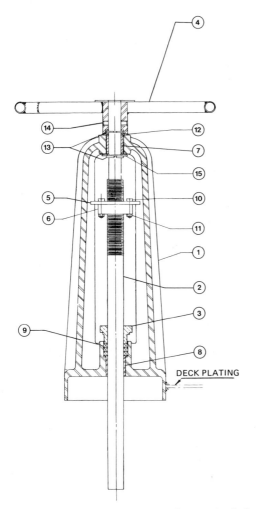

| NO. | PART |
|-----|------|
| 1 | BODY |
| 2 | STEM |
| 3 | GLAND |
| 4 | HANDWHEEL |
| 5 | INDICATOR PLATE |
| 6 | INDICATOR NUT |
| 7 | BUSHING |
| 8 | BUSHING |
| 9 | PACKING |
| 10 | HEX HEAD SCREW |
| 11 | LOCKNUT |
| 12 | THRUST WASHER |
| 13 | RETAINER |
| 14 | TENSION PIN |
| 15 | WASHER |

DECK PLATING

Fig. 5-8. Valve-operating stand on main deck. A metal reach rod connects the hand-wheel to a valve inside the tank. Each turn of the handwheel produces a corresponding turn on the valve. A threaded indicator, or *telltale,* registers the approximate number of turns the valve has been opened. Hayward Manufacturing.

**Heating coils.** Certain cargoes (heavy fuel oils, for example) must be heated during the voyage to the discharge port. Steam heating coils are used for this purpose. As tanks top off, the chief mate may want the watch officer to turn on the heating coils. Check with him if in doubt.

**Logbook entries.** The logbook is an important document. Tanker companies rely on it as a vital source of information, and officers can be certain

Fig. 5-9. Proper alignment of loading arms is essential to prevent damage to connecting flanges. Exxon.

their entries receive careful scrutiny in the main office. In that regard be sure to make entries required by government and company regulations. Include the following *times:* hoses connected/disconnected; start/ finish of each product; any delays in the loading operation and their cause.

**Smoking.** Make sure crew members smoke in authorized areas only. Be particularly wary of visitors and workers from ashore who may "light up" without thinking.

**Vessel security** has become an important consideration in recent years. Be careful not to allow unauthorized individuals aboard, and stay alert for suspicious activity on (or under) the water adjacent to the ship.

### OFFSHORE MOORINGS

With the steady increase in the size of tankers, a need developed for deep-water terminals to accommodate them. Many of these terminals are off-

Fig. 5-10. Safe loading requires accurate ullaging. Shown here is a mimic diagram from the Saab MaC/501 monitoring and control system (also illustrated in figure 5-6). Saab Marine Electronics.

shore moorings, where a ship ties up to one or more buoys in deep water well off the land. (When necessary, VLCCs can also be lightered to smaller vessels; see figure 5-11.)

Cargo is loaded/discharged through a special hose attached to a submerged pipeline. The pipeline runs along the sea bottom to a terminal or tank farm on the adjacent shore. There are basically two types of offshore moorings: multipoint and single-point.

**Multipoint moorings** have been in use for years and are common off the coast of the United States. A ship moors by dropping both anchors—one at a time and carefully spotted—and backing into a nest of five or more buoys (fig. 5-12). A mooring line is run from the ship to each buoy. The ship is thus held in position by the balanced tension of mooring lines and anchor chains.

Cargo is loaded through a submerged hose that descends to a pipeline on the seabed. Prior to loading, the hose is hauled aboard by means of a cable attached to a hose buoy in the mooring.

**Single-point moorings (SPMs).** Figure 5-13 illustrates a typical SPM. The ship makes her bow fast to the buoy, after which a floating hose is brought aboard and fastened to the manifold. Swivels allow the ship to pivot freely around the buoy with changes in wind and tide.

**Loading at an offshore mooring.** At an offshore mooring, proper communication is crucial, and the radio becomes a vital link between ship and terminal.

On nonautomated tankers, where the mate on watch spends most of his time on deck, portable radios are used. These can be carried from tank to tank. Automated vessels are normally equipped with a permanent radio installation in the cargo control room. (In addition, portable radios are often used for onboard communication between mate and sailors.)

The radio should be tested at regular intervals during each watch. Messages to the terminal should be spoken slowly and clearly. After each message, have the terminal repeat your instructions, especially when shutting down or changing the loading rate.

Radios sometimes malfunction, and so there should always be a prearranged emergency shutdown signal: usually one long blast of the ship's whistle.

At offshore moorings it is also important to keep an eye on the hose connection at the manifold. As a ship loads, she settles in the water; this

Fig. 5-11. Lightering operation at sea. A 209,000-dwt VLCC discharges part of her cargo to a smaller vessel (71,000 dwt). For the VLCC, this is basically a discharging operation; for the smaller vessel, a loading operation. Lightering is often used when VLCCs must enter shallow ports that cannot accept them fully loaded. Shell International Petroleum.

sometimes puts a kink in the hose. Should this happen, shut down until the hose can be cleared.

Another thing to watch is the pilot or accommodation ladder rigged for launch crews. This must be tended at frequent intervals to prevent submerging and resultant damage.

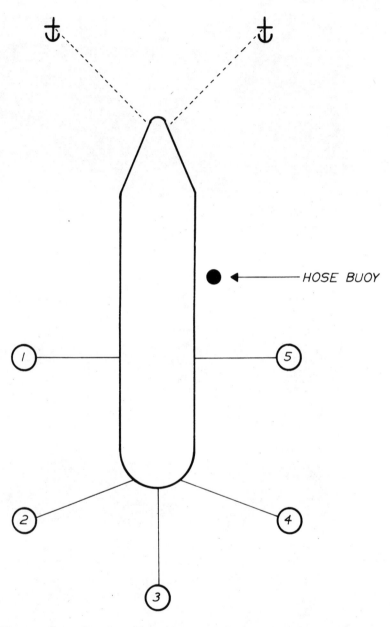

Fig. 5-12. Diagram of a multipoint offshore mooring. The ship's anchors are carefully positioned and dropped, one at a time, prior to backing into a nest of buoys.
A mooring line is run to each buoy. The ship is thus held in position by the balanced tension of mooring lines and anchor chains. A cable attached to the hose
buoy runs to a submarine hose, which is hauled up from the seabed with the ship's
hose boom.

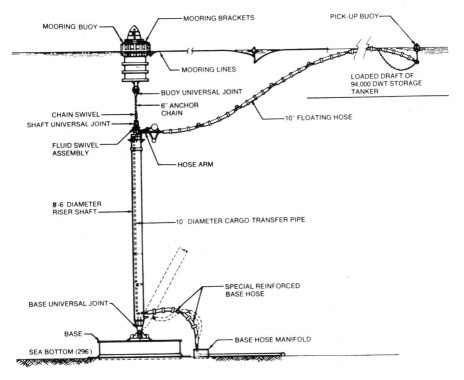

Fig. 5-13. Diagram of a single-point mooring used in the South China Sea.

## LINE DISPLACEMENTS

During the final phase of loading, the terminal may want to fill their pipe-line with another product, possibly in preparation for the next ship due at the dock. This is called a *line displacement.*

For example, if the pipeline from shore tank to ship holds 3,000 bar-rels, the terminal will ask to be notified when the ship's gauges indicate 3,000 barrels to go. At this point they will stop their pumps and switch tanks (or they may do a "flying switch"). By the time loading is completed, 3,000 barrels of new product will displace the old product and push it aboard the ship.

Generally speaking, the two products involved must be similar (two grades of gasoline, for example) so that a few barrels of mixing, which is inevitable, won't matter. On the other hand, lines containing heavy crude or fuel oil are often displaced with a light product, such as diesel. This is particularly true at offshore moorings where submerged hoses would otherwise become clogged by the heavier products.

Fig. 5-14. Portable radios are often used for communicating with the terminal and for onboard communication between mate and sailors. Chevron Shipping.

**Gauging a line displacement.** Let's assume the terminal has asked you to gauge a 3,000-barrel line displacement. You will have no trouble doing this as long as you load the last 3,000 barrels in one tank (the chief mate has probably specified which one).

Let's assume this tank is number 1 center, with a final ullage of 8′ 2″. With the calibration tables you determine that this ullage corresponds to 44,447 gross barrels (you need not be concerned with net barrels when figuring line displacements).

Since you want to stop the cargo 3,000 barrels short, you subtract this amount from the final figure for the tank: 44,447 − 3,000 = 41,447.

Referring to the calibration tables once again, you select the ullage that most nearly corresponds to 41,447 barrels: 11′ 9″ (see figure 5-15). Armed with this information, you watch the ullage at number 1 center until it reads 11′ 9″ (trim corrections can be ignored). At this point you signal the dock, indicating 3,000 barrels to go.

After the terminal switches tanks, you load the remaining cargo, bringing number 1 center to the final ullage of 8′ 2″. By the time you give the final signal to shut down, the shore line will be full of new product.

SS *Shasta Valley*

CARGO TANK #1 CENTER

| Ullage | Barrels | Ullage | Barrels |
|---|---|---|---|
| 8′ 00″ | 44586 | 10′ 00″ | 42914 |
| 01″ | 44517 | 01″ | 42843 |
| 02″ | 44447 | 02″ | 42774 |
| 03″ | 44377 | 03″ | 42705 |
| 04″ | 44308 | 04″ | 42635 |
| 05″ | 44238 | 05″ | 42565 |
| 06″ | 44168 | 06″ | 42495 |
| 07″ | 44099 | 07″ | 42426 |
| 08″ | 44029 | 08″ | 42356 |
| 09″ | 43959 | 09″ | 42286 |
| 10″ | 43889 | 10″ | 42217 |
| 11″ | 43820 | 11″ | 42147 |
| 9′ 00″ | 43750 | 11′ 00″ | 42077 |
| 01″ | 43680 | 01″ | 42008 |
| 02″ | 43611 | 02″ | 41938 |
| 03″ | 43541 | 03″ | 41868 |
| 04″ | 43471 | 04″ | 41798 |
| 05″ | 43402 | 05″ | 41729 |
| 06″ | 43332 | 06″ | 41659 |
| 07″ | 43262 | 07″ | 41589 |
| 08″ | 43192 | 08″ | 41520 |
| 09″ | 43123 | 09″ | 41450 |
| 10″ | 43053 | 10″ | 41380 |
| 11″ | 42983 | 11″ | 41311 |

Fig. 5-15. Gauging a 3,000-barrel line displacement. Loading is stopped at 11′ 9″, or 2,997 barrels short of the final amount. (A small discrepancy of 3 barrels is caused by rounding off to the nearest inch.)

## LOADING TO FINAL DRAFT

Unlike some types of merchant ships, tankers—most notably crude carriers—frequently load to the maximum draft permitted by law. In other words, many petroleum cargoes are heavy enough to load a ship "down to her marks."

Classification societies (such as the American Bureau of Shipping, Lloyd's Register of Shipping, and Norske Veritas) place draft marks on newly built vessels. When the chief mate draws up his cargo plan, he calculates the exact amount of cargo needed to submerge the ship to her marks. He must, however, work with information that may not be completely accurate. For example, final values for gravity and temperature often differ significantly from initial estimates. Then again, the chief engineer may have a few extra tons of fuel oil "up his sleeve."

With these potential inaccuracies in mind, it would not be surprising for the final draft to differ by several inches from the calculated value. Such a discrepancy causes one of two things: an overloaded ship, which is illegal, or an underloaded ship, which is less profitable for the company.

To avoid these pitfalls it is a practice on many tankers to monitor the draft from the dock during the final minutes of loading, signalling the terminal to shut down just as the ship submerges to her marks. As a rule, the chief mate does this while one of the other officers keeps track of the ship's tanks. (It is usually impossible to take an accurate draft at offshore moorings; the common practice is to rely on the calculated values.)

Before loading to draft, it is necessary to determine the specific gravity of the water alongside the ship. This value can often be obtained as a direct readout on the control console or computer terminal. On ships where such a readout is not available, it is necessary to take a sample of the water; the sample is then tested with a hydrometer to determine the specific gravity. The water sample should be taken within the final hour of loading, because the salinity of the water can change significantly with the tide. (For a discussion of fresh and dock water allowance, see chapter 7.)

## TRIMMING THE SHIP

Trim is often a vital consideration on tankers. For example, the master may want the ship flat for crossing a shallow bar. Then again, anticipating a large burnoff from after bunker tanks on a long voyage, he may want considerable stern trim.

In most cases the chief mate's calculations for trim are accurate. However, he must anticipate some variation, just as he did in loading to draft. It may therefore be necessary to adjust the final trim, in one of several ways: 1) by loading more cargo forward or aft, 2) by shifting cargo when loading has finished, 3) by shifting bunkers, or 4) by ballasting.

The last method would not be used on a fully loaded ship, but it could be used in the case of a partial load. In most situations the second method of shifting cargo is the easiest. This can often be done by *gravitation,* a technique that uses the natural tendency of oil to flow from a full tank to an empty or slack tank.

For example, if the ship has too much stern trim, simply open one or more full tanks in the after end of the ship, plus one or more empty or slack tanks in the midship or forward sections. Gravity will cause cargo to flow to the forward tanks. When the desired trim is reached, close the valves.

This technique is more apt to be used on a single-product ship where cargo separation is not a problem. On a multiproduct ship, the problem of shifting cargo may require a more complex lineup plus the use of one or more cargo pumps.

### AFTER LOADING

When the last tank has been topped off and secured, the vessel is made ready for sea. Hoses and loading arms are drained and disconnected. Cargo tanks are ullaged, and temperatures are taken. PV valves are closed, ullage covers are secured, and the inert gas system is pressurized.

The vessel is now ready to proceed to the next port and a different phase of the transfer operation—the discharge.

CHAPTER 6

# DISCHARGING

T HERE is a tendency among some officers to become complacent about discharging. Because cargo is flowing out rather than in, it seems less likely to spill. Unfortunately, this sense of security is unfounded. Discharging a tanker can be just as risky as loading one. To illustrate this fact, let's take a look at a hypothetical case that shows one way a spill might occur during discharging.

A small crude carrier arrives, fully loaded, at a refinery early one morning. Because of a problem in the terminal, there is a delay before discharging can begin. The third mate comes on watch at 0800. He confers with the terminal; they tell him they will be able to start receiving cargo at about 0900—they will let him know. With nothing better to do, the third mate leaves the deck and goes inside for some coffee. Taking the cue, the sailors on watch do the same.

In the meantime, the pumpman opens several tanks in preparation for the discharge. To save some time later, he also opens the manifold block valve. Then he, too, leaves the deck and heads for the engine room to do some work there. The deck is therefore deserted when crude oil begins to bubble out of number 8 center.

Although this case is hypothetical, quite a few such spills have actually occurred. Let's take a look at how it could happen. In our hypothetical situation, the shore tank is located on a hill above the ship. The valves to this tank are open, as are the valves on the dock. The oil thus can travel by gravity from the shore tank to the ship and, in this case, through the open manifold valve and into the tanks by means of a defective check valve in one of the pumps.

### PRETRANSFER CHECKOFF

As the foregoing story illustrates, a cargo watch while discharging demands as much vigilance as a loading watch. Devote as much care and effort to discharging as you would to loading and you will avoid serious problems. This effort starts with the pretransfer checkoff. As when loading, it pays to use a checkoff list (see chapter 5).

Fig. 6-1. Crew members prepare to hook up loading arms prior to discharging a VLCC. Shell International Petroleum.

Make sure scuppers are plugged, sea suctions closed and lashed, hoses securely bolted and supported, loading arms properly aligned, and warning signals displayed.

Check the lineup carefully. Drop valves must be closed; otherwise cargo could recirculate and cause a spill. In addition, check each tank valve and remove the handwheel lashings from tanks to be discharged. Mark the hoses and status board carefully, and sign the Declaration of Inspection.

Check with the terminal regarding cargo sequence, size of shore line, line displacements, and emergency shutdown signals. Will there be a booster pump on the shore line? If so, make sure they start it in the right direction (pumping oil *away* from the ship).

If your ship is equipped with an IG system, it must be operating before the discharge begins. The system will need to supply a steady pressure of inert gas to replace cargo drawn off during the discharge. Check the IG system carefully before pumping any cargo.

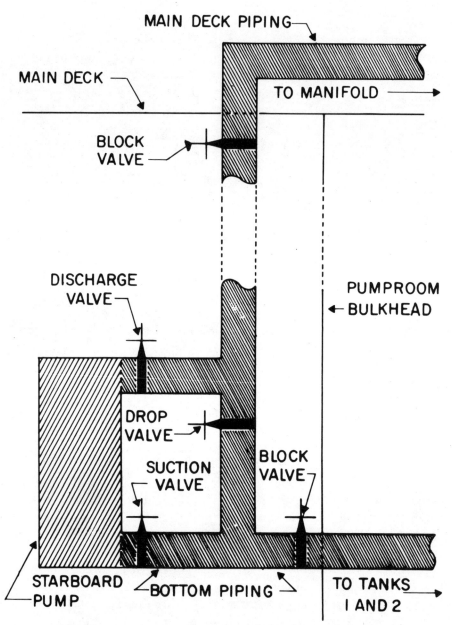

Fig. 6-2. Simplified diagram, side view, of the starboard pump, associated valves, and piping, as might be fitted in a three-pump pumproom. Bill Finhandler.

## THE PUMPMAN

As his title implies, the pumpman operates and maintains the cargo pumps. He goes into action anytime the pumps are used: while discharging, ballasting, tank cleaning, or whenever cargo is transferred between tanks.

His job is physically exhausting, and the hours are long. For this reason some ships carry two pumpmen. (Interestingly enough, with improved automation some ships now carry *no* pumpman—with a consequent increase in work for the deck officers.)

The pumpman must know the lineup intimately. He is potentially an excellent teacher. A new officer would do well to follow him through the cargo lineup, and stay by him during ballasting and tank cleaning. But a word of warning: No person is infallible, including the best pumpman. In the end, the officer on watch wields the authority and bears the final responsibility. If you suspect the pumpman is doing something unwise or illegal (like pumping bilge slops into the harbor at midnight), don't be afraid to speak up. He probably doesn't know the pollution regulations as well as you do. If a conflict should develop, call the chief mate and let him resolve it.

## TYPES OF CARGO PUMPS

Although the pumpman operates and maintains the pumps, it is important for the ship's officers to understand this equipment thoroughly. The following types of pumps are likely to be encountered on tankers: 1) reciprocating, 2) centrifugal, 3) rotary (such as gear or screw pumps), 4) jet (such as eductors), and 5) propeller.

Main cargo pumps are almost exclusively of the centrifugal type. Strippers are normally reciprocating or rotary pumps, or eductors. These pumps will be discussed in the following pages.

**Reciprocating pumps.** Until World War II, reciprocating pumps served faithfully as the primary means of discharging cargo. The subsequent development of efficient centrifugal pumps has largely eclipsed their use, but reciprocating pumps remain in service on many ships, mainly as stripping pumps.

A basic reciprocating pump consists of a piston—usually powered by steam—which slides back and forth in a cylinder. On the intake stroke the movement of the piston creates a vacuum, thus drawing oil into the cylinder through the intake valve. On the discharge stroke the piston forces oil

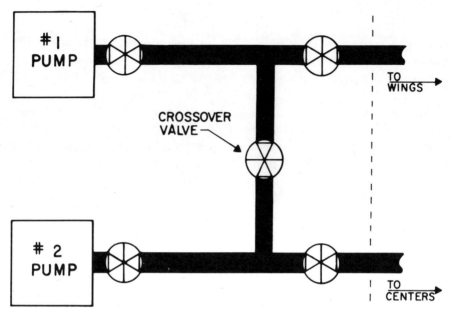

Fig. 6-3. Simplified diagram, top view, of a two-pump pumproom (bottom piping only). By opening or closing the crossover valve, pumps can be isolated or made "common." Thus, number 1 pump could be used in the center tanks or number 2 could be used in the wings. Similarly, both pumps could be made common and used to pump out a combination of wings and centers simultaneously. Note: A typical pumproom contains stripping pumps, bilge pump, ballast pump, and associated piping, valves, etc.—none of which are shown here. Bill Finhandler.

through the discharge valve, creating a pressure on the discharge side of the pump.

Early reciprocating pumps were of simple design, but eventually the more sophisticated duplex pumps came into use (fig. 6-5). These are essentially two pumps in one, designed so that the intake stroke of one synchronizes with the discharge stroke of the other. The result is greater capacity and smoother operation.

Reciprocating pumps are sometimes called *positive displacement pumps*. Unlike centrifugal pumps they need not be fed by gravity, and can pump a tank to the bottom until dry. This is an important advantage.

But reciprocating pumps have one serious drawback—they are slow. It would take days or even weeks to discharge a modern tanker with reciprocating pumps; time that translates into lost revenue. Today's tanker therefore requires a faster means of discharging cargo.

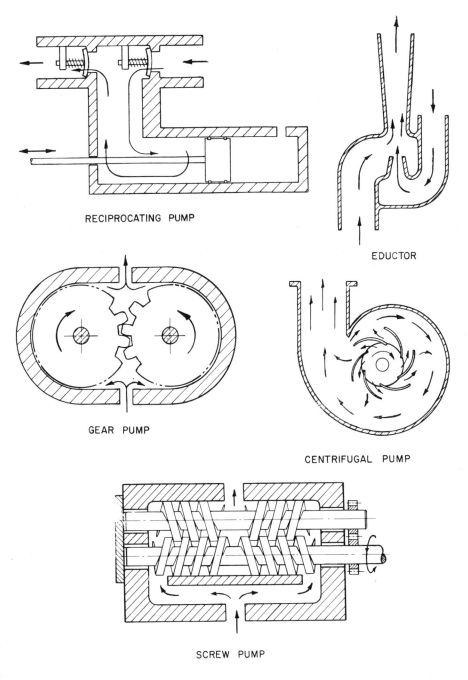

RECIPROCATING PUMP

EDUCTOR

GEAR PUMP

CENTRIFUGAL PUMP

SCREW PUMP

Fig. 6-4. Common types of pumps. U.S. Coast Guard.

**Centrifugal pumps** fill this need. These are continuous-flow, gravity-fed pumps, consisting of one or more spinning impellers. These impellers draw oil through a central inlet and hurl it outward by centrifugal force. This action creates a vacuum on the inlet side and pressure on the discharge side of the pump.

Centrifugal pumps cannot function without a continuous gravity flow of cargo. For this reason they are generally located in an after pumproom, thus using the normal stern trim to drain cargo more efficiently. From their position at the bottom of the pumproom, centrifugal pumps can draw cargo to within a meter or less of the tank bottom. If the pumps are *self-priming*—or if they are otherwise carefully primed by "cracking" a full tank—it is often possible to strip tanks with centrifugal pumps alone. Otherwise, it is necessary to remove the residue with a separate stripping pump. Centrifugal pumps are superior to reciprocating pumps in several important ways:

1. They pump more cargo in less time.
2. They are smaller, more compact, and easier to install.
3. They are less expensive.
4. They are more reliable and require less maintenance.
5. They produce a steady flow, rather than pulsating.
6. They produce less noise and vibration.
7. Since they are usually located in an after pumproom adjacent to the engine room, they can adapt to various power sources, including steam turbines, electric motors, and diesel engines. This is often accomplished as follows: a drive shaft runs from the engine room to each pump via a gastight gland in the engine room bulkhead, thus allowing the power source (an electric motor, for example) to be segregated from possible explosive vapors in the pumproom.

Centrifugal pumps are controlled in a variety of ways. For example, when steam turbines are used as the power source, the pumps are started and stopped by operating the turbine steam valves, either remotely from the cargo control room or manually at the turbine itself.

On some ships the pumps are controlled from the engine room; it is therefore necessary to call the engine room to start or stop a pump. This situation is one of many requiring good communication between deck and engine departments. Advise the engine room of your pumping plans well ahead of time.

When using centrifugal pumps always be careful to switch tanks in ample time to avoid losing suction. Learn the characteristics of your ship, and ascertain how low each tank can be taken before switching tanks

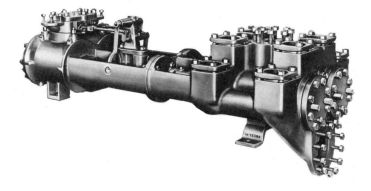

Fig. 6-5. Reciprocating pump. Worthington.

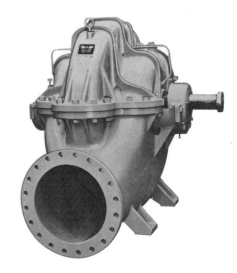

Fig. 6-6. Centrifugal pump. Worthington.

or—as is often done—priming the pump from a full tank. If allowed to run dry, a centrifugal pump will suffer serious damage in a matter of minutes; it might even explode. With experience, your ears will become sensitive to the high-pitched whine of a pump about to lose suction.

Many centrifugal pumps used on tankers are now *self-priming*. A typical system works in the following manner: When the pump loses suction, a venturi device automatically activates the system. The pump is primed from a recirculation tank as cargo is automatically recirculated through a special valve. At the same time, air is vented through an extraction line. When repriming is finished, the pump automatically resumes normal operation. These devices make it possible to take the tanks much lower with

Fig. 6-7. On this older automated tanker, pumps are operated from the console in the cargo control room. See figure 6-8 for comparison with a newer system. Shell International Petroleum.

the main centrifugal pumps, and when used carefully they virtually eliminate the need for stripping pumps.

**Deepwell pumps** are centrifugal pumps of special design used mainly on ships carrying a great diversity of refined products. Each pump is permanently installed above an individual cargo tank. The impeller is located at the end of a long vertical shaft extending to the bottom of the tank. The shaft is enclosed in a discharge pipe that carries oil from the impeller to the above-deck piping. This arrangement takes advantage of the speed and efficiency of a centrifugal pump while minimizing the disadvantages. Because the impeller operates so close to the bottom of the tank, it can discharge nearly all cargo before losing suction. Stripping is usually unnecessary. Cargo separation is therefore greatly enhanced in that only one pump is used for each tank so fitted.

Fig. 6-8. On some ships, the entire discharging operation can be controlled from a computer terminal. On the ship illustrated here, pumps and valves can be operated by touching a light pen to the screen, or by entering commands on the keyboard. Saab Marine Electronics.

**Eductors** work on a simple principle. A *driving fluid* is pumped down the main line, through a constriction, and past a relatively smaller opening, thus creating a vacuum (see figure 6-4). When eductors are used for clean ballast, the driving fluid is seawater. When used for stripping crude oil, the driving fluid is the cargo itself—delivered by means of a bypass from one of the main cargo pumps. When used for stripping tank washings, the driving fluid is often drawn from the slop tank—and then recirculated back to the slop tank in a closed system. In the latter case the driving fluid is either crude oil or seawater, depending on the tank cleaning method.

Eductors are simple and rugged, have no moving parts, and do not become air-bound like other types of pumps. They are widely used on tankers of all types and sizes.

## PRIMING THE PUMPS

Both reciprocating and centrifugal pumps occasionally become air-bound and fail to pick up suction on a tank. In such instances it is necessary to prime the pump from a full tank or, in some cases, to bleed air from the discharge side of the pump by opening a vent cock.

Centrifugal pumps will not operate properly unless a steady flow of cargo is provided. If air is allowed to get into the lines, pumps will lose suction in short order. Therefore, when tank levels get low, there is always the danger of losing suction. If suction is lost completely and a pump "trips," it is best to restart the pump in a full tank. It should regain suction again quickly. As previously noted, many pumps are now fitted with self-priming systems, which reduce this problem considerably.

As stated above, it is sometimes possible to strip tanks with centrifugal pumps by priming from a full tank which has been "cracked" open a few turns. At the same time, the tank suction valve should be closed down partially. This is a delicate task, requiring skill and practice. If done improperly, pumps can be damaged severely.

Reciprocating pumps are designed to operate efficiently at a given speed, with a typical maximum of 30 to 32 double strokes per minute. When stripping the last few barrels from a tank, the pump tends to draw in air from the surface of the oil. To avoid this—and resultant loss of suction—reduce pump speed and pinch down the tank valve. This will lower the gate of the valve below the level of the oil, thus excluding air from the valve aperture.

On smaller tankers without inert gas systems, a helpful trick is to listen at the ullage hole. A gurgling noise from inside the tank indicates the pump is sucking air. When you hear this noise, pinch down the valve until the gurgling stops. When it resumes, pinch down some more. In this manner you will keep the edge of the valve gate below the surface of the oil. (Of course, this technique cannot be used in ports where vapor emissions are prohibited, because all tank openings must be secured.)

There are times, however, when loss of suction is unavoidable. When this situation arises—and no full tank is available for a prime—slow the

Fig. 6-9. Cargo control console for a 90,000-dwt tanker (San Clemente Class). Level in the tanks is indicated on the top row instruments. Open and closed valve positions are shown by the lights on the ship's mimic diagram. The ballast and cargo and stripping pump speeds and pressures are regulated from the controls below the mimic area. Ballast and cargo valves are operated by push-button controls, which are also located on the mimic area of the console. Paul-Munroe Hydraulics.

pump and bleed air by opening the vent cock. In most cases the pump will regain suction immediately.

Reciprocating pumps, like centrifugal pumps, make a characteristic sound when losing suction. Each pump is a little different, but they all tend to race when sucking air. When you hear a reciprocating pump losing suction, quickly reduce the speed of the pump and begin pinching down the tank valve.

## DISCHARGING PROCEDURE

There are as many ways to discharge a tanker as there are to load one, and so no step-by-step instructions can be given. However, certain principles apply to all discharging watches.

These include:

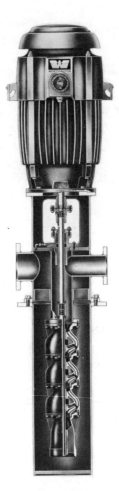

Fig. 6-10. Deepwell pump. Worthington.

**Get the bow up.** It is usually best to start the discharge in the forward tanks. This lifts the bow and provides a better suction head to the pumps. With increased trim, the tanks drain more effectively while stripping.

**Strip residual oil into a single tank.** Stripping pumps are not powerful enough to move cargo against the high pressure of large centrifugal pumps. Therefore, instead of trying to strip ashore against the main line pressure, it is standard practice to accumulate stripped oil in one tank on board the ship. Thus accumulated, most of it can be discharged with the main cargo pumps. The last few barrels can be stripped ashore after the main pumps shut down. Often, the aftermost center tank (which adjoins

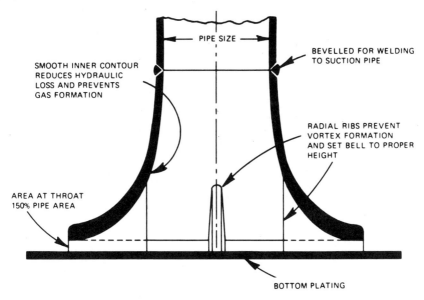

PIPE SIZE

BEVELLED FOR WELDING
TO SUCTION PIPE

SMOOTH INNER CONTOUR
REDUCES HYDRAULIC
LOSS AND PREVENTS
GAS FORMATION

RADIAL RIBS PREVENT
VORTEX FORMATION
AND SET BELL TO PROPER
HEIGHT

AREA AT THROAT
150% PIPE AREA

BOTTOM PLATING

Fig. 6-11. Tank piping flares into a suction bell-mouth at the end of each branch line. The bell-mouth allows pumps to draw suction very close to the bottom of the tank. This is vital during stripping, when air tends to leak into the line. The design of the bell-mouth also helps to prevent eddies, or whirlpools, from forming around the intake. Hayward Manufacturing.

the pumproom) is used for this purpose. A special filling line runs from the stripping system into the tank.

This tank is normally full at the start of discharging. It is therefore necessary to pump it down partway before stripping into it. Later in the discharge as the strippers pump residues into the tank, causing the level to rise, it may be necessary to pump out additional cargo with the main pumps. Always watch this tank carefully. If left unattended it could easily overflow and cause a spill when least expected.

**Check pumproom frequently.** Make regular inspections of the pumproom, checking for leaks and excessive vapor accumulation. (This is also a good idea while loading.) Check the pumps for smooth operation and make sure the drive-shaft seals, where the pump drive shafts enter the engine room, are not overheating.

A gassy pumproom can kill you. Before entering, always make sure the ventilation system is operating. Have a sailor stand by topside while you're below, in case you should be overcome by vapors (pumproom gassing is perhaps the most common serious accident on tankers). This simple precaution has saved numerous lives.

Fig. 6-12. Shifting tanks on a small, coastwise tanker. The smaller handwheel operates the stripping valve. Chevron Shipping.

**Two-valve separation.** If possible, keep at least two closed valves between systems containing unlike cargoes.

**Watch the pressure.** While discharging, pressure on the cargo system is normally much higher than it is while loading. As a typical example, a product carrier might discharge with a manifold pressure of 8.5 kg/cm$^2$ (121 psi). Later, while backloading at the same terminal, the manifold pressure might be 1.0 kg/cm$^2$ (14 psi).

Pressure should be monitored carefully, because it tends to change, sometimes appreciably, as tanks are topped off in the terminal. Be prepared to change pump speed or place additional or fewer pumps on the line.

**Chief mate's discharging orders.** The chief mate generally writes a set of discharging orders detailing sequence, pumps to use, maximum pressure, key valves to open or close, and anything else he thinks important. Study these orders carefully before taking charge of the deck.

**Logbook entries.** Pay the same scrupulous attention to logbook entries as you would while loading.

Fig. 6-13. Saab MaC/501 "cargo systems discharge" mimic diagram. Various mimic diagrams, accessed by means of a menu on the screen, allow the officer on watch to monitor and control the entire discharge from one location. Saab Marine Electronics.

**When in doubt, shut down.** Learn the location of the emergency shutdown switches, or similar controls, for each pump—and don't be afraid to use them.

**Tape floats.** After the discharge of heavy or sticky products such as bunker fuel, ullage tape floats tend to stick to tank bottoms. If your ship is fitted with a tape-float system—and you suspect the floats may stick—have the pumpman or another crew member roll up the tapes.

**Heating coils.** To avoid damage to the heating coils, turn off the steam to individual tanks well before each is empty.

**Mooring lines.** At most docks, mooring lines tend to tighten as the ship rises. A rapidly rising tide combined with a fast discharge could easily part one or more lines. Watch the mooring lines carefully and, if necessary, shut down while the sailors tend them.

**Stress.** In July of 1980 the VLCC *Energy Concentration,* while discharging a cargo of crude oil in Europort, the Netherlands, broke in half. The discharge had been started in the tanks amidships, leaving the forward and aft tanks full. As the middle of the ship was emptied, a dangerous hogging stress developed, with disastrous consequences. Luckily, only a small amount of oil was spilled, and the two halves of the ship were re-floated and salvaged.

As the foregoing illustrates, it is important to plan the discharge carefully to avoid excessive stresses on the hull.

**Booster pumps.** When a shore tank is located at a great distance from the ship, or on top of a hill, an additional pump or pumps are frequently put into use along the shore line. This helps to reduce pressure and increase the rate of discharge. In general, the terminal waits until the ship has started discharging before putting booster pumps on the line.

Whenever a booster pump is to be used, be sure to start the discharge slowly. Watch the pressure; it should drop sharply within a few minutes, indicating the booster pump is on the line. It is now safe to increase the discharging rate by speeding up the ship's pumps or placing more pumps in service. If, however, the pressure *rises* sharply when the booster pump is brought on the line, immediately shut down the ship's pumps and close the manifold valves. The terminal has lined up the booster pump in the wrong direction (a not unheard-of occurrence) and is pumping oil *toward* the ship.

**Draft, trim, and list.** As previously noted, it is generally helpful to get the bow up during the discharge. However, trim should not be excessive, and it should be monitored carefully. Often a direct readout of trim and draft is available in the control room or on the bridge (such as the mimic display shown in figure 6-14).

Control of list is essential during the discharge, especially while stripping. When a ship is allowed to list excessively, residual oil pools on the low side of the tanks, where it may not drain properly to the bell-mouths. As a result, an unacceptable amount of oil is left in the tanks. To avoid such pitfalls, list must be carefully controlled. This is done mainly by keeping each pair of wing tanks even, a task that requires careful observation and adjustment. However, this in itself may not be enough to keep the ship from listing. For example, a temporary list is often induced when the engineers shift bunkers or water from one side of the ship to another. Then again, some tankers are built with a natural list (caused by a slight imbalance in the arrangement of engine room machinery). In such situations, you must compensate by counterbalancing a single pair of wing tanks. For example, you might choose number 5 wings to eliminate a port list. This would be accomplished as follows:

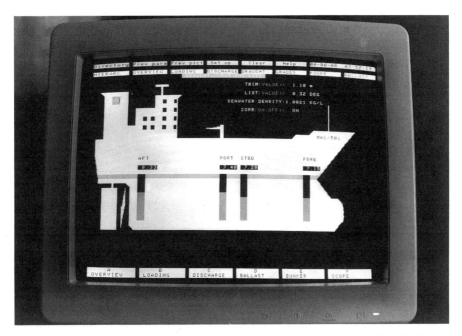

Fig. 6-14. Trim and list should be monitored carefully throughout the discharge. Often a direct readout of draft, trim, and list is available in the cargo control room or on the bridge. Saab Marine Electronics.

Pump out number 5 port until the ship straightens herself; then close number 5 wings, port and starboard. If a new list should develop, use these two wing tanks to straighten the ship by pumping cargo from the low side. Save number 5 wings to be discharged last, so that positive list control can be maintained throughout the discharge.

**Inert gas systems.** During the discharge the inert gas system operates continuously. As cargo leaves each tank, an equal amount of inert gas must take its place; otherwise a vacuum will form, drawing air into the tanks. IG systems are designed to maintain a given pressure of inert gas inside the tanks. *Watch the pressure carefully.* If it falls too low, it may be necessary to slow down the cargo pumps until the IG pressure builds back up to an acceptable level. Carefully monitor the oxygen indicator in the cargo control room. Make sure the oxygen content does not exceed permissible limits for your ship (generally below 5 percent). For a discussion of inert gas systems, see chapter 13.

**Controlling vapor emissions.** If discharging at a port where the venting of hydrocarbon vapors is prohibited, it is important that all ullage

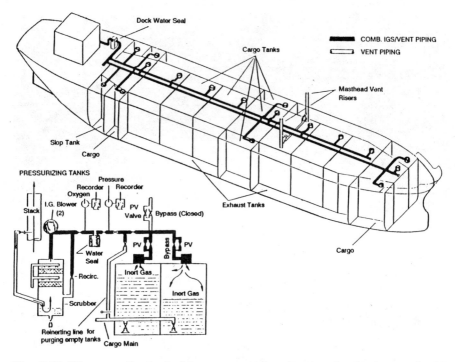

Fig. 6-15. Diagram of a typical inert gas system. During the discharge, the IG system operates continuously. Inert gas pressure and oxygen content must be monitored carefully throughout the discharge. Reprinted with permission from *Controlling Hydrocarbon Emissions from Tank Vessel Loading*, 1987. Published by National Academy Press, Washington, DC.

covers and other tank openings be secured. As cargo is discharged, it is typically replaced by inert gas supplied by the IG system. However, if the ship is loading and discharging at the same time, or—more commonly— ballasting and discharging at the same time, the situation becomes more complicated. One technique that has been used successfully is called "vapor balancing," in which vapors displaced from tanks being ballasted are transferred to tanks that are being discharged (fig. 6-16). However, the decision to use such a technique should only be made by an officer who is familiar with company procedures and local regulations. See chapter 14 for a detailed discussion of vapor control systems.

## SPILLS

Spills are less common while discharging than while loading, but they still occur. Several situations can lead to a spill:

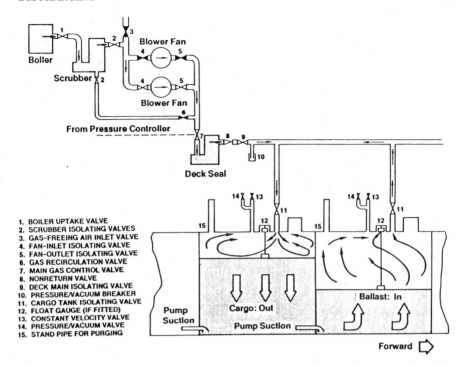

1. BOILER UPTAKE VALVE
2. SCRUBBER ISOLATING VALVES
3. GAS-FREEING AIR INLET VALVE
4. FAN-INLET ISOLATING VALVE
5. FAN-OUTLET ISOLATING VALVE
6. GAS RECIRCULATION VALVE
7. MAIN GAS CONTROL VALVE
8. NONRETURN VALVE
9. DECK MAIN ISOLATING VALVE
10. PRESSURE/VACUUM BREAKER
11. CARGO TANK ISOLATING VALVE
12. FLOAT GAUGE (IF FITTED)
13. CONSTANT VELOCITY VALVE
14. PRESSURE/VACUUM VALVE
15. STAND PIPE FOR PURGING

Fig. 6-16. When discharging and ballasting at the same time, vapors displaced by incoming ballast can be transferred to tanks discharging cargo. Reprinted with permission from *Controlling Hydrocarbon Emissions from Tank Vessel Loading*, 1987. Published by National Academy Press, Washington, DC.

**Broken hose or loading arm.** This is a too-common occurrence, caused by defective equipment, improper support, or excessive pressure.

**Improper lineup.** An open drop valve on a discharge line will cause cargo to recirculate to the tanks—where it could overflow.

**Defective check valve.** Centrifugal pumps are fitted with check valves to prevent oil from gravitating through the pumps and into the tanks. These check valves are not infallible and they sometimes stick. If the manifold valves are opened several minutes before starting the pumps, back pressure from the shore line could force cargo through the pump and into the tanks. A slight backflow to a full tank could easily cause a spill. With this in mind, *always leave the manifold block valves closed until ready to start discharging.*

**Gravitation.** When a tanker is trimmed by the stern, cargo tends to gravitate toward the after tanks. Thus, if full tanks forward and aft are opened several minutes before starting the pumps, cargo will have time to flow aft and could cause a spill. Therefore, *leave tank valves closed until ready to start discharging.*

**Overflow of stripping fill tank.** Keep a careful watch on the tank used to accumulate stripping residues. Never allow it to fill above a safe level.

### LINE DISPLACEMENTS

On light-oil product carriers, the first phase of the discharge sometimes occurs while still docked at the loading port. This is the pump and line flush. A small amount of oil is discharged with each pump (into the terminal slop line), thus flushing the discharge piping and assuring that each pump and its system are full of the correct product. If the pumps are to discharge more than one product, care should be taken to flush with the first product in the discharging sequence. When a ship arrives at her port of discharge, the terminal sometimes asks for an initial line displacement. This procedure clears the shore line of other products. In order to facilitate gauging, it is best to restrict the discharge to a single tank during the line displacement. (Chapter 5 describes the procedure for gauging a line displacement). Line displacements are also common at the end of the discharge, particularly on black-oil ships. Many heavy fuel oils and some crudes solidify to the consistency of shoe polish when allowed to cool; they can clog pipelines unless flushed clear. A ship loaded with such a cargo will therefore carry on board a tank of diesel or other light stock for the final line displacement. After all cargo has been discharged and stripped, the light stock is flushed through the ship's pumps and pipelines and is then pumped ashore. This clears the heavy oil from all lines, both on board and in the terminal.

CHAPTER 7

# PLANNING THE LOAD

How many tankers have been lost as a result of improper cargo planning? Nobody knows. But this much is clear: Tankers show an alarming tendency to break in half during heavy weather. An improperly distributed load greatly augments this tendency.

Cargo planning is essential on tankers, just as it is on other types of merchant ships. But while transverse stability is a constant concern on—for example—containerships, it is not generally a factor on tankers. (By virtue of their design, most tankers are inherently stable.) However, another important factor comes into play—*stress*. Loads must be carefully spread through the tank range to minimize the shear and bending stresses on the hull. A tanker's steel hull will bend with remarkable elasticity, but if bent too far, it will break. Stress is not the only consideration. In addition, the ship must be loaded to a proper draft and trim. Unlike cargoes must be assigned to separate tanks and, if necessary, to separate systems.

## THE VOYAGE ORDERS

The chief mate normally decides how these problems are to be dealt with, and it is his responsibility to draw up the final loading plan. The decision is not his alone, however. The ship's owner or charterer specifies (by radio or satellite) how much cargo to load and, frequently, which tanks to put it in. Experienced cargo planners in the company's main office work out each load in advance.

Voyage orders are often sent to the ship in code for the purpose of speed and economy. After decoding, a typical set of orders might read as follows:

SS *Shasta Valley,* voyage 21. Proceed Barber's Point, Hawaii. July 1 load approximately 62,000 tons low sulphur fuel oil. API 21.5, temperature 145. Tanks 1 across, 2 across, 4 across, 5 center, 6 across. Oncarry 1300 tons clean ballast in afterpeak and after clean ballast tanks. Bunkers 1400 tons. Water 210 tons. Discharge entire cargo Long Beach, California. Tentative orders voyage 22: load Drift River, Alaska; discharge Los Angeles.

Fig. 7-1. Heavy weather generates tremendous bending stresses on a tanker's hull.

These orders should never be followed blindly, because cargo planners are human and make mistakes. The chief mate must check their figures; he bears the final responsibility for the load.

At this point we should note the role of junior officers in cargo planning. Although the chief mate shoulders most of the responsibility, it is important for the second and third mates to develop a thorough understanding of the procedures involved.

As a junior officer, you should make every effort to learn about cargo planning. First of all, this knowledge will help you to perform your own duties more efficiently. For example: stress, draft, and trim must be checked at frequent intervals—even hourly—during loading and discharging on many ships. This task must be performed by the mate on watch, usually a second or third mate. In addition, a thorough knowledge of cargo planning is essential for eventual promotion to chief mate, and finally, to master.

## LOAD LINES AND ZONE LIMITATIONS

Early in the history of seafaring, sailors and shipowners recognized the importance of cargo planning, which included strict limits on the total weight carried each voyage. These early seafarers realized that an overloaded ship, although carrying more potential revenue, rode dangerously low in the water.

As long ago as 2500 B.C., Greek vessels were required to undergo loading inspections before venturing into the Mediterranean. During the Middle Ages, the city-state of Venice enforced similar laws on her vessels—each marked her load line with a cross painted on the hull. The Scandinavians were equally careful; in the fierce gales of the North Sea their lives depended on it. A Swedish law written in 1288 declares: "If goods are loaded above the load line, the owner must either put the excess goods ashore or pay a fine."

But it was not until the nineteenth century that a universal standard for load lines began to emerge. Samuel Plimsoll, a member of the British Parliament and an ardent crusader for seamen's rights, pushed for the adoption of stringent load line regulations. Against stiff opposition, he succeeded.

The first of these laws came from Parliament in 1876, and by the time of Mr. Plimsoll's death in 1898 virtually every maritime nation had followed Great Britain's example. Today we still refer to a vessel's load line as her "Plimsoll mark" in remembrance of Samuel Plimsoll.

Standards for today's ships are set by the International Convention on Load Lines, 1966. (A recent protocol to the 1966 convention, not yet ratified at this writing, will make slight changes to the requirements.) These international standards, drawn up by the maritime nations of the world, have been incorporated into federal laws, which are enforced by the U.S. Coast Guard. When a ship is new, the appropriate load line markings are

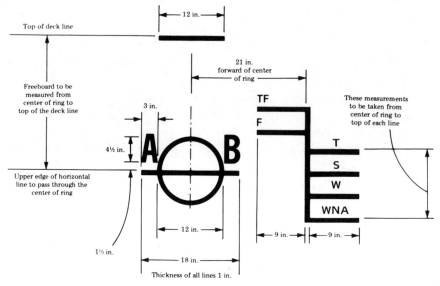

The center of the ring is to be placed on each side of the vessel at the middle of the length as defined in the Load Line Regulations. The ring and lines are to be permanently marked, as by center punch, chisel cut or bead of weld.

| A B | American Bureau of Shipping |
| T F | Tropical Fresh Water Allowance |
| F | Fresh Water Allowance |
| T | Load Line in Tropical Zones |
| S | Summer Load Line |
| W | Winter Load Line |
| W N A | Winter North Atlantic Load Line |

Fig. 7-2. Load line markings for oceangoing vessels. These are placed amidships on both sides of the hull. The American Bureau of Shipping is authorized to assign load lines to vessels registered in the United States and other countries. American Bureau of Shipping.

etched permanently on her hull (both sides, amidships) by an authorized classification society. In the United States this task is performed by the American Bureau of Shipping (ABS). In the United Kingdom it is done by Lloyd's Register of Shipping. Each mark corresponds to a given *displacement,* or total tons of water displaced by the vessel. This tonnage is exactly equal to the weight of the loaded ship. Marks are provided for Tropical, Summer, Winter, and Winter North Atlantic zones for fresh and salt water. (Because salt water is more buoyant than fresh, allowance is made for the extra sinkage in fresh water—the *fresh water allowance.*)

Fig. 7-3. American Bureau of Shipping inspectors check a vessel's load line markings. American Bureau of Shipping.

This system permits vessels to load more deeply in regions of predominantly fair weather and during seasons when good weather can be expected (see figure 7-5). For example, a tanker loading in Valdez, Alaska (Winter Seasonal Zone) on December 1st would load to her winter marks.

In contrast, a ship loading in Rio de Janeiro, Brazil (Tropical Zone) would be allowed to load to her tropical marks.

**Zone allowance.** However, a ship that has loaded to her tropical marks in Rio de Janeiro is unable to venture north or south into the Summer Zone without violating the law. She is governed not only by the zone in which she loads, but also by those through which she must sail. If her course takes her through the Summer Zone, *she must not be loaded below her summer marks at any time while inside that zone.*

The trick is to load maximum tonnage allowable while making sure the ship will not be overloaded as she sails from one zone to another. Allowance can be made for the burnoff of bunker fuel and consumption of fresh water while steaming toward the *controlling zone* (that is, the strictest zone through which the vessel must sail).

Thus the *zone allowance* represents the extra tonnage a vessel may load beyond that permitted by the controlling zone. This figure is easily calculated on the basis of bunker fuel burnoff and water consumption. For example:

A tanker loads at a terminal within the Tropical Zone. She will enter the Summer Zone approximately nine days after departing the loading port, and the approximate burnoff at sea speed is 50 tons/day. Water consumption is 10 tons/day. How many tons may she load beyond that allowed by her summer load line? By simple arithmetic:

$$\text{Zone allowance} = 9 \text{ days} \times 60 \text{ tons/day}$$
$$= 540 \text{ tons}$$

Note that a ship sailing in the other direction (that is, from Summer Zone to Tropical Zone) would not require this calculation; she would already be in the controlling zone.

## IMPORTANT TERMS

In order to provide a clear understanding of cargo planning on tankers, a few terms should be explained at the outset:

**Deadweight.** This is the total weight of cargo, plus crew, stores, water, fuel, and ballast on board at a given time.

**Displacement.** When a ship floats freely in the water, the weight of water displaced by her hull is exactly equal to the weight of the ship. Thus

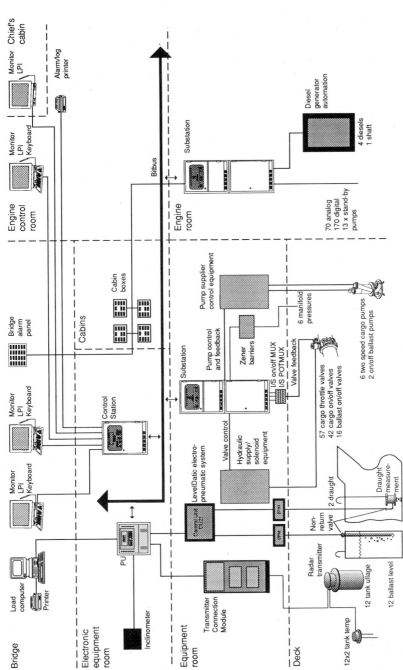

Fig. 7-4. Schematic of an integrated monitoring and control system installed on a tanker in 1989 (Saab MaC/501 system). Note that, because of an interface to the centralized microcomputer system, the loading computer can not only be used to precalculate the load, but can also provide virtually instantaneous updates of draft, trim, and stress throughout all phases of the ship's operation. Saab Marine Electronics.

the term *displacement* is used to denote a vessel's weight in tons at a given draft.

**Deadweight scale.** Figure 7-6 shows the deadweight scale of a typical tanker. This is a handy device for determining the mean draft corresponding to a given deadweight or displacement. Important hydrostatic values, such as tons per inch immersion (TPI), are also listed for various drafts.

**Light ship.** This is the displacement, or weight in tons, of a vessel minus cargo, crew, stores, fuel, water, and ballast; in plain words, the weight of the empty ship.

**Tons per inch immersion (TPI).** Change in draft is proportional to the amount of weight loaded or discharged. The number of tons required to submerge a vessel one inch amidships, or TPI, varies with the draft. Values for TPI can be found on the deadweight scale or in tables drawn up from this data.

This information is valuable when computing changes in mean draft caused by weights loaded or discharged. The following formula is used:

$$\frac{\text{Weight loaded (or discharged)}}{\text{TPI}} = \text{change in mean draft}$$

Let's illustrate with an example:

A tanker's mean draft is 25′ 00″. At this draft the value for TPI is 150 tons/inch. What will be her new draft after loading 900 tons?

Using the formula:

$$\frac{900 \text{ tons}}{150 \text{ tons/inch}} = 6'' \text{ increase in draft}$$

$$
\begin{array}{r}
25' \ 00'' \\
+ \quad 6'' \\
\hline
25' \ 06''
\end{array} = \text{new mean draft}
$$

**Trim** is simply the difference between forward and after drafts. On American ships it is expressed either in feet or inches.

**Tipping center, or center of flotation,** could be described as a hinge about which a vessel rotates longitudinally. This hinge is not fixed in a single position but slides forward and aft with changes in draft and trim.

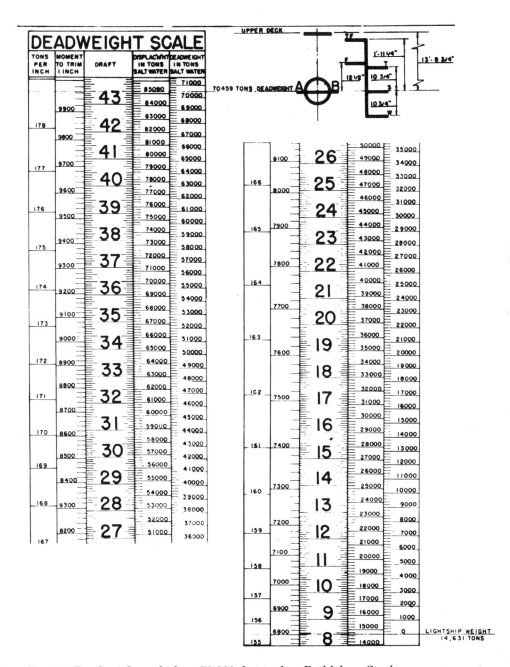

Fig. 7-6. Deadweight scale for a 70,000-dwt tanker. Bethlehem Steel.

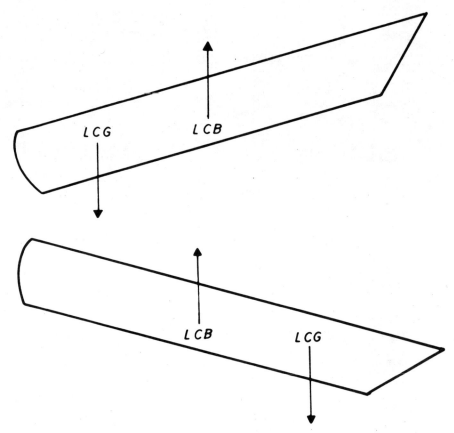

Fig. 7-7. *Top,* trim by the stern; LCG aft of LCB. *Bottom,* trim by the head, LCG forward of LCB.

**Longitudinal center of buoyancy (LCB)** is the center of volume of the underwater part of a vessel's hull, and is the point through which all upward forces of buoyancy are assumed to act.

**Longitudinal center of gravity (LCG)** is the counterpart of LCB, or the point through which all *downward* forces of a vessel's weight are assumed to act. More precisely, LCG represents a vessel's center of mass (as viewed longitudinally, or from the side).

As we will discuss later in this chapter, LCB and LCG act together to form a trimming lever, or arm, which trims a vessel about her tipping center. The position of LCB and LCG relative to each other determines the amount of the final trim and whether it will be by the head or by the stern (fig. 7-7). Values for LCB are found in tables or hydrostatic curves supplied by the naval architect. LCG is calculated by a method we will discuss shortly. When both values are known, trim can be computed by simple arithmetic.

**Trimming moment.** When a weight is loaded or discharged at a given distance forward or aft of the tipping center, a *trimming moment* is created. Likewise, a moment is created when a weight already on board is shifted forward or aft. Moments are expressed in foot-tons and are computed by the formula:

$$\text{Trimming moment} = \text{weight (tons)} \times \text{distance (feet)}$$

**Moment to change trim one inch (MT1)** is used in conjunction with trimming moment to determine change in trim. MT1 varies with the draft; values are found on the deadweight scale or tables derived from it. Let's illustrate the use of MT1 with an example:

A tanker has a draft of 25′ 00″ forward and aft (vessel on even keel). MT1 at this draft is 1,000 foot-tons. Suppose 100 tons is moved aft 100 feet; what are the new drafts?

$$\text{Trimming moment} = 100 \text{ tons} \times 100 \text{ feet}$$
$$= 10,000 \text{ foot-tons}$$

$$\text{Change in trim} = \frac{10,000 \text{ foot–tons}}{1,000 \text{ foot–tons}}$$
$$= 10″ \text{ by the stern}$$

$$\begin{array}{r} 25′\ 00″ \\ -\quad 5″ \\ \hline 24′\ 07″ \end{array} = \text{new draft forward}$$

$$\begin{array}{r} 25′\ 00″ \\ +\quad 5″ \\ \hline 25′\ 05″ \end{array} = \text{new draft aft}$$

Note that the new drafts are determined by applying *half* the change in trim to forward and after drafts respectively. Because the weight has moved aft in this case, we add 5 inches to the after draft and subtract the same amount from the forward draft.

When a weight is loaded or discharged, we encounter a slightly different problem. The first step is to determine the new mean draft produced by the change in displacement. Change in trim can then be computed and applied to the new mean draft to determine the new drafts forward and aft.

Let's go back to the ship used in the preceding example. Once again, let's give her an initial draft of 25′ 00″ forward and aft, plus an MT1 of 1,000 foot-tons. TPI at this draft is 50 tons/inch.

Suppose 100 tons is loaded 100 feet aft of the tipping center; what are the new drafts?

$$\text{Increase in mean draft} = \frac{100 \text{ tons}}{50 \text{ tons/inch}} = 2''$$

$$\begin{array}{r} 25' \ 00'' \\ + \quad 2'' \\ \hline 25' \ 02'' = \text{new mean draft} \end{array}$$

$$\begin{aligned} \text{Trimming moment} &= 100 \text{ tons} \times 100 \text{ feet} \\ &= 10{,}000 \text{ foot-tons} \end{aligned}$$

$$\begin{aligned} \text{Change in trim} &= \frac{10{,}000 \text{ foot-tons}}{1{,}000 \text{ foot-tons}} \\ &= 10'' \text{ by the stern} \end{aligned}$$

$$\begin{array}{r} 25' \ 02'' \\ - \quad 5'' \\ \hline 24' \ 09'' = \text{new draft forward} \end{array}$$

$$\begin{array}{r} 25' \ 02'' \\ + \quad 5'' \\ \hline 25' \ 07'' = \text{new draft aft} \end{array}$$

**Fresh and dock water allowances.** As we noted earlier, fresh water is less buoyant than salt water; a vessel therefore requires less tonnage to submerge her applicable load line in fresh water. The load line regulations allow for this fact, and each ship is assigned a *fresh water allowance* equal to the number of inches her mean draft will change when moving from fresh to salt water in a fully loaded condition.

Merchant ships rarely sail in completely salt-free water, but it is not uncommon to enter a harbor formed by a mixture of salt and fresh water (as at the mouth of a river). Here the term *dock water allowance* comes into play.

Dock water allowance is the number of inches a ship may load below her marks in water of a given specific gravity. A water sample is taken during the last hour of loading, and the specific gravity is measured with a simple hydrometer.

The specific gravity of fresh water is 1.000; of salt water, 1.025. Dock water often falls somewhere in between. Thus the dock water allowance is found by a simple proportion. This is best shown by example:

On a ship with a fresh water allowance of 10 inches, a water sample is taken and the specific gravity is found to be 1.010. What is the dock water allowance?

We know this: at specific gravity 1.000, the allowance would be 10 inches; at 1.025, zero inches. Our value of 1.010 falls 10/25 of the way between 10 inches and zero or, going the other way, 15/25 of the way between zero and 10 inches.

Thus:

$$\text{Dock water allowance} = \frac{15}{25} \times 10'' = 6.0''$$

Many people find this calculation confusing and, for this reason, a table of dock water allowances such as the one shown in Table 7-1 is normally used.

Table 7-1

DOCK WATER ALLOWANCES
(Fresh water allowance = 10″)

| Specific Gravity | Allowance |
| --- | --- |
| 1.000 (fresh) | 10″ |
| 1.005 | 8″ |
| 1.010 | 6″ |
| 1.015 | 4″ |
| 1.020 | 2″ |
| 1.025 (salt) | 0″ |

## LOADING PLAN AND CALCULATIONS

Earlier in this chapter we used a set of voyage orders for the *Shasta Valley* as an example. Let's look over the chief mate's shoulder as he calculates the load and fills out the loading plan for Voyage 21 (see figure 7-9).

His first problem is to find out which load line must be used. Barber's Point lies within the Seasonal Tropical Zone (tropical marks in July). Long Beach, on the other hand, is in the Summer Zone. The ship must therefore load to the summer displacement, plus a small amount for zone allowance.

At summer marks the *Shasta Valley* displaces 79,863 tons. The mate knows from experience that she will require about 43 hours, or 1.79 days, to reach the Summer Zone at sea speed. He also knows that fuel and

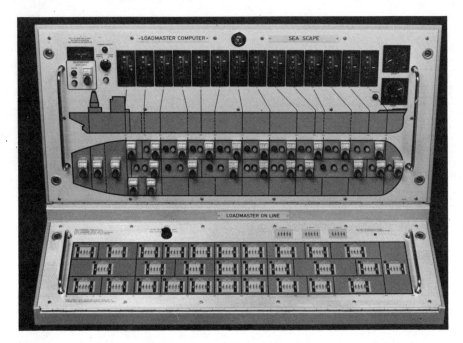

Fig. 7-8. The Kockums Loadmaster Computer can be used to precalculate cargo distribution and can also be connected to the automated gauging system. In the latter mode it provides a continuous automatic readout of stress, trim, and draft. Kockumation.

water consumption at sea speed equals about 100 tons per day. He therefore calculates zone allowance as follows:

$$\text{Zone allowance} = 1.79 \text{ days} \times 100 \text{ ton/day}$$
$$= 179 \text{ tons}$$

He adds this tonnage to the summer displacement to ascertain the maximum displacement to which the *Shasta Valley* may load at Barber's Point.

$$
\begin{array}{ll}
79{,}863 & \text{(summer displacement)} \\
+\quad 179 & \text{(zone allowance)} \\
\hline
80{,}042 & = \text{loaded displacement}
\end{array}
$$

Referring once again to the deadweight scale, or tables, the mate finds that a displacement of 80,042 tons corresponds to a mean saltwater draft of 41′ 02″. This will be the *Shasta Valley*'s loaded draft at Barber's Point.

S.S. SHASTA VALLEY          Voyage # _21_

| Product | API | T° | Gross | m | Net | BPT | Tons |
|---|---|---|---|---|---|---|---|
| Low Sulphur Fuel Oil | 21.5 | 145 | 444,824 | .9668 | 430,056 | 6,925 | 62,102 |
|  |  |  |  |  |  |  |  |
|  |  |  |  |  |  |  |  |
|  |  |  |  |  |  |  |  |
|  |  |  |  |  |  | Total | 62,102 |

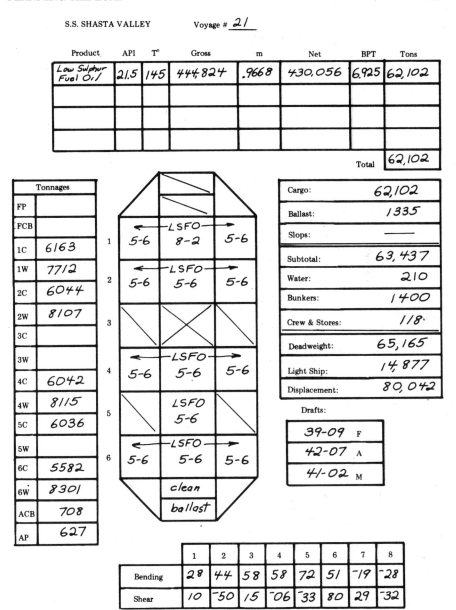

| Tonnages | |
|---|---|
| FP |  |
| FCB |  |
| 1C | 6163 |
| 1W | 7712 |
| 2C | 6044 |
| 2W | 8107 |
| 3C |  |
| 3W |  |
| 4C | 6042 |
| 4W | 8115 |
| 5C | 6036 |
| 5W |  |
| 6C | 5582 |
| 6W | 8301 |
| ACB | 708 |
| AP | 627 |

1  LSFO  5-6  8-2  5-6
2  LSFO  5-6  5-6  5-6
3
4  LSFO  5-6  5-6  5-6
5  LSFO  5-6
6  LSFO  5-6  5-6  5-6
clean ballast

| Cargo: | 62,102 |
|---|---|
| Ballast: | 1335 |
| Slops: | — |
| Subtotal: | 63,437 |
| Water: | 210 |
| Bunkers: | 1400 |
| Crew & Stores: | 118· |
| Deadweight: | 65,165 |
| Light Ship: | 14,877 |
| Displacement: | 80,042 |

Drafts:

| 39-09 | F |
|---|---|
| 42-07 | A |
| 41-02 | M |

|  | 1 | 2 | 3 | 4 | 5 | 6 | 7 | 8 |
|---|---|---|---|---|---|---|---|---|
| Bending | 28 | 44 | 58 | 58 | 72 | 51 | ⁻19 | ⁻28 |
| Shear | 10 | ⁻50 | 15 | ⁻06 | ⁻33 | 80 | 29 | ⁻32 |

Fig. 7-9. Loading plan.

How many tons of cargo must be loaded to reach this draft and displacement? From the voyage orders, the mate knows this figure should be somewhere around 62,000 tons, but he must come up with the exact tonnage. His first step is to figure total noncargo tonnage, as follows:

| | |
|---|---|
| Light ship | 14,877 |
| Fuel | 1,400 |
| Water | 210 |
| Crew and stores | 118 |
| Ballast | 1,335 |
| Total | 17,940 = noncargo tonnage |

Since cargo must make up the remaining tonnage, the mate simply subtracts noncargo tonnage from displacement to determine cargo tonnage to load:

$$\begin{array}{ll} 80,042 & \text{(loaded displacement)} \\ -17,940 & \text{(noncargo tonnage)} \\ \hline 62,102 & = \text{tons of cargo to load} \end{array}$$

Using the values given for API and temperature, the mate can now figure total net and gross barrels (for a review of this procedure, see chapter 3). This accomplished, he must distribute the gross barrels of cargo throughout the tanks in such a manner as to produce an acceptable stress and trim. To simplify this task, the mate searches through old cargo plans in the hope of finding a similar load to use as a model. Luckily, he finds one in which the same cargo, at approximately the same tonnage, was loaded. He discovers that number 3 across and number 5 wings were left empty (3 and 5 wings are clean ballast tanks), number 1 center slack, and the remaining tanks full. Using this distribution as a guide, the mate fills out a tentative plan (fig. 7-9). How about stress and trim? The *Shasta Valley* is equipped with a loading calculator (see figure 7-11) and these values are easily determined.

The mate enters the tonnages for each tank into the calculator; he then reads off values for forward and after drafts, plus stress, directly from the face of the machine. Draft: 39′ 09″ forward, 42′ 07″ aft, 41′ 02″ mean. The mean draft is correct, since it corresponds to the desired displacement. The trim, 34″, is also satisfactory.

The calculator indicates shear and bending stress numerals for each of 8 points along the hull. None of these may exceed 100 (the maximum stress numeral permitted on the *Shasta Valley*).

The mate checks each of the points and finds them all within acceptable limits. The plan can therefore be used as it stands.

Table 7-2

SS *HILLYER BROWN*
(17,000 dwt)

| Displacement | LCB | MT1 | Draft |
|---|---|---|---|
| 6,000 | 257.55 | 1542 | 9-04½ |
| 6,500 | 257.5 | 1561 | 10-01 |
| 7,000 | 257.42 | 1576 | 10-09 |
| 7,500 | 257.36 | 1591 | 11-05 |
| 8,000 | 257.3 | 1610 | 12-01 |
| 8,500 | 257.25 | 1621 | 12-09 |
| 9,000 | 257.2 | 1632 | 13-04 |
| 9,500 | 257.09 | 1650 | 14-01 |
| 10,000 | 257.0 | 1660 | 14-09 |
| 10,500 | 256.89 | 1672 | 15-04½ |
| 11,000 | 256.8 | 1685 | 16-00½ |
| 11,500 | 256.7 | 1694 | 16-08½ |
| 12,000 | 256.6 | 1711 | 17-04½ |
| 12,500 | 256.49 | 1721 | 18-00 |
| 13,000 | 256.38 | 1737 | 18-08½ |
| 13,500 | 256.23 | 1749 | 19-04½ |
| 14,000 | 256.1 | 1761 | 20-01½ |
| 14,500 | 255.93 | 1780 | 20-09 |
| 15,000 | 255.81 | 1791 | 21-05 |
| 15,500 | 255.7 | 1808 | 22-00½ |
| 16,000 | 255.55 | 1822 | 22-08½ |
| 16,500 | 255.33 | 1840 | 23-04½ |
| 17,000 | 255.18 | 1857 | 24-00 |
| 17,500 | 255.01 | 1873 | 24-07½ |
| 18,000 | 254.89 | 1890 | 25-02 |
| 18,500 | 254.65 | 1910 | 25-11 |
| 19,000 | 254.5 | 1928 | 26-05½ |
| 19,500 | 254.3 | 1945 | 27-02 |
| 20,000 | 254.09 | 1965 | 27-09½ |
| 20,500 | 253.92 | 1983 | 28-06 |
| 21,000 | 253.73 | 2000 | 29-00½ |
| 21,500 | 253.48 | 2020 | 29-08½ |
| 22,000 | 253.32 | 2040 | 30-04 |
| 22,500 | 253.05 | 2063 | 30-11 |
| 23,000 | 252.87 | 2082 | 31-07 |
| 23,500 | 252.65 | 2102 | 32-02 |
| 24,000 | 252.43 | 2127 | 32-10 |

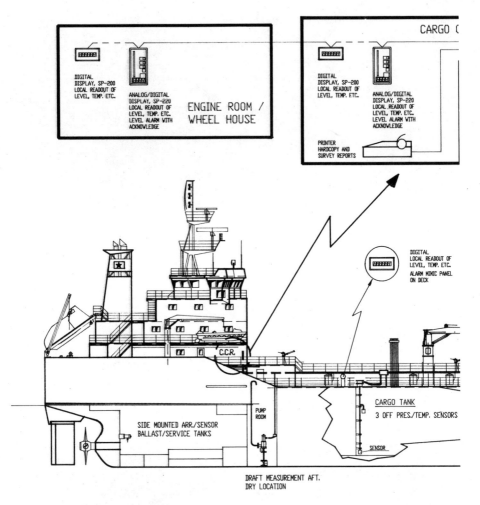

Fig. 7-10. CARGOMASTER monitoring and control system. The loading computer can be operated on-line for instantaneous updates of draft, trim, stress, etc.; it can also be operated off-line for load planning. (For comparison with another integrated system, see figure 7-4.) Skarpenord Data.

## COMPUTERS AND LOADING CALCULATORS

Cargo planning calculations can be made in a variety of ways. Many ships are equipped with a loading calculator or computer which has been pre-programmed with the ship's characteristics. In some installations, the loading computer/calculator includes an interface with the gauging system or with a centralized microcomputer system (for examples, see figures 7-4 and 7-10).

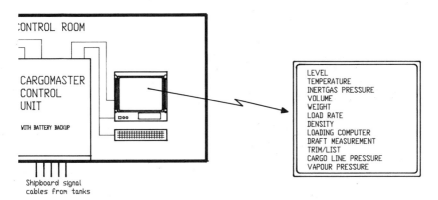

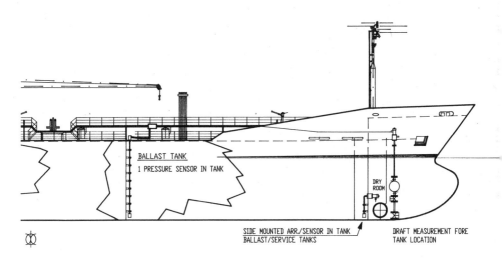

Fig. 7-10 *(cont.)*

Calculations can also be made by using a personal computer, along with software specifically designed for the ship. Once again, it is possible to interface a personal computer with the gauging system or other ship's systems.

### FORMS FOR CALCULATING STRESS AND TRIM

If, for some reason, a ship is not equipped with a functioning computer or loading calculator, then stress and trim must be computed manually.

A form such as the one shown in figure 7-12 is normally used, along with a hand calculator, and the procedure is a relatively simple one. (A very general description of the procedure is given in the following paragraphs.)

**Trim.** As we discussed earlier, the longitudinal center of buoyancy (LCB) and longitudinal center of gravity (LCG) act together to trim a ship (fig. 7-7). When LCG falls aft off LCB, trim is by the stern; when LCG is forward of LCB, trim is by the head.

If calculating the final trim without the aid of a computer or loading calculator, the first step is to locate LCB and LCG. LCB is a hydrostatic value that changes with draft and trim; it can be found in tables or curves provided by the naval architect (see table 7-2). The location of LCB is given in feet forward or aft of the centerline (or other fixed part of the vessel, such as the forward perpendicular).

LCG is another matter. In order to make this calculation, LCGs for each tank (taken from tables) are multiplied by their tonnages to determine a moment for each. The same calculation is made for light ship, fuel oil, fresh water, etc. The sum of all moments is divided by displacement to determine the distance of LCG forward or aft of the centerline (or whichever reference point is used).

The *trim arm* is the longitudinal distance between LCG and LCB. It is multiplied by the ship's displacement to find the total trimming moment. This total moment can then be divided by MT1 to find the trim.

Simply stated:

$$\text{Trim arm} = \text{longitudinal distance between LCG and LCB}$$

$$\text{Trim (inches)} = \frac{\text{displacement} \times \text{trim arm}}{\text{MT1}}$$

By another method, the total trimming moment is determined by adding up the moments for the various tanks, light ship, fuel oil, fresh water, etc. This total is subtracted from the product of LCB times displacement. The resultant trimming moment is, as before, divided by MT1 to determine trim. Therefore, by the second method:

$$(\text{LCB} \times \text{displacement}) - (\text{sum of moments}) = \text{total trimming moment}$$

$$\text{Trim} = \frac{\text{total trimming moment}}{\text{MT1}}$$

**Stress** can be divided into several constituents. *Shear stresses* occur when two forces act in opposite directions parallel to one another, as at a bulk-

Fig. 7-11. The Sperry-Sintep Loading Calculator. Sperry Marine.

head between an empty tank (pushed up by buoyancy) and a full tank (pushed down by the weight of cargo).

*Hogging* occurs when a ship loads too heavily at the ends, causing the middle to bend upward. *Sagging* occurs when a ship loads too heavily in the middle, causing it to bend downward (fig. 7-13). When a ship puts to sea, such stresses are greatly augmented by the action of the swells, which can create a dangerous condition in a poorly loaded tanker. Stress can be computed mathematically when no loading calculator is available. A form similar to the one used for trim is generally used. As a rule, stresses are resolved into a *stress numeral* for each tank or point along the hull. None of these numerals may exceed the maximum allowed for the vessel.

## LOADING TO FINAL DRAFT

As we discussed in chapter 5, the loading plan serves as an initial guide or approximation of the final loaded condition. Ullage readings, draft, and trim rarely turn out exactly as calculated. For this reason, it is often necessary to make adjustments in the ullage of the final tank or tanks to be loaded. (For example, if the cargo temperature turns out to be higher than anticipated, a greater volume of cargo will have to be loaded.)

If the ship is loading down to her marks, it is also the practice on some ships to do the final loading to draft by observing the ship's draft marks from the dock. When the ship reaches the appropriate draft, the final shutdown signal is given, and the loading operation is complete.

# TANKER STRESS AND TRIM DETERMINATION C-96
## FOR USE WITH STRESS AND TRIM TABLES

| OUTAGES | | GROSS | TEMP | TANK | PRODUCT | NET | °API | LONG | STRESS NUMERALS | | MOMENT |
| FEET | INCHES | BARRELS | °F | | | BARRELS | GRAV | TONS | HOG | SAG | |
|---|---|---|---|---|---|---|---|---|---|---|---|
| | | | | | | | | | | | |
| | | | | | | | | | | | |
| | | | | | | | | | | | |
| | | | | | | | | | | | |
| | | | | | | | | | | | |
| | | | | | | | | | | | |
| | | | | | | | | | | | |
| | | | | | | | | | | | |
| | | | | | | | | | | | |
| | | | | | | | | | | | |
| | | | | | | | | | | | |
| | | | | | | | | | | | |
| | | | | | | | | | | | |
| XXXXXXXX | | | | TOTALS FOR CARGO | | | XXX | | | | |

| OTHER THAN CARGO | | XXXXXXXX | XXX | XXXXXXXXXXX | XXXXXXXXXX | XXXXXXXXXX | XXXXXXXXXXXXXXXXXX |
|---|---|---|---|---|---|---|---|
| BUNKERS | | | | | | | |
| FRESH WATER | | | | | | | |
| MISCELLANEOUS | CREW AND STORES | | | | | | |
| | SUB-TOTALS | | | | | | |
| LIGHT SHIP | LIGHT SHIP | | | | | | |
| | TOTALS | | | | | | |

STRESS

SUBTRACT STRESS DEADWEIGHT CORRECTION (.0____ TIMES SUB-TOTAL)

RESULTANT STRESS NUMERALS (MUST NOT EXCEED 100, EXCEPT 12 FOR T-1's)    XXXXXXXXXXXXXXXXXXXXX    XXXXXXXXXXXXXXXXXXXXX

TRIM

TOTAL LONG TONS _____ TIMES _____ LONGITUDINAL CENTER OF BUOYANCY

REPEAT "TOTAL" SHOWN ABOVE IN "MOMENT" COLUMN AND MAKE SUBTRACTION

RESULTANT TRIM MOMENT (IF INVERTED SUBTRACTION, TRIM IS BY THE HEAD)

DIVIDE RESULTANT TRIM MOMENT

BY MOMENT OF TRIM PER INCH AT DRAFT _____ = _____ INCHES OF TRIM BY _____ STERN _____ HEAD

DRAFT

TOTAL LONG TONS (DISPLACEMENT) EQUALS SALT WATER MEAN DRAFT OF _____ FEET _____ INCHES

COMPUTED DRAFT:    FORWARD; _____ AFT: _____ MEAN. _____

OBSERVED DRAFT:    FORWARD; _____ AFT: _____ MEAN. _____    DENSITY ALLOWANCE _____ INCHES

| VESSEL | VOYAGE NO. | LOADING PORT | DATE | DESTINATION |
|---|---|---|---|---|
| | | | | |

C-96 (5M-CD-10-65)
PRINTED IN U.S.A.

Fig. 7-12. If, for some reason, a ship is not equipped with a functioning computer or loading calculator, a form such as this one could be used to calculate stress and trim. Chevron Shipping.

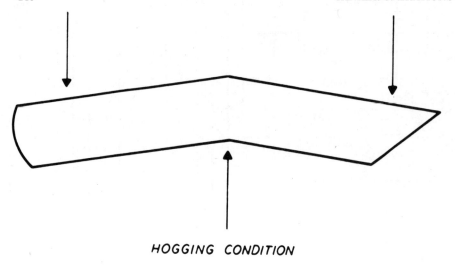

HOGGING CONDITION

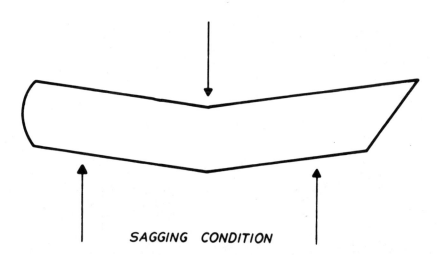

SAGGING CONDITION

Fig. 7-13. *Top,* hogging condition is caused by too much weight in the extreme ends, too little amidships to counter the buoyant force of water beneath the hull. *Bottom,* sagging condition is caused by too much weight amidships.

# CHAPTER 8

# BALLASTING

F IFTEEN centuries ago, a tribe from northern Germany—the Saxons— invaded England. The Saxons were a seafaring people; they brought a colorful vocabulary of nautical terms with them to England. The word *barlast* (literally, "bare load") referred to heavy weights (or cargoes carried because of their heaviness) which, when stowed in the hold of an empty ship, greatly increased stability. This is the probable origin of our own word *ballast*.

The Saxons were good sailors and recognized an important fact: an empty ship is often less seaworthy than a loaded one. Fifteen hundred years later this fact is no less true. Ballast is still used and the reasons are basically the same: 1) to increase seaworthiness and stability, 2) to equalize stresses on the hull, and 3) to increase maneuverability and speed.

## THE NEED FOR BALLAST

An empty tanker rides high in the water. Instead of slicing through the swells, the bow tends to bounce along on top of them. This action creates dangerous stresses on the ship's structure. The ship is also less maneuverable; the propeller and rudder—only partially submerged when a tanker is "light"—lose much of their efficiency.

One obvious solution (the one tanker companies prefer) is to make sure a tanker always sails with cargo in her tanks. This not only makes her more seaworthy but more profitable too. This arrangement is ideal but often impractical. For example, the typical VLCC can only carry cargo in one direction: from the oil fields to the refinery or receiving terminal. The long voyage outbound to the oil fields must be made with no cargo in the tanks at all.

Ballast—seawater—must take the place of the missing cargo. Seawater is the logical choice because it is abundant and readily available. Seawater ballast has traditionally been carried in empty *cargo tanks*. This practice is still the rule—to a greater or lesser degree—on most tankers. However, two things have changed significantly over the years: the method of cleaning tanks before ballasting and the method of *deballasting* and slop disposal. For many years, tankers disposed of dirty ballast and slops simply by pumping them into the sea. This is no longer the case—to the contrary, discharges of oil at sea are now strictly limited. New tank-cleaning and ballast-handling techniques have greatly reduced oily discharges. Specifically, we will discuss *crude oil washing* (COW), *load-on-top* (LOT), and multistage slop separating systems.

Segregated ballast tanks (SBT) are now required on virtually all new tankers. A separate pump and pipeline are provided for ballast—thus keeping oil out of the ballast and (in theory) seawater out of the cargo system. SBT offers at least a partial answer to the problem of *dirty ballast,* which we will discuss shortly.

### PLANNING THE BALLAST LOAD

Ballasting involves more than just filling tanks with seawater; it must be carefully planned. The following factors must be considered when planning the distribution of ballast.

**Stress.** Generally speaking, ballast must be spread evenly through the tanks, taking care not to concentrate it in the middle or at the ends. Since more tanks are left empty when ballasting than when loading cargo, these empty tanks must be distributed carefully. Additional empty tanks increase the possibility of creating a dangerous hog or sag condition. Stress should therefore be calculated for each ballast plan used. (Methods for checking stress are discussed in chapter 7.)

**Draft, trim, and propeller immersion.** Before departing on the ballast passage, and at all times during the passage, draft and trim must be kept within established limits. These limits are specified in MARPOL and Coast Guard regulations, and they are summarized in the following paragraphs.

The minimum draft amidships (in meters) that is allowed during the ballast passage is found by using the following formula:

$$dm = 2.0 + .02L$$

where L is equal to the length overall (in meters).

Tanks are routinely cleaned during the ballast passage, and an adequate amount of stern trim is needed for proper stripping. However, trim by the stern may not exceed the permissible maximum, which is determined as follows:

$$t = .015L$$

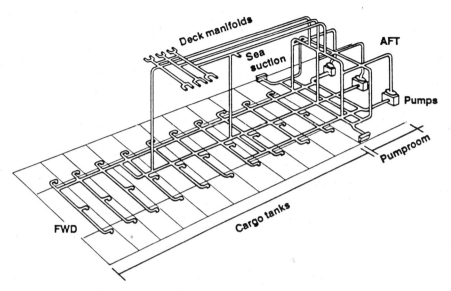

Fig. 8-1. General piping and pumping arrangements for an older tanker. No segregated ballast system is provided, so all ballast must be pumped through the cargo system. Reprinted with permission from *Controlling Hydrocarbon Emissions from Tank Vessel Loading,* 1987. Published by National Academy Press, Washington, D.C.

Besides the above requirements, an adequate after draft must be maintained at all times to ensure full immersion of the propeller throughout the passage.

**Weather expected on the ballast passage.** Weather is a vital consideration in ballast planning. Bad weather can force a tanker to take on as much as 60 percent of her loaded deadweight in ballast; sometimes even more. In good weather this amount is naturally much less.

One of the most important things is to prevent *pounding,* which occurs when the bow crashes over oncoming swells instead of slicing through them. Enough forward draft must be maintained to keep the bow well submerged.

**Tank cleaning.** Whenever repairs or inspections must be made inside the tanks, they must first be cleaned and gas-freed (see chapter 9). This operation is a routine part of the ballast passage. Tanks to be cleaned must, of course, be empty when the cleaning is performed. Ballasting should be planned with this in mind.

Fig. 8-2. A 119,000-dwt tanker leaves port in ballast. A number of tanks have been cleaned and gas-freed (note the open tank lids). Also visible in this photograph: fore-and-aft walkway, cargo and steam piping on deck, ullage tapewells, fire main, tank vents, and cargo manifold (near aft house). Note: Since this photo was taken, the ship has been retrofitted with inert gas and crude oil

Fig. 8-3. Proper ballasting of tankers increases maneuverability and speed. Kock-umation.

When more than a few tanks are to be cleaned, it is usually necessary to shift or discharge ballast from some of the ballasted tanks. This is also the case when using the load-on-top technique for ballast handling (discussed later in this chapter and in chapter 11).

Fig. 8-4. Ballasting involves more than just filling tanks with seawater; it must be carefully planned. Chevron Shipping.

## CHOOSING THE PLAN

After considering the requirements for a particular ballast load, old ballast plans should be consulted; one of these should prove adequate for the present voyage. This is generally the chief mate's job, although the master may want to choose the plan himself.

Many ships keep a book of standard ballast plans that cover the whole spectrum of ballast conditions. For example, figure 8-5 illustrates a plan that might be used by a 65,000-ton tanker in moderate weather. In fair weather an arrangement such as the one shown in figure 8-6 might be used. Here, only tanks on the clean ballast system are used (forepeak, forward and after clean ballast tanks, afterpeak, three wings, five wings).

The exact figures for trim, draft, and displacement will vary each time a plan is used, depending on the amount and position of bunkers, water, and stores. Most of the time these differences are insignificant.

## CLEAN BALLAST VERSUS DIRTY BALLAST

At this point we should make an important distinction between clean ballast and dirty ballast. The U.S. Coast Guard defines *clean ballast* as follows:

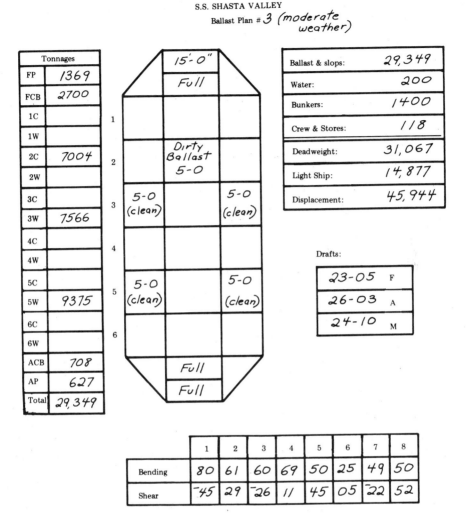

S.S. SHASTA VALLEY
Ballast Plan # 3 (moderate weather)

| Tonnages | |
|---|---|
| FP | 1369 |
| FCB | 2700 |
| 1C | |
| 1W | |
| 2C | 7004 |
| 2W | |
| 3C | |
| 3W | 7566 |
| 4C | |
| 4W | |
| 5C | |
| 5W | 9375 |
| 6C | |
| 6W | |
| ACB | 708 |
| AP | 627 |
| Total | 29,349 |

15'-0"
Full

Dirty Ballast 5-0

5-0 (clean)    5-0 (clean)

5-0 (clean)    5-0 (clean)

Full
Full

| Ballast & slops: | 29,349 |
|---|---|
| Water: | 200 |
| Bunkers: | 1400 |
| Crew & Stores: | 118 |
| Deadweight: | 31,067 |
| Light Ship: | 14,877 |
| Displacement: | 45,944 |

Drafts:

| | |
|---|---|
| 23-05 | F |
| 26-03 | A |
| 24-10 | M |

| | 1 | 2 | 3 | 4 | 5 | 6 | 7 | 8 |
|---|---|---|---|---|---|---|---|---|
| Bending | 80 | 61 | 60 | 69 | 50 | 25 | 49 | 50 |
| Shear | ¯45 | 29 | ¯26 | 11 | 45 | 05 | ¯22 | 52 |

Fig. 8-5. A moderate weather ballast plan for a 65,000-dwt tanker.

. . . ballast in a tank which, since oil was last carried in it, has been so cleaned that ballast, if discharged from a stationary vessel into clean, calm water on a clear day, would make no visible traces of oil on the water surface or adjoining shore lines or cause a sludge or emulsion to be deposited beneath the water surface or on adjoining shore lines.

It takes very little oil to produce a trace on the water's surface; therefore, ballast containing even a small amount of oil must not be pumped overboard in areas where this is illegal. Laws forbid the discharge of dirty

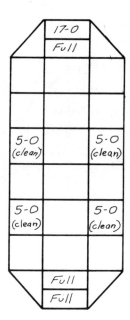

Fig. 8-6.

ballast within the *prohibited zones,* which normally extend 50 miles from shore (farther in some areas). Limited amounts of ballast may be discharged on the high seas beyond the prohibited zones, but this is strictly regulated too. (The amount of oil that may be discharged on the high seas is specified by the MARPOL Convention; see chapter 11.)

In order to comply with local and international regulations, careful ballast-handling techniques must be used. New tankers are built with segregated ballast systems that virtually eliminate the possibility of oily discharges. Most other ships use the load-on-top system (ships with segregated ballast tanks also use this system when ballast must be introduced into the cargo tanks, as in heavy weather). These and other methods of handling ballast are discussed on the following pages.

### SEGREGATED BALLAST TANKS (SBT)

Most new tankers must now be fitted with SBT, complete with pumps and piping systems for clean ballast only. Typically a number of these tanks are *protectively located* to shield the cargo tanks in the event of a collision or grounding.

Ballast and cargo systems are completely separate: no oil can find its way into the ballast unless a pipeline or bulkhead leaks. Therefore, ballast from segregated systems can normally be discharged in coastal waters or in port with no problem.

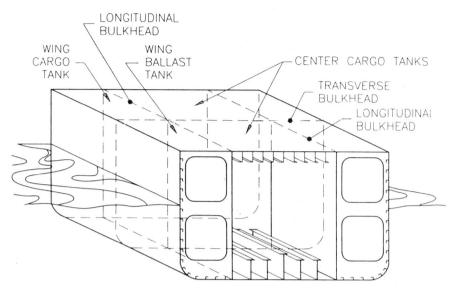

Fig. 8-7. A "MARPOL" tanker, which is fitted with protectively located segregated ballast tanks (PL/SBT). Reprinted with permission from *Tanker Spills, Prevention by Design,* © 1991 by the National Academy of Sciences. Published by National Academy Press, Washington, D.C.

In heavy weather the capacity of clean ballast systems may prove insufficient, making it necessary to pump additional ballast into the cargo tanks (see figure 8-5). This becomes dirty ballast and must be treated accordingly. As an alternative to taking on large amounts of dirty ballast in heavy weather, some masters prefer to slow down their ships. This action is often enough to prevent pounding.

### BALLAST-HANDLING TECHNIQUES

Many older ships do not fall under the requirement for SBT. These ships must use special techniques to avoid accumulating large amounts of slops and dirty ballast. These techniques include crude oil washing (COW) and load-on-top (LOT). Crude oil washing is discussed in chapter 9. Load-on-top is discussed in this chapter and in chapter 11.

Loading dirty ballast requires all the precautions that would normally be devoted to loading cargo. A spill involving dirty ballast is no less serious than one involving cargo; in addition, the risks of fire and explosion are as great with dirty ballast as they are with cargo—if not greater.

**Sea valves.** Seawater is introduced into the cargo system by opening the sea valves (or *sea suctions,* as they are sometimes called). This is a critical operation because it exposes the cargo system directly to the sea. If done incorrectly it can result in a bad spill; there is always a risk that oil will flow *out* instead of seawater flowing *in* (fig. 8-8). Normally one sea valve is located on each side of the pumproom, port and starboard. These valves sit right at the skin of the ship. When taking on ballast, only one of these valves need be opened in most cases. Before opening the sea valve, however, it is important to check the lineup carefully. Make sure each tank valve is open in the tanks designated to receive ballast.

When ballasting through the cargo system, the main object is to prevent oil in the line from escaping as the sea valve is opened. Therefore, *always start the pump first,* before opening the sea valve. This creates a vacuum that immediately draws seawater into the line as the valve is opened. Consequently, no oil is allowed to escape.

Ballast is sometimes loaded by gravity without using the pumps. Tanks cannot be topped off in this manner, however, since water will stop flowing into the tanks when it reaches the level of the water surrounding the vessel. At this point the pumps must be used to take the level higher.

In any event, whether ballasting with the pumps or by gravity, the sea valve should be the last valve opened and the first valve closed.

**Controlling vapor emissions.** If ballasting in a locality where vapor emissions are prohibited, make sure that ullage covers and all other tank openings are secured. As ballast enters the tanks, inert gas and petroleum vapors in the tanks are forced out and must have a place to go. When vapor control is in effect, the vapors are dealt with in one of several ways. First of all, they can be sent ashore via the vapor line for recovery or incineration. Secondly, they can be routed to an empty tank on the ship (fig. 8-9). A third technique, which has been used effectively in some situations, is "vapor balancing"—transferring displaced vapors from ballast tanks to tanks from which cargo is being discharged (see figure 6-16).

The technique used will depend on company policies, local regulations, and the availability of recovery facilities ashore. It goes without saying that clear communication with the terminal regarding vapor control is crucial. (See chapter 14 for a discussion of vapor control systems.)

**Load-on-top (LOT)** is a ballast-handling technique—first introduced in the 1960s—that has proven extremely effective in reducing the amount of

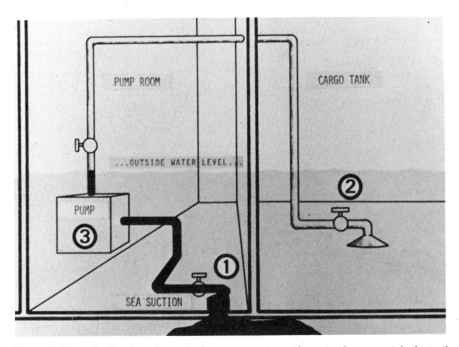

Fig. 8-8. When ballasting through the cargo system, there is always a risk that oil will escape through the sea suction. This can be prevented with careful ballast-handling techniques. Chevron Shipping.

slops generated during the ballast passage. To get a general idea of how this system works, let's watch it in action on a hypothetical ship—a 100,000-ton crude carrier—beginning at the discharge port.

Our ship is fitted with a crude oil washing system; therefore, ballast preparations begin during the discharge as each designated ballast tank is washed with crude oil. (On ships fitted with COW, any cargo tank to receive ballast must first be crude washed—see chapter 9.)

After the *departure ballast tanks* have been crude washed and stripped, they are filled with seawater. This is considered dirty ballast. Certain designated *clean ballast tanks* are also crude washed during the discharge. These tanks will not be ballasted until later, however.

The ship departs the discharge port and begins the ballast passage. It is now necessary to prepare the clean ballast tanks (the *arrival ballast tanks*) for clean ballast. Each of these tanks is washed with seawater and stripped carefully. The slops are transferred to the slop tank, and the tanks are filled with clean seawater. This is considered clean ballast.

In the meantime, the dirty ballast has had time to settle—that is, oil residues have floated to the surface. The clean bottom water is pumped

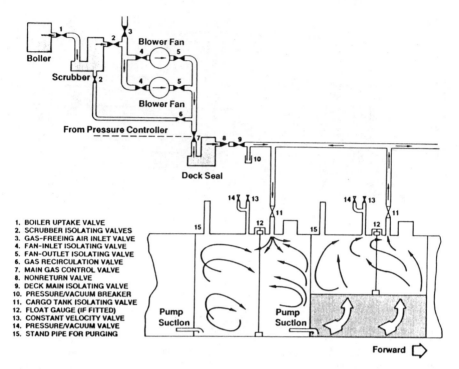

1. BOILER UPTAKE VALVE
2. SCRUBBER ISOLATING VALVES
3. GAS-FREEING AIR INLET VALVE
4. FAN-INLET ISOLATING VALVE
5. FAN-OUTLET ISOLATING VALVE
6. GAS RECIRCULATION VALVE
7. MAIN GAS CONTROL VALVE
8. NONRETURN VALVE
9. DECK MAIN ISOLATING VALVE
10. PRESSURE/VACUUM BREAKER
11. CARGO TANK ISOLATING VALVE
12. FLOAT GAUGE (IF FITTED)
13. CONSTANT VELOCITY VALVE
14. PRESSURE/VACUUM VALVE
15. STAND PIPE FOR PURGING

Fig. 8-9. When loading ballast in a locality where vapor emissions are prohibited, vapors can be dealt with in several different ways. One method (shown here) is to transfer and compress vapors in empty tanks. Reprinted with permission from *Controlling Hydrocarbon Emissions from Tank Vessel Loading,* 1987. Published by National Academy Press, Washington, D.C.

overboard, and the remaining oil-water mixture is stripped to the slop tank. In the same manner, the slop tank is allowed to settle; then the clean bottom portion is carefully pumped overboard. This process is most effective on ships using multistage slop tanks (see figure 11-5).

It is important to note that the "clean" bottom water from dirty ballast and slop tanks should not be pumped overboard in a prohibited zone. It is bound to contain some oil. It should therefore be discharged on the high seas, making sure the oil content falls within MARPOL guidelines, as discussed in chapter 11.

By following the load-on-top procedure carefully, our ship arrives at the loading port with nothing but clean ballast in her tanks—the only exception being a small amount of slops. The slops can either be pumped ashore or commingled with the new cargo (which is literally *loaded-on-top*).

## DEBALLASTING

Ballast must naturally be removed from a ship's tanks before cargo can be loaded. Clean ballast can normally be pumped overboard on the approach to the loading port or in the harbor itself, providing it produces no traces of oil on the water's surface. Unfortunately, not all ships are able to arrive with clean ballast in their tanks. For this reason many terminals have improved their capacity to receive dirty ballast water. This has greatly simplified the task of deballasting. Ballast is pumped ashore (into the terminal's slop line) as if it were cargo. Each tank is stripped in the usual manner by accumulating residues in a single tank. This tank is discharged last and stripped into the shore line.

CHAPTER 9

# TANK CLEANING

${E}$ARLY in my career as a deck officer, it was my good fortune to observe a complete tank-cleaning operation on board a T2 tanker. I joined the ship in Honolulu, where she began her voyage, in ballast, to a West Coast dry dock. I took charge of the four-to-eight watch on the bridge, thus freeing the chief mate to supervise the tank cleaning. This operation was carried out round-the-clock during the nine-day passage to the shipyard. During the previous year and a half, the ship had been in the black oil trade. Thick, waxy residues of past cargoes clung to every inner surface of her tanks.

Petroleum residues produce vapors that are both explosive and poisonous; the idea now was to clean the tanks so that upon our arrival they could be certified gas-free, "safe for entry, safe for fire." This would make it possible for shipyard workers to enter and make repairs.

To me it seemed an impossible task. I watched from my vantage point on the bridge as crew members dragged hoses and portable tank-cleaning machines across the foredeck. These were lowered into the tanks, tied off securely, and charged with hot seawater from the fire main. Each night I went to sleep listening to the distant echo of water cascading off bulkheads in the tanks below the midship house.

But washing with machines was only the first step in the process. Next began the dreaded *mucking*. I watched from the bridge as the sailors descended, one by one, into the darkness of a forward center tank. Blowers mounted in special deck openings kept a stream of fresh air flowing into the tank, making it possible for the men to work and breathe in safety.

One sailor remained on deck to operate a pneumatic hoist, which he positioned over the hatch. He sent down buckets and scoops. A short time later, he began hauling up the buckets, now full of "muck" from the tank bottom.

After mucking, the tanks were washed again with hot, high-pressure seawater. It all added up to a dirty, exhausting, time-consuming process— but it worked. When the ship arrived at the dry dock, a marine chemist came aboard, tested each tank, and issued the appropriate "gas-free" certificate. Welders entered the tanks in short order and were soon busy making repairs.

Fig. 9-1. Birth of a VLCC: Wing tank modules are positioned for final hull erection. Gigantic tanks such as these present formidable cleaning problems. Ralph M. Parsons.

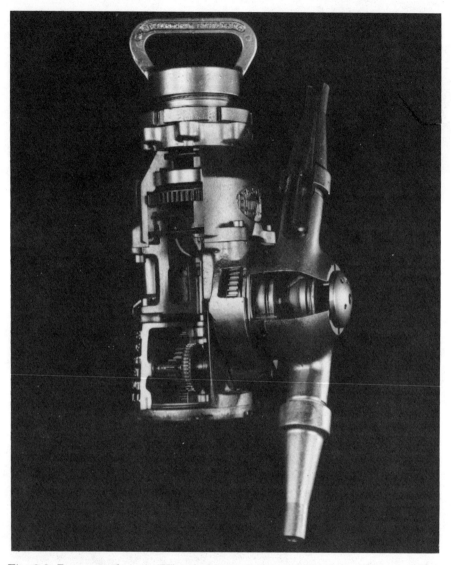

Fig. 9-2. Butterworth type "K" portable tank-cleaning machine (cutaway view). Butterworth.

### WHY CLEAN TANKS?

These days it is unlikely that a new tankerman, going to sea for the first time, will ever witness an operation quite like the one just described. Things have changed considerably. Many tankers are now fitted with powerful, permanently mounted machines, and most crude carriers are equipped for crude oil washing (COW). Inert gas systems have become standard equipment on most tankers over 20,000 dwt. We will discuss these and other developments in the following pages.

But first it is perhaps appropriate to ask a question: *Why clean tanks?* The reasons for cleaning tanks include: 1) change in cargo, 2) repair work or inspection, 3) prevention of sludge accumulation, 4) preparation for clean ballast, and 5) preparation for shipyard.

Like any other operation on board a tanker, the cleaning of tanks must be planned and executed carefully. An improperly cleaned tank can cause severe problems. Suppose, for example, that a consignment of stove oil is mixed with a small amount of gasoline inadvertently left in a tank. The resultant mixture could cause an explosion in somebody's home.

### METHODS AND EQUIPMENT

Mechanical tank-cleaning machines were first developed in the late 1920s. Prior to their introduction, and for some time afterward, tanks were cleaned by hand-hosing with salt water. Today this method is still used occasionally by ships in special trades. However, the vast majority of tank cleaning is now accomplished with machines, either fixed or portable.

Tank-cleaning machines are designed to deliver seawater (or crude oil) under high pressure in a rotating stream that arcs through every possible angle. Thus nearly all surfaces in the tank are exposed to the stream. Those not struck directly are hit by water splashing at high velocity from other parts of the tank (although it is sometimes necessary to spot clean problem areas, either by lashing a portable machine nearby or installing a special machine permanently in that area).

A special pump delivers seawater into the system (often employing the fire main) at pressures ranging from 7 to 13 kg/cm$^2$ (100 to 185 psi). Pressures are adjusted according to the type of product being cleaned from the tank. The pump is often located in the engine room; when this is the case it is necessary to call the engineers to start or stop the cleaning water or change the pressure. (On many tankers—those fitted for crude oil washing, for example—the cargo pumps can deliver into the tank-cleaning system. Crude oil washing techniques are discussed later in this chapter.)

Seawater can either be used cold or heated to temperatures up to 190°F. (by means of a heat exchanger in the engine room). This, too, depends on the previous product and the degree of cleanliness required.

On ships carrying heavy fuel oils, for example, tanks might be washed at "180-180"; that is, 180 psi and 180°F. (12.7 kg/cm$^2$ and 82°C.). A ship

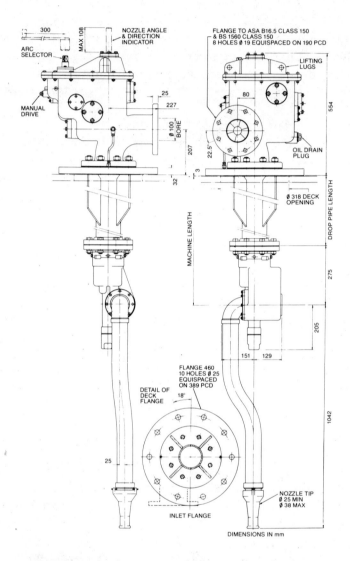

Fig. 9-3. Butterworth P-60 deck-mounted machine is suitable for crude oil washing (COW). This machine is normally programmed at the factory for three standard downward washing arcs. For a full wash, the nozzle travels in an arc from 140° to 0°. For a top wash, it travels from 140° to 50°. For a bottom wash, the arc is from 50° to 0°. Selection of the desired washing arc is made by an *arc selector* on top of the power/control housing. After a washing cycle, the selected washing arc is automatically repeated until the unit is turned off or another washing arc selected. Butterworth.

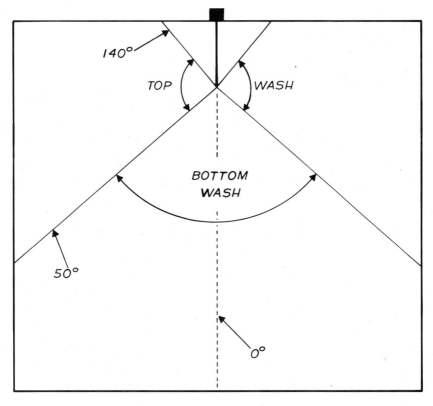

Fig. 9-4. A typical two-stage crude oil washing (COW) operation starts with a top wash and ends with a bottom wash. In this case, the top wash covers a downward arc from 140° to 50°. The bottom wash covers an arc from 50° to 0°. Some units provide an "overlap" between stages.

carrying refined products, on the other hand, might use cold seawater at 120 psi. This depends, once again, on the type of product carried and the reason for cleaning the tanks.

An increasingly popular practice is to coat the insides of cargo tanks with a special paint, thus reducing the amount of time and effort required for tank cleaning. This makes the job of tank cleaning much easier.

A certain amount of caution must be used when cleaning coated tanks, however. Epoxy coatings can be damaged by using excessive pressures or temperatures in the wash water. For example, 120 psi and 120°F. might be the maximums used on a typical ship. Generally speaking, washing times are greatly reduced when cleaning coated tanks.

Fig. 9-5. Gumclean fixed tank-cleaning machine in action. Hudson Engineering.

**Gas-freeing.** Crew members must often enter tanks for inspection or repairs, in which case the tanks must be thoroughly ventilated after washing. On smaller tankers, several types of portable blowers are used for this purpose (fig. 9-8). These are powered by steam, air, or water. Special openings in the main deck are fitted in various positions over each tank. When the covering plates are removed, blowers can be placed into the openings. (These openings are also used for portable tank-cleaning machines.)

Larger ships are equipped with permanent fans designed to ventilate tanks by blowing air through the inert gas system (portable blowers may also be used—see chapter 13).

**Portable tank-cleaning machines.** Although permanent, fixed-in-place tank-washing systems are now standard equipment on many tankers, portable machines are still used on small vessels.

Portable machines are used in conjunction with 2½-inch rubber hoses, which are connected to the tank-cleaning line (usually the fire main). The machines are screwed onto the hoses, then hung through tank-cleaning openings in the deck. The hoses are secured in special saddles on deck or, in some cases, special hose reels are used (fig. 9-9).

Although each hose supports the full weight of its machine, a separate safety line is also attached to the machine. This prevents the machine from dropping into the tank in the event of a broken or uncoupled hose and is helpful when hauling the machine out of the tank.

The tanks are washed in a series of drops, often three, beginning near the top of the tank and working downward. The hoses are marked in 5-foot intervals to facilitate the accurate positioning of machines.

The exact height of each drop is dictated by the inner structure of the tank. On ships that have been in service for a few years, experience has shown how many machines to use in a given tank, for a given length of time, to clean a given product—and at what pressure, temperature, height, and number of drops.

For example, a 16,000-ton tanker in black oil service might use two machines at 180 psi and 180°F. in the following pattern:

1st drop:    7 feet, ½ hour
2nd drop:  17 feet, ½ hour
3rd drop:  30 feet, 1 hour

These figures are meant as examples only; they would vary considerably from ship to ship and in differing circumstances. Generally speaking,

Fig. 9-6. Main deck components of the Gunclean 5000 R fixed tank-cleaning machine. Shipbuilding and Marine Engineering International.

Fig. 9-7. Lavomatic fixed tank-cleaning machine. Butterworth.

the number of minutes a machine is used at each drop depends on the amount of time required to complete one or more full cycles.

**Fixed systems.** Over the years the world has witnessed a magnificent increase in the size of tankers. Ships are built bigger, but with fewer tanks. This development has spurred important changes in tank-cleaning methods.

Cleaning the cavernous tanks of a VLCC with portable machines would be little more effective than sending the crew inside with garden hoses. In short, a much larger machine is required, a machine too heavy and awkward to drag vast distances across a VLCC's deck. The logical solution is to mount these machines permanently inside the tanks.

Such a system has numerous advantages. Machines can be put on or taken off the line simply by turning a valve; therefore, fewer crew mem-

Fig. 9-8. Portable high-capacity blower (shown with adapter) used for gas-free-ing cargo tanks. Portable blowers are placed over tank openings on the main deck. They are normally driven by steam, compressed air, or water. Coppus Engineering.

bers are required. This eliminates much dirty, exhausting, dangerous work—with attendant risk of dropped machines, broken feet, and bruises.

**Cleaning charts.** Most tanker companies provide detailed instruction manuals and cleaning charts outlining cleaning procedures; these indicate the exact requirements for making the transition from one product to another.

For example, let's assume the last cargo carried in a tank was automobile gasoline; the new cargo, aviation gasoline. The cleaning chart might indicate that no washing is necessary between these particular products (provided that no exotic additives were used in the automobile gasoline). On the other hand, the transition to a sensitive product like insulating oil might require extensive tank cleaning, hand mopping, and flushing. Such procedures would be outlined on the cleaning chart.

Fig. 9-9. Hose reel systems are sometimes used when washing with portable machines. Gamlen Chemical.

## STRIPPING AND DISPOSING OF SLOPS

Effective stripping is a vital part of tank cleaning. Wash water must be removed continuously as it enters the tanks; otherwise it quickly pools up and prevents the water stream from hitting the bottom. The bottom is the dirtiest part of a tank, with the greatest accumulation of sludge. It is therefore essential to keep the bottom dry, and thus exposed to the water stream, during the entire washing cycle.

Eductors have proven particularly effective for this task (see chapter 6). They are basically immune to the excessive wear and occasional loss of suction that may plague other types of pumps in the same situation. Nevertheless, when no eductor is available one of the stripping pumps must be used. The pump must be set at a speed equal to or slightly greater than the input of water.

Fig. 9-10. Gamajet II portable tank-cleaning machine. Gamlen Chemical.

Pumps have a tendency to lose suction during tank cleaning, so it is important to watch them carefully. If water begins to pool up on the bottom of a tank, it is a fair bet the pump has lost suction. In such cases the pump must be primed from a full ballast tank. Plenty of stern trim is required for effective stripping.

At this point a problem arises—what to do with the slops? In the past it was common, during a ballast passage, to pump slops directly into the sea (except in prohibited areas near coastlines). This practice has ended, however. The MARPOL Convention places strict limits on the amount of oil that may be discharged on the high seas (see chapter 11). Slops must therefore be retained on board. The aftermost center tank has traditionally been used for this purpose. However, an increasing number of tankers now use a two- or three-stage slop separating process in which several slop tanks are used. The purpose of these systems is to separate oily residues from water—by the simple process of allowing them to float to the surface. When the procedure is carried out properly, much of the bottom water is clean enough to pump overboard. As a result much less slop water is accumulated.

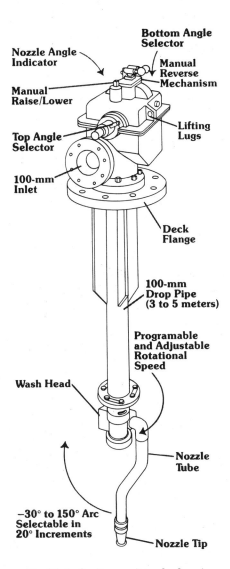

Fig. 9-11. The Lavomatic SA (selective arc) tank-cleaning machine is specifically designed for crude oil washing. As with other types of equipment, COW is carried out while cargo is being discharged. However, with this unit the operation can begin as soon as the cargo level is below the wash head.

The initial stage of washing covers a downward arc from 140° to 90°. As the discharge progresses, the washing arc can be changed in 20° increments to keep pace with the falling cargo level. In the final stages, a −30° "overlap" is provided for more effective bottom washing. Butterworth.

As an example, let's examine a system using the two aftermost wing tanks for slops. One of these is the *dirty* slop tank and the other is the *clean* slop tank. Slops are introduced into the dirty slop tank about mid-level in the tank (both tanks are first filled partway with clean seawater). The *bottom* portion of the dirty slop tank continuously gravitates, through a special line, to the *midlevel* of the clean slop tank. The *bottom* portion of the clean slop tank is either: 1) recirculated to the tank-cleaning machines or 2) pumped overboard after adequate settling (see figure 11-5).

After tank cleaning is completed, the slop tanks are allowed to settle for a given period of time. Then the clean bottom portion is pumped overboard. The remaining slops can be discharged in port or mingled with the next cargo. This entire process is called *load-on-top;* it has proven particularly effective on ships using COW.

The amount of oil that can be pumped overboard on the high seas is strictly limited. To make sure that discharges fall within regulatory guidelines, many tankers are now fitted with monitors that measure the oil content of ballast discharged at sea. Also, oil-water *interface detectors* are used to locate the interface in slop and dirty ballast tanks. The pumping of bottom water can thus be stopped in ample time to prevent discharge of oil.

### CRUDE OIL WASHING (COW)

Most crude carriers have now adopted a tank-cleaning technique that greatly reduces the amount of slop water accumulated. Tanks are washed with a *crude oil spray* drawn from the ship's cargo and delivered with the fixed tank-cleaning machines.

This method takes advantage of the solvent properties of crude oil, which are greatly augmented by delivery in a high pressure spray. Crude oil washing is particularly effective against built-up sludge on tank surfaces, and it significantly reduces the need for manual mucking. It also increases the amount of crude recovered during the discharge, by as much as 1 percent of the total load. On a 250,000-ton ship, this represents an additional 2,500 tons of cargo recovered—which otherwise would be left clinging to tank surfaces.

COW is normally used only while a tanker is discharging her cargo. Crude is routed from the discharge side of the cargo system into a special line that carries it to the tank-cleaning machines. The cargo pumps supply the necessary pressure and no special pump is required. A pressure of 10 kg/cm$^2$ (142 psi) might be considered typical—although this may vary considerably, even on the same ship. It is important to note that the COW technique requires a certain minimum pressure (as specified in each ship's COW manual) in order to operate effectively. At some discharging ports it is necessary to "pinch down" the manifold valves to achieve the desired pressure on the system.

**Twin-nozzle machines.** In order to wash tanks with crude oil, only fixed machines specifically designed for crude oil washing may be used. These may either be twin-nozzle or single-nozzle machines. Both work effectively, but require different methods of operation. Twin-nozzle machines are nonprogrammable; that is, no specific arc can be selected. They run through a complete cycle, washing all tank surfaces in a given period of time. For this reason, crude oil washing with this type of machine is not started until the tank is nearly empty. In this manner no time is wasted "washing" the surface of the cargo.

**Single-nozzle machines** are deck-mounted and programmable. Tanks are washed in stages. As the tank level drops, the arc of the cleaning spray is varied to "follow" the oil level downward. If *selective arc* machines are being used, the operation can begin as soon as the cargo level is below the wash head. With less sophisticated machines, the process usually begins with a *top wash* when the tank is about 60 percent empty.

The *bottom wash* begins when the tank is almost completely empty. This step is important, because the largest amount of sludge, wax, and sediment tends to accumulate on the bottom. Strategically located twin-nozzle machines, mounted near the tank bottom, are often called into play at this point. These machines are used to wash trouble spots or "shadow areas" behind beams, platforms, etc., which are missed by the deck-mounted machines.

**Stripping** is of vital importance when crude oil washing. The purpose of COW is to reduce residues left on board the ship—therefore, if stripping is not done carefully the process is a waste of time. Discharge and suction piping must be drained and stripped, and the COW lines on deck must be drained as well. This is done by opening a COW nozzle at the forward end of the ship and another at the aft end. The line then drains into the aft tank by gravity.

The initial crude oil wash can be followed by a water rinse, if necessary. This is done, for example, when a tank is needed for clean ballast or when crew members must enter for repairs, inspections, etc.

**Prerequisites for using COW.** In order to use COW, several conditions must be met. First of all, only ships with inert gas systems, properly oper-

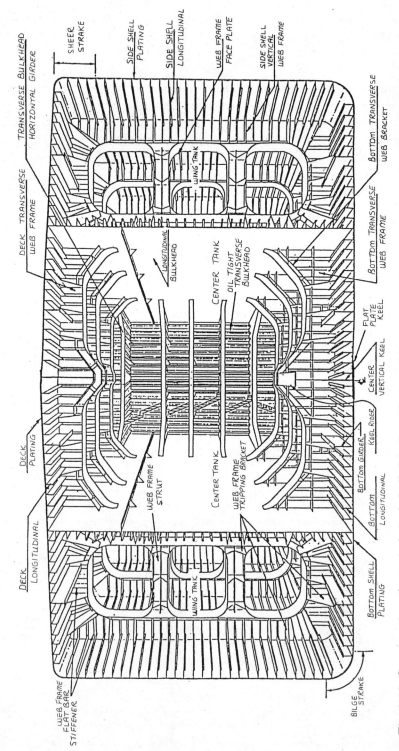

Fig. 9-12. Cross section of a typical single-hulled tanker. The complex structure of cargo tanks makes tank cleaning a challenging task. Chevron Shipping.

ating, may use the technique. Also, because not all types of crude oil are adaptable to COW, the type of crude on board must be taken into account. A positive means must be provided to check tank bottoms and confirm that they are clean and dry. And because COW usually lengthens the total discharge time, an allowance must be made for this extra time when planning a vessel's stay in port.

The tank-cleaning machines must be permanently mounted and of a type suitable for crude oil washing. Each machine must be supported in a manner that will enable it to withstand the vibration and pressure surges associated with crude oil washing. If portable drive units are being used, there must be at least one unit available for every three machines. Single-nozzle machines mounted on deck must each have an indicator showing arc and rotation of the machine. Twin-nozzle machines mounted on deck must have an indicator showing that each machine is actually moving when in use. In addition, regulations specifically state that bottom-mounted machines must *not* be programmable.

**Which tanks, and how often?** The International Maritime Organization (IMO) requires the following on ships using COW: 1) no ballast may be pumped into a cargo tank unless the tank has first been crude washed and 2) all tanks must be crude washed periodically for sludge control. The basic requirement is that enough tanks be crude washed to permit adequate ballasting during the ballast passage, taking into account normal weather, draft, and trim requirements. (For a discussion of draft and trim requirements during the ballast passage, see chapter 8.) Of the remaining tanks approximately 25 percent must be crude washed each voyage on a rotating basis—although an individual tank need not be washed more than once every four months.

**Hectic, but effective.** The addition of COW and inert gas systems to crude carriers has increased the complexity of ship operation tremendously. To say that the average discharge is hectic is an understatement. It is not uncommon to discharge, crude oil wash, and ballast—all simultaneously.

Great pressure is put on the ship's officers—the chief mate in particular—to keep the systems operating efficiently and in accordance with the plethora of regulations currently provided by local, national, and international authorities. A system failure often results in costly delays. For example, if the COW system (or IG system) fails, the ship is unable to crude wash her tanks. If she can't crude wash her tanks, she can't ballast them—which in turn means she can't sail.

Despite these difficulties, crude oil washing has proven to be an effective technique. Cargo recovery is improved; less slops are accumulated; sludge is controlled. But to achieve these results, sincere and careful effort is required of the ship's officers and crew.

## LINE, PUMP, AND BOTTOM FLUSHES

When cleaning tanks it is important to remember that cargo piping is also dirty and must be flushed. This is done in a variety of ways, depending on the degree of cleanliness required.

Before washing tanks in preparation for clean ballast, it is essential to flush the branch lines by pumping a little water into each tank with the main cargo pumps. Otherwise the clean ballast will push the dirty contents of each branch line into the tank as it is loaded, thus contaminating the ballast. This initial flush is often performed alongside the dock before sailing on the ballast passage.

It is also wise to flush the bottom piping before pumping clean ballast overboard. Some ships are fitted with a line drop at number 1 tank for this purpose. A tank-cleaning hose is hooked up to the drop, by means of a special adapter, and hot water is flushed through the system. Master valves and crossovers are arranged so that the whole lower piping system can be flushed aft into the slop tank.

The piping can also be flushed with the main cargo pumps. Seawater is pumped forward through the bottom lines and—by means of a special crossover at number 1 tank—back to the slop tank via the stripping line. This method forms an improvised loop, with water travelling forward through the main lines and returning aft through the stripping line. It can only be used, unfortunately, on ships fitted with a forward crossover between main and stripping lines.

On light-oil ships, mainly those carrying water-sensitive cargoes, another situation sometimes arises at the loading port. Just prior to loading, the tank bottoms are occasionally flushed with the product to be loaded. An inch or two of product is loaded into each tank, then pumped ashore via the terminal's slop line. This assures that the ship's pipelines and tank bottoms are clear of water, which might contaminate the cargo. After loading has finished, the pumps can also be flushed by discharging a small amount of cargo with each. This clears the pumps and the piping between them and the manifold.

These procedures are important, especially when handling water-sensitive products. Refinery technicians take product samples before and after the ship is loaded. Specifications (such as flash point and gravity)

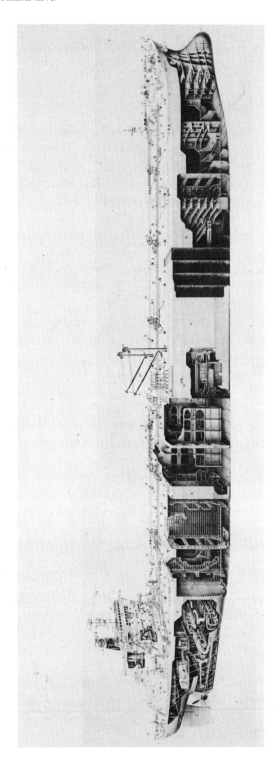

Fig. 9-13. Cutaway diagram of a VLCC. The immense size of cargo tanks makes washing with portable machines impractical. Instead, fixed machines much larger than portable models are installed inside the tanks. Exxon.

are checked for each product. When the final "specs" fall off their initial values, the ship's officers—the chief mate in particular—usually take the blame. Careful tank cleaning and flushing help to prevent this.

## THE TANK-CLEANING TEAM

It is the chief mate's job to plan the tank-cleaning operation, including number and position of machines, number of drops, temperature and pressure of wash water, and flushing procedures. The practice on many ships is to outline the tank-cleaning strategy on a blackboard. Each tank is marked off with an appropriate symbol after it is washed, gas-freed, and (if necessary) mucked.

On vessels equipped with portable machines, the operation is carried out by the pumpman (who lines up the system and strips the tanks), the bos'n (who acts as foreman on deck), and two or more sailors. In port, the mate on watch is usually in charge; at sea, the chief mate directs the operation.

The procedure is different on tankers with permanent, fixed-in-place machines, in that much less physical work is required. One or two crew members can normally do the job.

## DANGERS

Tank cleaning is a routine part of tanker life and there is a temptation to become complacent about it. This is a mistake; *tank cleaning is hazardous and should be regarded as such.* Here is an example:

The crew of a tanker was cleaning tanks when one of the portable machines became fouled on an obstruction. It was necessary for a man to enter the tank and free the machine—a routine operation, no problem. He donned a fresh-air breathing apparatus and lifeline, then started down the ladder. One of his shipmates, who was tending the lifeline, leaned over the hatch to check his progress. Inadvertently, the line tender allowed his cigarette lighter to slip out of his shirt pocket.

It tumbled into the tank, which —like a powder keg with no fuse—was brimming over with explosive vapors. There was a tiny spark and then, in an instant, the tank became an incinerator. The lifeline and air hose disintegrated in the flames. The men topside could do nothing to save their shipmate. They stood by helplessly while he burned to death.

Crew members, especially officers, must never develop an easygoing attitude toward tank cleaning. It is one of the riskiest operations tanker crews must perform, with the ever-present danger of: 1) explosion; 2) gas-

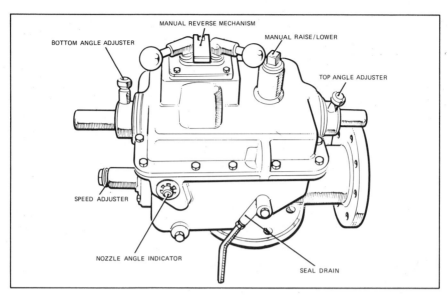

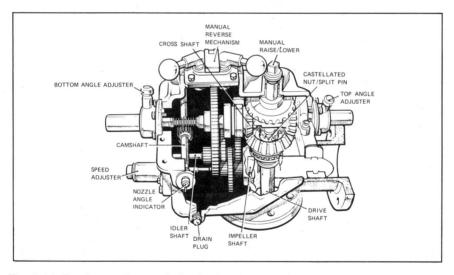

Fig. 9-14. Gearbox and controls for the Lavomatic SA deck-mounted tank-cleaning machine. This model contains a selective arc control for use with multistage crude oil washing. The gearbox contains: 1) the in-line washing fluid turbine that powers the machine and 2) the system of gears controlling the speed and direction of nozzle rotation. Butterworth.

sing or asphyxiation of crew members entering tanks; 3) injuries caused by falls inside tanks; and 4) broken feet and toes, hot water burns, and bruises suffered by crew members while handling portable machines.

The first two dangers—explosion and gassing—are the most serious, but the others should not be ignored. I have seen enough burns, bruises, and smashed toes to attest to that. It was also my sad misfortune to be on board a tanker in dry dock when one of the yard workers fell and broke his neck inside a tank. In short, tank cleaning is a time when all hands must remain alert and cautious.

## EXPLOSION

Tankers have been prone to explosion since their development in the latter part of the 1800s. Risk of explosion is particularly great during tank cleaning. Empty tanks—especially those in the process of being cleaned—are more often inhabited by explosive vapor mixtures than full tanks, where vapors are normally too "rich" to ignite. (See chapter 10 for a discussion of *explosive range.*)

In general, officers and crew must strive to prevent explosive mixtures from contacting sources of ignition. One way to accomplish this is by eliminating sources of ignition (fires, sparks, burning cigarettes, static electricity) inside and in proximity to cargo tanks.

It is also possible to alter the atmosphere inside the tanks. Most tankers are now fitted with inert gas systems which dilute tank atmospheres with incombustible gases. On the following pages we will explore these explosion-prevention procedures in more detail.

### STATIC ELECTRICITY

During an 18-day period in December of 1969, a chain of three supertanker explosions shocked the shipping world. One ship, the 206,000-ton *Marpessa,* sank as a result of the damage to her hull. At the time, she was the largest ship ever lost through sinking. The other two ships, the *Mactra* and the *Kong Haakon VII,* were salvaged and repaired at tremendous expense. All three ships were new at the time of the explosions. In addition, all three were about the same size, all were steaming through the tropics in a ballasted condition, and *all were cleaning tanks at the time of the explosions.*

A few months after these explosions occurred, I was in San Francisco at a company meeting for ship's officers. An executive showed our group an aerial photograph taken after the explosion on board the *Mactra.* The steel deck had peeled back, like a giant sardine can, through half the length of the ship.

"This," he said, pointing at a small outline superimposed on the photograph, "indicates the approximate size of a T2 tanker. Most of you gentlemen have sailed on a T2 so you are familiar with the size. As you can see, a T2 would fit inside the hole in the *Mactra*'s deck."

What had caused these disasters?

Shipowners, with millions of dollars and the lives of their crews at stake, launched an extensive investigation. Although the exact cause of the explosions will, in all likelihood, never be known, the investigation revealed evidence pointing to *static electricity* as a probable cause of ignition. The effects of static electricity are familiar to virtually everyone. Try shuffling across a carpet and touching somebody with your fingertip. More often than not, you will each receive a tiny shock. This is static electricity. It is caused by the tendency of electrons to transfer between molecules of unlike charge. The molecules on the soles of your shoes pick up extra electrons as you shuffle across the carpet, giving your body a negative charge. These electrons immediately want to flow toward a neutral or positively charged object, such as your unsuspecting friend across the room. The same process takes place in the molecules of tank wash water. The water rushes through an intricate system of pipes, ejects from a whirling nozzle, and collides at tremendous velocity with the bulkheads and decks of the tank. In the process it picks up an electrical charge and leaves an opposite charge on surfaces it has contacted, such a tank-cleaning machines. This action is greatly exaggerated in large tanks with huge, permanently installed machines.

When electrons jump from one object to another, they create a *spark*. This generates heat—enough to ignite a flammable mixture. However, *two* things are required before a tank explosion can occur: 1) a flammable mixture of vapor and oxygen and 2) a source of ignition.

A number of years after the *Marpessa-Mactra-Kong Haakon explosions,* lawmakers decided the first condition was easier to control. As a result most tankers of 20,000 dwt and above are now required to have inert gas systems. Nevertheless, it is important to control the second condition—sources of ignition—whether a ship is fitted with inert gas or not. Certain precautions are strongly recommended for eliminating static electricity as a source of ignition while tank cleaning; these precautions are outlined in the following paragraphs.

**Keep machines grounded.** A clear electrical pathway must be maintained between portable machines and ground, in order to neutralize any charges that might accumulate.

Portable tank-cleaning hoses contain one or more internal bonding wires for this purpose. As long as these wires remain intact and the hose

Fig. 9-15. Proof that tank cleaning is dangerous; the VLCC *Kong Haakon VII* exploded while cleaning tanks off the coast of Africa in 1969. U.S. Salvage.

remains securely coupled to the hydrant, electrical charges will flow freely to ground. If, on the other hand, the electrical continuity is interrupted (as by a defective bonding wire or uncoupled hose) the electrical charge may flow the other way by *sparking into the tank.*

Crew members must not be allowed to uncouple hoses while machines are still inside the tanks. Unfortunately, some sailors are in the habit of uncoupling hoses as an easy way of draining them. *This is extremely dangerous—don't allow it.* Instead, have crew members loosen the hose coupling just enough to break the vacuum, then retighten after the hose has drained. Better yet, install bleeder valves at each deck connection to permit draining of hoses without loosening couplings.

**Charged steam and mist.** Steam that has been injected into a tank is likely to contain a strong electrostatic charge. No objects, grounded or otherwise, should be lowered into a tank containing steam. The same precautions should be observed immediately after cleaning a tank with water, when the charged mist suspended inside could easily spark to a foreign object. Ventilate the tank thoroughly before lowering sounding rods or other objects.

**Crude oil washing.** Before washing tanks with crude oil, the tank (or tanks) to be used as the source for driving the tank-cleaning machines must first be *debottomed.* At least one meter (three feet) should be discharged from the tank, thus eliminating residual water. This precaution is important, because oil-water mixtures generate large static charges when used for tank cleaning. Also, any ship using COW must have an operating inert gas system, which we will discuss in the following paragraphs.

### INERT GAS SYSTEMS

Until comparatively recent times, tanker crews had little or no control over the atmosphere within cargo tanks. This is one of the reasons why tankers have been vulnerable to explosions since their early history.

Tanker owners have sought to remedy this situation through the use of tank-inerting systems which pipe the ship's flue gases to the cargo tanks (fig. 9-16). These systems are expensive, but they work.

In a ship's boiler, air (approximately 79 percent nitrogen, 21 percent oxygen) mixes rapidly with fuel oil to produce heat and the following residual gases:

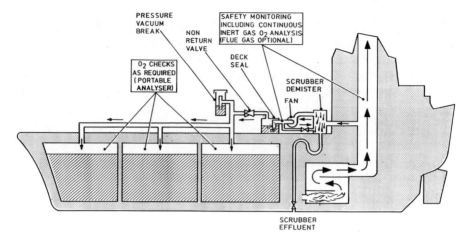

Fig. 9-16. Simplified diagram of a basic inert gas system. Flue gases are drawn off, cooled, cleansed of impurities, and piped to the ship's tanks. Servomex.

| Oxygen | 3 to 4 percent | Water vapor | 5 percent |
| Carbon dioxide | 13 percent | Nitrogen | 77 percent |
| Sulphur oxides | 0.3 percent | Other gases | 1 to 2 percent |

This residual mixture is, for all practical purposes, inert and will not promote combustion. On ships fitted with inert gas systems, these gases are drawn off, filtered of impurities, and cooled (fig. 9-17). The result is a mixture of nitrogen, carbon dioxide, and about 3 percent oxygen. A fan blows this gas into the tanks by means of a special inert gas line on the main deck. Entering gas dilutes and displaces the tank atmosphere until it falls below 8 percent oxygen. Thereafter, the system maintains a slight, constant pressure of gas. No air can enter, and chances of explosion are close to nil.

Quite a few vessels are now equipped with inert gas generators, which supplement or take the place of flue gas systems. Still others are equipped with nitrogen membrane separators, which provide inert gas—nitrogen— of high purity and dryness. This might be the case, for example, on a chemical carrier where cargo contamination is a consideration. For a detailed discussion of inert gas systems, see chapter 13.

### ENTERING THE TANKS

Every time a seaman descends into a tank, there is a chance he won't come out alive. The ill-informed and the foolhardy are the most likely to

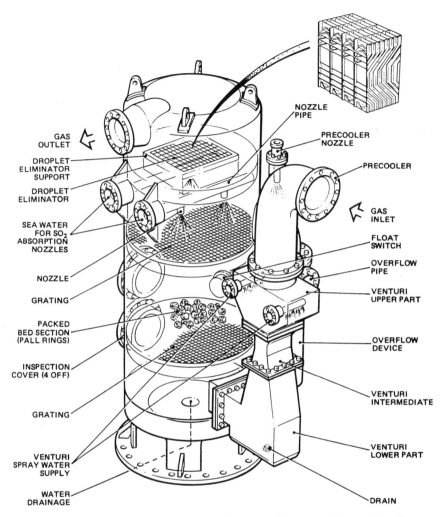

GAS
OUTLET

DROPLET
ELIMINATOR
SUPPORT

DROPLET
ELIMINATOR

SEA WATER
FOR SO$_2$
ABSORPTION
NOZZLES

NOZZLE

GRATING

PACKED
BED SECTION
(PALL RINGS)

INSPECTION
COVER (4 OFF)

GRATING

VENTURI
SPRAY WATER
SUPPLY

WATER
DRAINAGE

NOZZLE
PIPE

PRECOOLER
NOZZLE

PRECOOLER

GAS
INLET

FLOAT
SWITCH

OVERFLOW
PIPE

VENTURI
UPPER PART

OVERFLOW
DEVICE

VENTURI
INTERMEDIATE

VENTURI
LOWER PART

DRAIN

Fig. 9-17. The inert gas *scrubber* cools the gas and removes impurities. Permea Maritime Protection.

perish. It is therefore essential to understand both the risks and precautions involved.

Besides the risk of fire and explosion that we have already discussed, two basic dangers lurk inside empty cargo tanks: 1) *gassing*—caused by breathing poisonous hydrocarbon vapors and 2) *asphyxiation*—caused by lack of oxygen.

**Gassing.** Petroleum vapors are poisonous. Even low concentrations can kill a human being in minutes. The gassing victim first feels a slight dizziness, followed by a mild elation. He quickly loses his sense of smell, begins to feel drunk, slurs his speech, staggers, becomes increasingly confused, loses consciousness, and—unless removed to fresh air in short order—dies.

This all happens *very* quickly. Some gases, such as hydrogen sulfide. can render a person unconscious after two or three inhalations. Hydrogen sulfide, which is found in Arabian crude and other so-called "sour" crudes, is characterized by a "rotten egg" odor in small concentrations. However, in higher concentrations it has virtually no odor, because *hydrogen sulfide, like all hydrocarbon vapors, quickly deadens the sense of smell.*

Before entering a tank, always check the vapor content with a combustible gas indicator (figs. 9-19 and 9-24). The indicator draws a sample of the tank atmosphere by means of a "sniffer" attached to a long tube.

This sample should be taken close to the bottom of the tank, where petroleum vapors (which are heavier than air) are most likely to accumulate. Concentrations of vapor should also be suspected near bell-mouths, corners, beam faces, and puddles of oil or sludge.

Combustible gas indicators are designed to detect *explosive* concentrations of vapor. However, petroleum vapors are *poisonous* in concentrations well below the lower explosive limit (the L.E.L., about 1 to 2 percent for most products).

*Therefore, the slightest movement of the needle indicates an unsafe condition.*

Important notes on combustible gas indicators follow.

1. They detect vapor at the point of the sample only. Pockets of vapor may be present in other parts of the tank.

2. Some models do not work properly in oxygen-deficient atmospheres. They may indicate a safe condition when, in fact, a high concentration of vapor is present along with a deficiency of oxygen. Therefore, always test with an oxygen indicator before entering a tank.

Tanks should be retested at frequent intervals, hourly if necessary, while crew members are working inside. In addition, *tanks must be ventilated continuously while crew members are below.*

Muck, sludge, and scale give off vapors which can quickly gas up a tank. Crew members walking through puddles of oil or sludge may accelerate this process. Leaky fittings such as pipelines, valves, and heating coils can also introduce vapors. If you suspect a tank is gassing up, get out immediately. But remember—don't rely on your nose for warning.

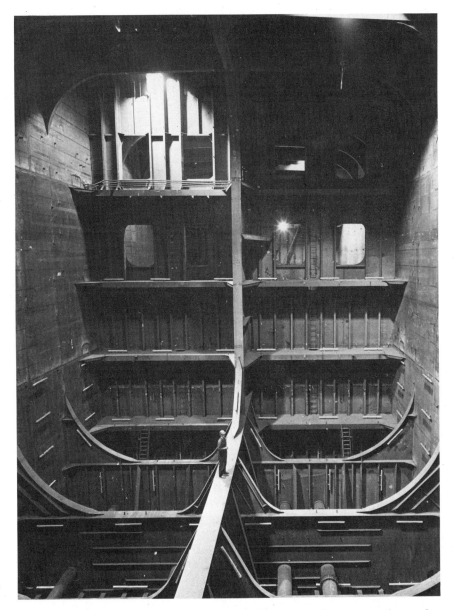

Fig. 9-18. Both man and machine are dwarfed by the dimensions of a modern cargo tank. Salen & Wicander.

After working in the tanks, it is not uncommon for crew members' boots and clothing to be covered with oil and sludge. It is important that crew members not store this oily clothing in their quarters or other living

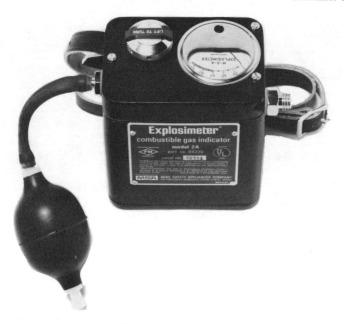

Fig. 9-19. Combustible gas indicator (Explosimeter). The readout indicates the amount of hydrocarbon vapor as a percentage of the lower explosive limit. (Note that this model is not designed for use in oxygen-deficient atmospheres.) Mine Safety Appliances.

spaces. Vapors given off by such clothing can be a serious health hazard, particularly in a small room with poor ventilation. Furthermore, the risk of fire—even explosion—is all too real, especially if crew members smoke. Oily clothing should therefore be laundered promptly and kept out of living quarters in the meantime.

As a final note on gassing, it is important to understand that a crew member can be gassed even while wearing a breathing apparatus. This has happened more than once after someone has gone into a partially full tank to fix a piece of equipment, such as a broken reach rod. Needless to say, a person who passes out and falls into a tank full of cargo is in a very bad place indeed. Therefore, the foolish practice of entering tanks with cargo in them should *never* be allowed.

**Asphyxiation.** Human beings quickly perish without oxygen. A compartment containing less than 21 percent oxygen by volume is unsafe.

Permanent ballast tanks, cofferdams, chain lockers, peak tanks, and other sealed spaces may become deficient in oxygen as a result of the rusting process, which consumes oxygen.

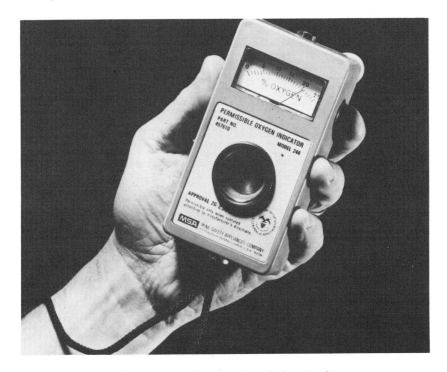

Fig. 9-20. Oxygen indicator. Mine Safety Appliances.

*Tanks that have been inerted are especially dangerous.* They should be thoroughly ventilated and tested with an oxygen indicator before entering. Any reading under *21 percent* oxygen is unsafe. Always use *extreme caution* when entering a tank. Pockets of inert gas and hydrocarbon vapors may still be present.

**Precautions.** The following precautions should be observed when entering tanks:

1. Check for petroleum vapors before entering. Don't rely on smell; use an *Explosimeter* or similar device. The slightest movement of the needle denotes an unsafe atmosphere.

2. Make sure oxygen content is adequate (21 percent).

3. Operate blowers continuously while crew members are below.

4. Have rescue equipment close by the tank entrance and ready for immediate use.

5. Assign somebody to remain topside and keep an eye on workers below. Should trouble develop in the tank, his job is to *sound the alarm first,* before attempting a rescue.

6. If at any time while working in a tank you begin to feel dizzy or giddy, leave the space immediately. Have other crew members do the same.

## RESCUE

The following equipment should be available for tank and pumproom rescues: 1) lifeline, 2) harness, 3) large tripod or similar device from which to rig the lifeline, and 4) self-contained breathing apparatus.

The pumproom is the most frequent source of gassing accidents. One set of equipment should therefore be kept at the top of the pumproom at all times. Another set should be available for tank rescues.

Practice using the rescue equipment before you run into an emergency. When one of your shipmates passes out in a tank or pumproom, seconds count. Don't waste them reading instructions on the breathing apparatus or trying to figure out how to rig the lifeline. Learn these things beforehand. Speed is essential. If the victim remains below longer than 4 to 6 minutes, he will suffer brain damage and, in all probability, death. Four minutes is not much time. Even a well-trained rescue team working with good equipment laid out ahead of time (not always the practice, unfortunately) may have only a poor chance of success.

The situation is particularly bleak on VLCCs. A person climbing around in a VLCC center tank is little more conspicuous than a flea and, if unconscious, just as hard to find. Noel Mostert paints an apt picture in his book, *Supership:*

> . . . to reach someone lying in the remoter regions of the tank, lost from sight and with only a rough idea where he might be, was tantamount, surely, to being told atop the dome of a darkened Gothic cathedral to descend an eighteen-inch-wide stairway pinned to its walls and buttresses and to find somewhere at the bottom among the naves, bays, chapels, colonnades, and apses a senseless form that had to be brought aloft, all within four minutes.

The breathing apparatus is an essential part of any rescue; don't go down without one. To illustrate: try climbing out of a tank sometime while holding your breath; then imagine what it would be like with a 200-pound man on your back. It would be virtually impossible. You would have to breathe and, in all likelihood, would also succumb to the vapors. Don't try to be a hero. Too many people have died that way.

Along the same lines, don't remove your air mask to give air to the victim unless an unavoidable delay makes it necessary. The important thing is to get him out quickly.

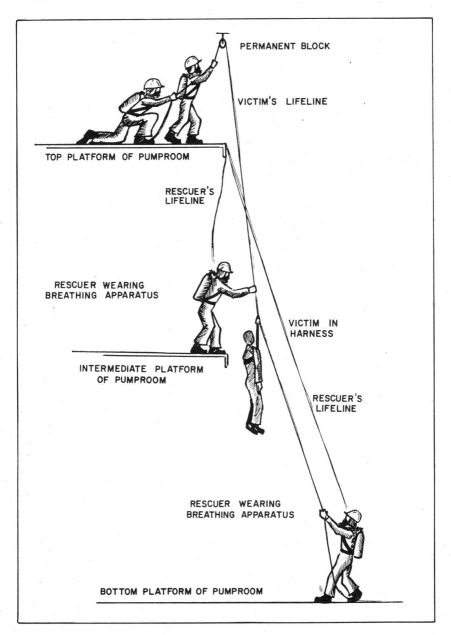

Fig. 9-21. Proper method of making a pumproom rescue. Speed is essential in both pumproom and tank rescues: The victim must be removed to fresh air within 4 to 6 minutes to prevent permanent brain damage or death. U.S. Coast Guard.

Fig. 9-22. The compressed air type of breathing apparatus has become increasingly popular on tankers. It is fast and simple to use. Mine Safety Appliances.

Check the victim's pulse and breathing as soon as you are clear of the tank. If his heart has stopped or if he has stopped breathing, administer cardiopulmonary resuscitation immediately. When he begins breathing on his own, have him lie face downward with his head slightly downhill if possible. This position will prevent him from gagging if he vomits. It will also keep his lungs clear and minimize the chance of pneumonia.

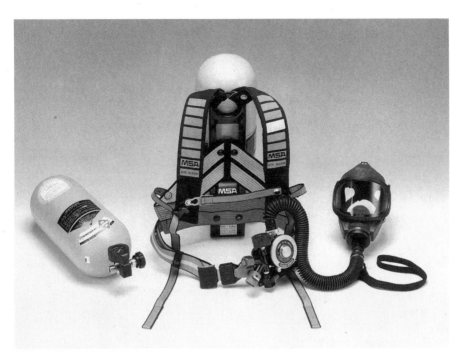

Fig. 9-23. Compressed air breathing apparatus, shown with spare tank. It is important to learn how to use the breathing apparatus before an emergency occurs. During an emergency, such as the gassing of a crew member, speed is essential. Mine Safety Appliances.

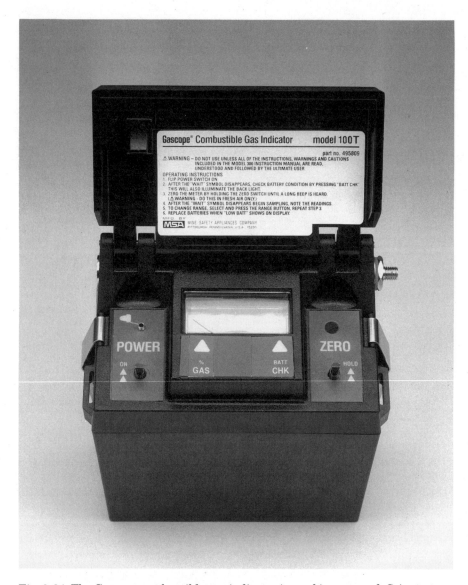

Fig. 9-24. The Gascope combustible gas indicator is used in oxygen-deficient atmospheres. The readout indicates total percentage of hydrocarbon vapor present (as opposed to the Explosimeter, which indicates vapor as a percentage of the lower explosive limit). This model features an electric pump, which replaces the aspirator bulb used on the older model (Tankscope). Mine Safety Appliances.

# CHAPTER 10

# FIRE FIGHTING AND FIRE PREVENTION

THE word *fire* strikes fear in the hearts of seamen, especially those who have seen a ship burn. These individuals have felt the panic and desperation that only a fire at sea can cause. But a shipboard fire need not end in tragedy. Calm, resolute, and intelligent action can defeat the most terrible conflagrations. An amazing example of this was provided by the crew of the 8,000-ton British tanker *San Demetrio* during World War II. While steaming in an Atlantic convoy, the *San Demetrio* was shelled and badly damaged by the German pocket battleship *Admiral Scheer.* Fire engulfed the tanker, which was carrying a full cargo of gasoline. It is not surprising that the crew quickly decided to abandon ship. They drifted in the Atlantic for 20 hours. No help arrived; they had been given up for lost. Then the badly scarred hull of the *San Demetrio,* still ablaze, drifted back into view. Faced with a lack of other alternatives, the crew decided to reboard the burning vessel in the hope of saving her. They climbed aboard with tremendous difficulty and, after two harrowing days, succeeded in extinguishing the fire. Eventually the *San Demetrio* limped into port and delivered most of her cargo.

More than one tanker crew has chosen to abandon ship before making a serious attempt to fight a fire. Abandoning ship is a perilous undertaking in itself, especially in rough weather. The safer alternative is often to stand fast and fight the fire. As the crew of the *San Demetrio* demonstrated, even a serious fire can, with calmness and courage, be fought successfully.

Modern tankers are supplied with fire-fighting equipment which is at once sophisticated and reliable. But even the most expensive equipment is useless if crew members are ignorant of its operation. Each officer should learn the location and function of every piece of fire-fighting equipment. This knowledge is crucial on any ship, and especially so on a tanker.

## WHAT IS FIRE?

Fire cooks our food, warms our homes, and powers our machines. Without it, civilization could not exist as we know it. But fire can be a danger as well as an asset, as the caveman who discovered it undoubtedly learned.

Fig. 10-1. Crew members practice with portable foam equipment during fire drill. British Petroleum.

Fire burns people, too. It burns their homes, their farms, their cities. It is dangerous in other ways as well. It uses oxygen and causes asphyxiation; creates carbon monoxide, thick smoke, and toxic gases, all of which can quickly kill.

**Fire, a chemical reaction.** When vapors given off by a flammable substance combine rapidly with oxygen, we witness the phenomenon we call "fire." For example, the wax in a candle—the fuel—must first melt and then vaporize before it can be drawn into the flame and burned. Fire is, in effect, a chemical reaction. Molecules of hydrocarbon gas join violently with molecules of oxygen to form carbon dioxide, water vapor, and most importantly, heat.

### THE ELEMENTS OF FIRE

Every fire owes its existence to four indispensable elements:

Fig. 10-2. This tanker, the *Salem Maritime,* was gutted by fire in 1956. U.S. Salvage.

**1. Fuel.** This is the vapor from petroleum or other combustibles that combines with the oxygen to produce fire.

**2. Heat.** Hydrocarbon molecules must be heated substantially before they will combine with oxygen. For example, a piece of wood left lying in a cold fireplace will not ignite, but apply a sufficient amount of heat (as with burning newspapers) and it bursts into flame.

Heat need not be applied with an open flame, however. Heat can transfer through a steel bulkhead and ignite a tank of fuel oil without the aid of an open flame. This process is known as *conduction.* Heat also spreads by *convection*—the tendency of hot air to expand and move from one location to another—and by direct *radiation* (much as the sun heats a sandy beach on a hot summer day). Once ignited, a fire produces its own heat and continues getting hotter, often reaching temperatures above 2,000°F. (1,100°C.).

**3. Oxygen.** People and fires both need oxygen to survive. The earth's atmosphere contains approximately 21 percent oxygen by volume. Lower this figure far enough (to 10 to 15 percent) and you literally "suffocate" the most tenacious fire.

Fig. 10-3. Kings Point midshipmen attack a blaze at fire-fighting school. National Maritime Union of America.

**4. Chain reaction.** Molecules must pass through several steps in the oxidation process, one after another, in a regular progression. This is a little like building a tower out of toy blocks. Remove one of the blocks, and the whole structure collapses. Similarly, remove one step from the molecular chain reaction, and a fire ceases to burn.

To extinguish a fire, therefore, at least one of four elements—fuel, heat, oxygen, chain reaction—must be removed. Modern fire-fighting equipment and methods have been developed with this in mind.

### IMPORTANT TERMS

To aid in preventing fires and, when necessary, in extinguishing them, it is important to understand the following terms:

**Flash point.** The temperature at which petroleum vapors form a flammable mixture with air is called its flash point. For many petroleum products (such as gasoline), the flash point is below the average temperature found in cargo tanks. In other words, you can assume explosive vapors are present when such products are carried.

**Explosive range, or flammable limits.** Hydrocarbon vapors will not burn in an atmosphere containing less than 10 percent oxygen. In addition, the vapors must fall within a given volumetric percentage or no reaction can take place. As shown in figure 10-5, a mixture containing too much or too little vapor will not burn (see also table 10-1).

Table 10-1

FLAMMABLE LIMITS
(Percent by Volume in Air)

| Product | Lower Limit | Upper Limit |
|---|---|---|
| Crude oils (average) | 1.0 | 10.0 |
| Gasoline | 1.3 | 7.6 |
| Kerosene | 0.7 | 6.0 |
| Propane | 2.1 | 9.5 |
| Methane | 5.0 | 15.0 |
| Benzene | 1.4 | 8.0 |
| JP4 (military jet fuel) | 1.4 | 7.6 |
| Ethylene oxide | 2.0 | 100.0 |

Fig. 10-4. Applying dry chemical to a Class B fire. Seafarers International Union.

When vapors are present in amounts above the upper flammable limit, the mixture is said to be too *rich* to burn. If below the lower limit, it is too *lean*. Oddly enough, an empty tanker is more likely to fall within these dangerous limits than a full one. In fact, most tank explosions occur in empty or ballasted vessels. On vessels with full tanks, the mixture is generally well above the upper flammable limit: too rich to ignite.

This was apparently the case when, in October of 1970, the *Pacific Glory* collided with the *Allegro* off the Isle of Wight. The *Pacific Glory,* a 77,000-ton tanker fully laden with Nigerian crude, suffered severe engine room explosions. Fire engulfed and destroyed her superstructure and spread to the surrounding water. Nevertheless, her cargo remained untouched; it was eventually delivered to its destination in Europe.

**Ignition temperature.** Any flammable substance will ignite when heated sufficiently. The point at which this happens is called the ignition temperature. For petroleum products this temperature is anywhere from 490° to 765°F. (255° to 405°C.) When heated to its ignition temperature, a product will ignite without the aid of a spark or other external source of ignition. Once ignited, a fire produces its own heat and continues to get hotter,

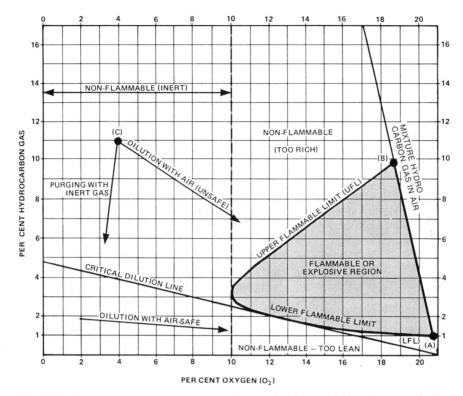

Fig. 10-5. The diagram shown above indicates the flammability of oxygen/hydro-carbon gas mixtures which might be expected in the ullage space of a cargo tank (in a wide range of conditions). Note that, as the oxygen level drops, the explosive region decreases dramatically—finally disappearing at 10 percent oxygen content. Permea Maritime Protection.

reaching temperatures hundreds of degrees above the ignition temperature. This fact underlines the paramount importance of *speed* in fighting fires. An incipient, relatively cool fire is much easier to extinguish than a white-hot blaze several hours in the making.

## THEORY OF FIRE FIGHTING

Every fire must be attacked by removing one of the four elements previously described: fuel, heat, oxygen, or chain reaction. The extinguishing method chosen depends on the size and location of the fire, and the combustible material involved.

Table 10-2 lists the various classes of fire and the preferred extinguishing methods for each.

Table 10-2

CLASSES OF FIRE

| Class | Material | Extinguishing Method / Agent |
|---|---|---|
| A | Ordinary combustibles such as wood, paper, and canvas | Cooling with water or water fog. Foam, $CO_2$, and all-purpose dry chemical are less effective but can be used. |
| B | Flammable liquids such as fuel oil, kerosene, and gasoline | Smothering with foam, $CO_2$, inert gas, or steam. Dry chemical is also effective. |
| C | Live electrical equipment | Extinguishing agent must be non-conducting: $CO_2$, dry chemical. *Water and foam must not be used.* |

**Removing fuel.** In theory, removal of fuel is an excellent method of fighting fires, but on tankers carrying thousands of tons of petroleum it is usually impractical. Nevertheless, certain situations demand that this method be used.

For example, a fire on deck is fed by an overflowing tank. This situation obviously calls for an immediate cessation of loading. Other, less obvious circumstances sometimes arise when the removal of fuel is indicated. Therefore, never dismiss this method as a possible means of fighting a fire.

**Removing heat.** Water is one of the most effective cooling agents known. When sprayed on a fire, it quickly turns to steam, thereby absorbing and carrying away heat. Water is most useful on *Class A* fires since it can penetrate to the hot core of burning material. Aqueous film forming foam (AFFF) also has considerable cooling properties. Other types of foam, however, provide only minimal cooling.

**Removing oxygen.** Fires, like people, perish without oxygen. It follows that a fire can be extinguished by: 1) diluting the oxygen content until it falls below the amount necessary for combustion (10 to 15 percent) and 2) smothering the surface of the flame so oxygen cannot enter. Generally speaking, the first method employs carbon dioxide, steam, or inert gas; the second, mechanical foam.

Fig. 10-6. Spraying foam on an oil fire. Seafarers International Union.

**Interrupting the chain reaction.** Fire remains something of a mystery to scientists. They have theorized that combustion involves a rapid chain of chemical reactions without which no fire could burn. This theory seems to explain the success of dry chemical and halogenated extinguishing agents in fighting fires. These agents somehow interrupt the vital chain reaction in a fire, thus bringing on its quick demise.

## FIRE PREVENTION

Fires are easy to start but extremely difficult to extinguish; therefore, the obvious solution is to prevent them from starting. The first step in fire prevention is to *remain fire conscious at all times while on board a tanker.*

**Smoking.** This is the number one cause of fires at sea. Many of these fires occur in the living spaces where they are extinguished before much damage is done. Some are serious, however, and one example is a tanker's captain who went to bed one night with a bottle of whisky and a lighted

Fig. 10-7. The $CO_2$ room. The gas is released by remote control, then carried by pipes to the protected areas. The device in the upper right-hand corner is a time release mechanism, which gives crew members time to evacuate spaces before $CO_2$ is released. Ansul.

cigarette—a bad combination. Some time later, crew members noted a large quantity of smoke billowing out of the bridge voice tube leading to the master's cabin. They rushed below, but were too late. The "old man" was dead from asphyxiation and smoke inhalation.

Never allow yourself or the people working with you to become lax about smoking rules. Encourage crew members to leave their cigarettes in their rooms or other safe areas. This precaution prevents an individual from lighting up a cigarette in an unsafe area. Only safety matches should be used; cigarette lighters should not be allowed on board.

Areas considered safe for smoking while at sea may be extremely hazardous in port. An example is the fantail. Vapors from the dock make smoking in such places a definite hazard—something crew members may not realize. The risk is particularly great after a long voyage during which the crew has become accustomed to smoking in these areas. Be alert for crew members who may "light up" without thinking.

**The pumproom.** If a single place on tankers can be labelled the most dangerous, it is the pumproom. Pumprooms are frequent sources of fire and explosion. In addition, many tankermen have died after being overcome by toxic pumproom vapors. Therefore, never allow yourself to become complacent about entering or working in the pumproom. Here is an example of a man who could have used this advice:

A new pumpman was packing a leaky valve in a tanker's pumproom. At the time, the ship was carrying a full cargo of casinghead gasoline, one of the most volatile products carried on tankers. The pumpman decided to take a break and moved to a corner well away from the leaky valve. He sniffed the air, detected no gassy smell, and lit a cigarette. A moment later he was engulfed in flames as the pumproom exploded. He was lucky, however; although badly burned, he lived to tell the tale.

There are two lessons to be learned from this episode:

1. Never trust your nose to detect petroleum vapors.
2. Always assume an explosive atmosphere exists in the pumproom.

Pumproom bilges are rarely dry, especially on older ships. It is a common practice to drain pumps and lines into the bilges; leaky fittings contribute their share as well. On very old ships the pumproom can become a tropical rain forest of dripping oil and leaky steam lines.

Gasoline and other volatile products evaporate quickly, especially when spread across the pumproom bilge plating. The resultant vapor is both toxic and explosive. It is therefore imperative to use great care when descending into the pumproom, and to make sure the ventilation system is operating while crew members are below.

**Cleaning with gasoline.** Never use gasoline as a cleaning solvent. The temptation is sometimes great, particularly with thousands of gallons readily available.

On one tanker, a crew member succumbed to this temptation and caused a catastrophe. He poured a bucket of gasoline into a washing machine (which was located inside the after house) and proceeded to do his laundry. Several men were smoking nearby. Soon the machine's turbulent action generated a large amount of vapor, which spread through the accommodation area. The subsequent explosion and fire killed four men and injured six.

**Vapor accumulations on deck.** When loading in calm weather, petroleum vapor leaving the vent lines may settle around the main deck. Being heavier than air, it tends to lie close to the deck in a stagnant, invisible pool until dissipated by the wind. This vapor may eventually find its way into living spaces, contact a source of ignition, and flash back to the tanks. The result would be explosion, fire, or both. The hazard is greatest when handling gassy products. One ship, for example, was loading butane blend when she suffered a massive explosion. Vapor had drifted into the crew quarters, contacted a burning cigarette, and flashed back through an open ullage hole to one of the tanks. The explosion and fire that followed killed thirteen crew members and completely destroyed the ship. Several precautions help to avert this kind of tragedy:

1. Make sure your ship's inert gas system is used properly (see chapter 13).

2. Keep all doors, portholes, and other accommodation area openings fronting the cargo deck closed during cargo or ballasting operations.

3. Stop loading operations whenever heavy concentrations of vapor accumulate in the cargo-handling area. This is most likely to happen on hot, humid days with no wind.

4. On older, smaller tankers without inert gas systems, ullage covers are often opened for gauging and sampling. On such ships, keep ullage covers closed whenever possible. When they must be left open for any length of time, use a *flame screen* (a piece of fine wire gauze that fits over the ullage hole). A flame screen permits the passage of vapor, but not of flame.

**Sources of ignition.** Watch for situations that could bring a spark or open flame in contact with flammable vapors. Keep a careful eye on visitors; people unfamiliar with tankers are liable to "light up" in nonsmoking areas. Make sure no unauthorized electrical equipment or other spark-producing devices are used around cargo tanks, in the pumproom, or in other gassy areas. Carefully watch all activities on the dock. An automobile or burning cigarette on the dock could ignite low-lying vapors. In turn, these could flash back to the ship's tanks and cause an explosion. The close approach of a tug or other vessel during cargo operations is equally hazardous. Hot, smoldering soot from the stack exhaust could trigger an explosion (it has happened).

In port, a serious fire hazard is sometimes presented by the crew themselves. Unfortunately, it is not unheard of for crew members to return to the ship intoxicated. To prevent such individuals from unwittingly lighting a cigarette in prohibited areas, and to prevent them from breaking their necks, they should be escorted to their quarters immediately upon their return to the ship.

**Electrical storms.** One of the first ships I worked on after getting my third mate's license was a small, multiproduct tanker. She was a delightful little ship and a lot of fun to work on. Unfortunately, about a year after I left her, she was struck by lightning while her tanks were being cleaned at sea. The ensuing explosion killed several men and injured several others. Lightning generates ample heat to ignite a flammable mixture. It is foolhardy (and illegal) to load, discharge, clean tanks, or transfer cargo during electrical storms.

**Spontaneous combustion.** Certain substances such as oily rags, oily sawdust, wet laundry, and oil-soaked rubbish are vulnerable to a process called spontaneous combustion. Slow oxidation generates heat, and over a period of days or weeks, or even months, a substance may eventually reach its ignition temperature. It then ignites *spontaneously.*

Such fires have been a problem at sea since the Phoenicians first sailed the Mediterranean thousands of years ago. More than one ship has gone to the bottom gutted by flames that started spontaneously. Joseph Conrad dramatized this danger in his story, *Youth,* in which the bark *Judea,* carrying a cargo of coal to the Orient, catches fire and sinks in the Indian Ocean:

> You see it was to be expected, for though the coal was of a safe kind, that cargo had been so handled, so broken up with handling, that it looked more

Fig. 10-8. Main deck fire station. Chevron Shipping.

like smithy coal than anything else. Then it had been wetted—more than once. It rained all the time we were taking it back from the hulk, and now with this long passage it got heated, and there was another case of spontaneous combustion.

Cleanliness is the best weapon against spontaneous combustion. Paint lockers, laundry rooms, and other enclosed spaces must be kept as clean as possible. The chief culprits are piles of rags, rubbish, or clothing that have been impregnated with paint, grease, or vegetable oil. Such items should be laundered or disposed of promptly.

## EXTINGUISHING AGENTS AND EQUIPMENT

The following extinguishing agents are used on tankers:

**Water** is highly effective against *Class A* fires where a cooling effect is valuable. Seawater is generally used for this purpose. One or more fire pumps draw from the sea and deliver water to the fire main, a system of pipes that carries seawater to fire stations at strategic locations throughout the ship. Stop valves are fitted between stations so that sections of damaged pipe can be isolated to prevent loss of pressure.

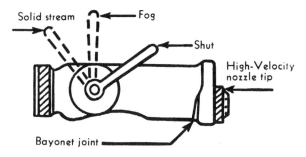

Fig. 10-9. All-purpose nozzle. U.S. Coast Guard.

Each fire station consists of a hydrant and fire hose (which is kept connected at all times, when practicable). In general, 2½-inch hose is used on weather decks, 1½-inch in confined spaces. Each hose is fitted with an all-purpose nozzle, which allows water to be delivered as a solid stream or in the form of high velocity fog (fig. 10-9).

Low velocity fog can also be produced with special applicators (fig. 10-10) that fit into the all-purpose nozzle. These break the water into a fine mist, thus presenting maximum surface area to the fire. Because of its superior cooling effect, low velocity fog is valuable as a protective "blanket" for fire fighters approaching a fire.

**Foam** is particularly valuable on tankers because of its ability to form a smothering blanket over burning petroleum. In addition, one type of foam (aqueous film forming foam, or AFFF) produces considerable cooling effect.

Foam is formed when air, water, and concentrated foam liquid are mixed together turbulently to produce the proper characteristics. Foam is generally mixed, or *proportioned,* by one of two methods on board ship (fig. 10-11). With the *balanced pressure* method, a proportioner mixes water and foam concentrate, which must enter the system at the same pressure. The second method is *line proportioning.* As water flows through a line proportioner, it creates a suction, or venturi effect, which draws foam concentrate into the water stream. (Foam discharge devices may be either aspirating or nonaspirating, as shown in figure 10-13).

On board tankers, foam is delivered either with portable foam nozzles or from fixed monitors. Portable nozzles (fig. 10-12) are fitted with pickup tubes which can be inserted into five-gallon containers of foam concentrate. Fixed monitors (fig. 10-18) are located strategically along the main deck.

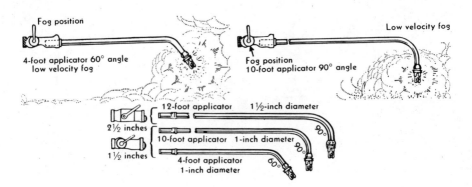

Fig. 10-10. Low velocity fog applicators are manufactured in various sizes and designs. U.S. Coast Guard.

**Carbon dioxide ($CO_2$)** is an inert gas approximately 50 percent heavier than air. It is an excellent smothering agent when used against *Class B* and *Class C* fires in confined areas. Carbon dioxide is applied by the following methods on board ship: 1) fixed systems, 2) semiportable extinguishers, and 3) portable extinguishers.

Fixed systems are most commonly used to protect the engine room, but spaces such as the pumproom and paint lockers can be fitted with their own separate systems as well (see figures 10-14 and 10-15). The gas is stored in batteries of tanks in a special room (fig. 10-7). Remote controls are provided in pull boxes for each space protected.

*Learn where these controls are located and which spaces they serve.*

Before activating a fixed $CO_2$ system, all ventilation to the area must be shut down and the space sealed to prevent entry of air. Fixed systems commonly contain only enough carbon dioxide for one application; they must therefore be used effectively the first time. Carbon dioxide smothers fires effectively, but it can also smother unwary crew members. The gas cannot be seen or smelled and gives no warning of its presence. For this reason, automatic alarms are installed on all fixed $CO_2$ systems. These alarms sound immediately throughout the protected spaces whenever the releasing controls are operated. A time-delay mechanism gives crew members time to leave the area before the gas is released.

Semiportable $CO_2$ extinguishers are often provided in the engine room, in addition to the usual fixed system. Tanks of carbon dioxide, bolted permanently to the bulkheads, are attached to portable hoses. These hoses are stored on reels and can be run out quickly to affected areas.

Portable $CO_2$ extinguishers (fig.10-16) are located in bulkhead holders throughout the vessel. They are provided in spaces where *Class B* and

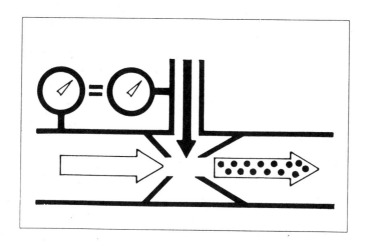

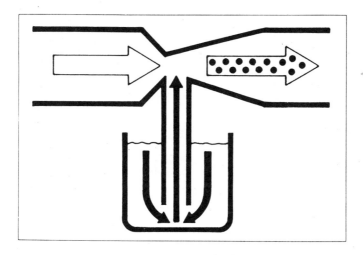

Fig. 10-11. One method of mixing, or proportioning, foam is the *balanced pressure* method *(top)*. A proportioner mixes water and foam concentrate during system discharge. The foam concentrate and water must enter the system at the same pressure.

Another method is *line proportioning (bottom)*. As water flows through a line proportioner (such as the portable foam nozzle shown in figure 10-12), it creates a suction, or venturi effect, which draws foam concentrate into the water stream. Ansul.

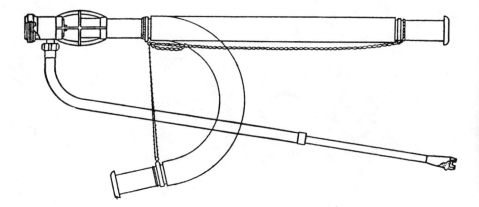

Fig. 10-12. Portable foam nozzle. Foam concentrate is syphoned from 5-gallon containers by means of the pickup tube. Inside the nozzle, concentrate combines turbulently with water and air to produce mechanical foam. U.S. Coast Guard.

*Class C* fires are most likely to occur, such as machine shop, radio room, galley, and pumproom. To operate a portable $CO_2$ extinguisher, lift it from its holder, pull the locking pin, and squeeze the handles together. Aim the horn toward the base of the fire and apply the $CO_2$ in intermittent, side-to-side sweeps.

**Dry chemical extinguishing agents** impede combustion by breaking up the molecular chain reaction. They are delivered with hand-held extinguishers (fig. 10-17), which are located strategically throughout the vessel.

Dry chemical is highly effective against *Class B* and *Class C* fires, and the all-purpose type extinguisher can also be used against *Class A* fires. Dry chemical should be applied across the base of the fire in a smooth, blanketing motion. If the fire is outside, it should be approached from windward. Dry chemical should be applied across the leading edge of the flame/fuel surface, using a side-to-side motion, and from a sufficient distance to avoid agitating (and thereby spreading) the fire.

**Steam.** With the exception of the fire main, steam-smothering systems are the oldest type of fire-fighting equipment found on tankers. Some older vessels are still fitted with steam-smothering systems, and it is important for officers to be acquainted with this equipment. The typical steam-smothering system consists of steam piping that leads from a master valve to a series of headers. A separate valve is fitted for each tank. When possible, these valves are left open; thus there is no delay in an emergency.

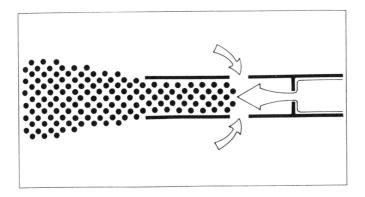

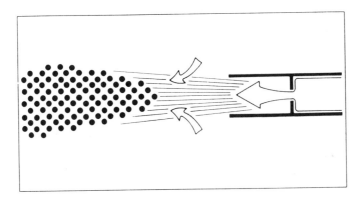

Fig. 10-13. Foam discharge devices may be either *aspirating* or *nonaspirating*. Aspirating discharge devices *(top)* are designed to mix air with the foam solution to form an expanded mass of bubbles. Nonaspirating discharge devices *(bottom)* may be used with certain low-expansion foam agents. With nonaspirating devices, the foam solution expands as it passes through the air enroute to the fire. Ansul.

When fire breaks out in one of the tanks, the master valve is opened; this allows steam to flow to all of the tanks. Valves to unaffected tanks are then closed, making certain to *leave steam on in tanks adjacent to the burning compartment.* This prevents the fire from spreading through heat conduction. After the fire has been extinguished, steam must continue to be applied until danger of reignition has passed. If turned off too soon, steam inside the tank will condense, create a vacuum, draw in air, and allow hot oil to reignite.

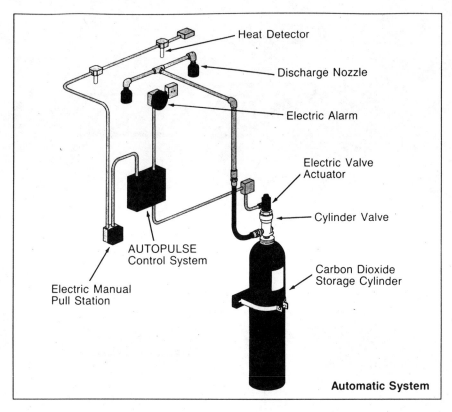

Fig. 10-14. Automatic $CO_2$ systems are used in spaces, such as paint lockers, which are often unattended. The most modern systems use an integrated detection and control package consisting of heat or smoke detectors, alarms, and an electronic control system. Ansul.

Every officer must know the location of the steam-smothering master valve. As a rule, this valve is located at main deck level in the forward end of the engine room or inside the athwartship passageway at the forward end of the after house. Except in case of fire, this valve is kept closed.

**Halogenated extinguishing agents, or halons,** are not new to merchant ships. In the past, carbon tetrachloride served as a popular extinguishing agent. It was banned, however, because it produces toxic vapors upon contacting fire. Two agents—Halon 1301 and Halon 1211—have proven safe when used on certain types of fires. Halon 1301 has been particularly effective against engine room fires.

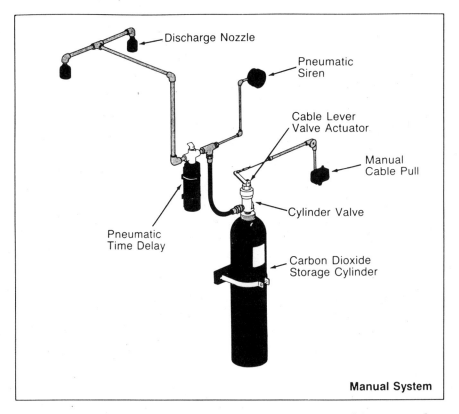

Discharge Nozzle

Pneumatic Siren

Cable Lever Valve Actuator

Manual Cable Pull

Manual Cable Pull

Cylinder Valve

Pneumatic Time Delay

Carbon Dioxide Storage Cylinder

**Manual System**

Fig. 10-15. Manual $CO_2$ systems have traditionally been used in spaces where personnel are present most or all of the time. Depending on the space protected, $CO_2$ is provided in a single tank or a battery of tanks (for example, for engine room installations). A time delay and alarm are installed to give personnel time to evacuate the area before release of $CO_2$. Ansul.

Unfortunately, the halons are ozone depletors. Because of environmental concerns about their use, it is likely that they will soon be eliminated as fire extinguishing agents on board merchant ships.

### FIGHTING THE FIRE

Early detection and prompt, resolute action are essential to fire fighting. After a fire has been detected, the following general procedure should be followed:

Fig. 10-16. Portable CO$_2$ extinguisher. General Fire Extinguisher.

1. *Sound the alarm.* A continuous sounding of general alarm and whistle will warn shipboard and shoreside personnel of danger and, equally important, will summon help.

2. *Evaluate the fire.* Above all, don't panic. Pause to think. How should this fire be fought? How can it be kept from spreading? How can sources of heat, fuel, and oxygen be eliminated? What is the greatest danger from this particular fire? How can this be blocked? A few seconds of clear, logical thought will prepare you to act decisively.

3. *Get the fire under control.* Isolate the fire by cooling surrounding bulkheads. Remove combustible material from adjacent compartments and, if possible, fill nearby cargo tanks with inert gas or steam. Cut off air to the fire by shutting down ventilation and by closing doors, portholes, hatches, and other openings.

4. *Extinguish the fire.* Take final steps to eradicate the fire completely: by cooling, smothering, breaking up the chain reaction, or a combination of these methods.

Fig. 10-17. All-purpose dry chemical extinguishers can be used on Class A, B, and C fires. General Fire Extinguisher.

5. *Guard against reignition.* Make sure the affected area has cooled completely before securing fire-fighting gear. This may take several hours.

Each fire must, of course, be attacked individually. The following pages outline a general course of action for specific types of fires.

**Fire in pumproom.** The pumproom presents the greatest risk of cargo fires. Most pumproom fires start near the bottom of the pumproom, where they are difficult to reach. Usually, if a small fire is caught immediately it can be put out with portable foam or $CO_2$ extinguishers; if not, it must be fought indirectly. One method is to hang hoses from the top of the pumproom. With all-purpose nozzles in the fog position, the fire is extinguished by a combination of cooling and smothering as water vaporizes and produces steam. Pumprooms on some vessels are fitted with fixed water fog systems that make lowering of hoses unnecessary.

Other ships are equipped with fixed $CO_2$ or foam systems. As a rule, these systems should be operated only after other methods have been tried. Should it become necessary to activate the fixed system, be sure the pumproom is sealed and all ventilation turned off. On some ships, the vent fans shut down automatically when controls to the fixed extinguishing system are operated.

Cool surrounding decks with water fog. If the pumproom adjoins the engine room, the bulkhead between them should also be sprayed with water. If the fixed system is not functioning or has been depleted, it may be possible to put out the fire by sealing the pumproom as thoroughly as possible. Provided that adjacent compartments are cooled or inerted, the fire will eventually burn itself out. After the fire has been extinguished, allow adequate cooling time before reopening. If possible, wait several hours. This precaution will avert possible reignition or explosion. Ventilate the compartment thoroughly before allowing crew members to enter.

**Fire on deck.** This type of fire is usually precipitated by a spill, as from a broken hose or overflow. Therefore, the first step is to cut off the fuel supply by shutting down transfer operations. Close ullage covers to prevent the fire from spreading to the tanks.

Foam is usually the most effective agent against fires on deck. Dry chemical, if available in sufficient quantities, is also effective against spill fires. It should be applied from upwind whenever possible.

**Fire in cargo tank.** A quantity of oil that has been on fire a short time is hot on the surface but relatively cool underneath. For example, fuel oil that has burned 10 to 12 minutes heats to its ignition temperature to a depth of only one inch. If extinguished quickly, it requires relatively little time to cool to a safe temperature.

A fire in an unruptured cargo tank should be fought in the following sequence.

1. Shut off the air supply by closing tank tops, ullage covers, tank cleaning openings, tapewells, and PV valves.

2. Activate the steam-smothering system, if fitted. After opening the master valve, close valves to unaffected tanks. Make sure, however, that tanks adjacent to the fire are protected.

3. Cool nearby decks, bulkheads, and equipment with high velocity water fog.

4. If the air supply cannot be cut off, direct foam through the tank top and allow it to spread over the fire. Unfortunately, this method is only effective in a full or nearly full tank. In an empty tank, it is necessary for the foam to coat every exposed surface where oil has been deposited: deck, keel, beams, frames, bulkheads, etc. This is virtually impossible. In such a case, high velocity water fog should be used.

Fig. 10-18. Foam monitor on deck. Exxon.

When a tank has been ruptured—as by explosion or collision—foam or water fog should be used. Water should be applied with caution. Be particularly careful not to agitate the surface of burning oil. If foam and water are used simultaneously, be careful not to break up, dilute, or wash away the foam blanket with the water.

**Fire in engine room.** Most engine room fires can be extinguished with portable or semiportable extinguishers (fig. 10-19). Larger fires should be fought with fixed or portable foam systems, plus water fog from the fire main. Fire fighters entering the burning area must wear a lifeline plus breathing apparatus for protection against asphyxiation and smoke inhalation.

Use the fixed $CO_2$ system as a last resort only. These systems often provide only one application; it must not be wasted. Before activating the fixed system, clear the area of personnel; close doors, hatches, and vents; secure boiler fires and vent fans. Controls for the $CO_2$ system and engine room ventilation are located outside the engine room. Learn the location

Fig. 10-19. This semiportable $CO_2$ system employs a hose reel and two fixed cylinders. The hose is reeled out, then charged with $CO_2$ by opening the cylinder
valves. The gas is directed at the fire by operating the control lever on the discharge horn. Ansul.

Fig. 10-20. Close-up of cylinder valves and attachments used with the semiportable $CO_2$ system. Ansul.

of these controls before you need them; don't be caught unprepared in an emergency. While the $CO_2$ is being released, spray water fog on outside decks and bulkheads. Remove combustible material, which could ignite through heat conduction, from neighboring areas. After the fire has been extinguished, allow adequate time for the compartment to cool before re-opening. Remember: If the fire flares up again, there may be inadequate $CO_2$ to put it out a second time.

**Fire on water adjacent to ship.** This type of fire often occurs after a collision. Foam is the most effective weapon. If no foam is available, solid streams of water may be sprayed between ship and fire. When conditions permit, this tactic will induce a surface current and move the fire clear of the ship.

**Fire in live electrical equipment.** If possible, de-energize the equipment. Should you have the slightest doubt, however, assume the equipment is "hot" and act accordingly. Never spray water on live electrical equipment. Salt water is an excellent conductor; fire fighters using it run the risk of being electrocuted. Foam is equally dangerous.

Carbon dioxide is the preferred agent against electrical fires. Dry chemical extinguishers can also be used, but they deposit a fine powder that may foul electrical contacts.

**Fire in living spaces.** This generally involves a *Class A* fire, making water the preferred extinguishing agent. Keep all doors to the compartment closed until equipment is assembled and ready for use. Cool outside bulkheads and doors with water. When ready to enter, fire fighters should use low velocity fog as a forward shield against heat and smoke. All crew members entering the compartment must wear lifelines and breathing apparatus (fig. 10-21).

**Fire on dock.** When a fire occurs on the dock or adjacent area, your first concern as officer in charge should be the safety of your ship. Take immediate steps to move her. Shut down the cargo, disconnect hoses and loading arms, single up lines, and have the engineers put steam on the engines. Call tugs if necessary. If a strong tide is running and no obstructions lie downstream, simply throw off mooring lines and allow the vessel to drift to safety. When well clear, drop the anchor.

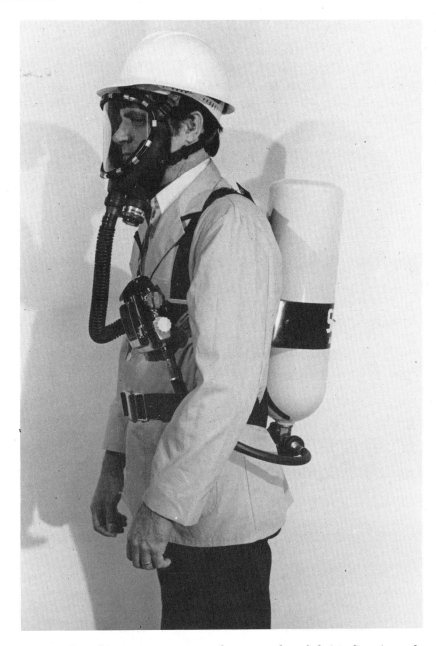

Fig. 10-21. Breathing apparatus must be worn when fighting fires in enclosed spaces. ATO.

## PREVENTION VERSUS CURE

The threat of fire, whether recognized or not, is always present on a tanker. Some crew members may go about their jobs in blissful ignorance, unmindful of the destructive force lurking beneath their feet, but you, as an officer, cannot afford to become complacent. A tanker fire is a terrifying thing, difficult and dangerous to put out. The crew of a tanker must always be prepared for the worst. But hopefully, if you and your shipmates remain alert and careful, the worst will never happen.

# CHAPTER 11

# POLLUTION PREVENTION

W HEN the *Exxon Valdez* ran aground on Bligh Reef in 1989, it resulted in the largest spill to date in U.S. waters. Other consequences of the grounding were costly repairs to the ship (fig. 11-1) and a monumental (and, once again, expensive) cleanup operation. (Still other ramifications of the spill——unforeseen at the time—have been perhaps even more profound than the damage to ship and environment. We will discuss some of these ramifications shortly.)

Spectacular accidents such as the grounding of the *Exxon Valdez* are a serious source of pollution, but they account for only a small percentage of the oil dumped into the world's oceans each year. In fact, a large percentage of oil discharges come from sources other than tankers. Shore terminals, naval vessels, and freighters are a few of the chief offenders on a very long list. However, these other sources of pollution are beyond the control of tanker crews, who have to concentrate on preventing discharges of oil from *tankers*.

The most important sources of tanker pollution are: 1) collisions and groundings, 2) accidental spills while loading and discharging, and 3) routine discharges while deballasting and tank cleaning. The last item—routine discharges—has been drastically reduced over the years as a result of improvements in equipment and techniques. Nevertheless, it is still a source of pollution.

In this chapter we will explore some of the ways in which oil pollution can be prevented. Improvements continue to be made in tanker design and equipment, but improved technology is not enough to solve the problem. Human beings control the machines, and the ultimate responsibility rests on their shoulders. The crew of every tanker, especially officers, share an important part of this responsibility.

## MINIMIZING ROUTINE DISCHARGES

Not that long ago, it was a common practice to pump tank washings and dirty ballast overboard at sea. As a result huge quantities of oil were dumped into the oceans of the world. It was normal, for example, while cleaning tanks en route to the shipyard, to pour a steady stream of "muck"

Fig. 11-1. In 1989, the *Exxon Valdez* ran aground on Bligh Reef, near Valdez, Alaska. This photograph, taken in dry dock, shows some of the extensive bottom damage caused by the grounding. Besides causing damage to the ship and environment, the grounding of the *Exxon Valdez* precipitated important changes in requirements for tanker design and operation. National Steel and Shipbuilding.

into the sea for days on end, leaving a trail of oil hundreds of miles long. At the time, tanker crews took this practice for granted as perfectly normal and legal (which it was). But those days are over.

The MARPOL convention places strict limits on the amount of oil discharged on the high seas. (MARPOL is discussed later in this chapter.) Slops are now retained on board for eventual discharge to shore facilities or, in some cases, are commingled with the next cargo. Only clean ballast is discharged along coastlines.

As discussed in chapter 8, tankers must often ballast their cargo tanks in order to remain seaworthy. Unfortunately, when seawater is pumped into cargo tanks it inevitably washes oil from tank surfaces. The resultant oil-water mixture is called *dirty ballast*.

Fig. 11-2. Bow-on view of a 326,000-tonner. The consequences of a collision involving such a ship could be disastrous. Improved navigation and collision avoidance systems, rigidly enforced sea lanes, and shore-based radar control may help to prevent such an occurrence. Gulf Oil.

Despite the stringent requirements dictated by MARPOL, ships must still ballast their tanks. And of course tanks still have to be cleaned periodically. The problem is to dispose of slops and dirty ballast without pumping them overboard. On the following pages we will explore some of the ways in which this problem is solved.

**Segregated ballast tanks.** One obvious solution to the problem of dirty ballast is not to create any. Most new tankers are now required to be fitted with segregated ballast tanks (SBT). These tanks incorporate a completely separate system of pumps and pipelines for clean ballast only.

**Load-on-top system (LOT).** In the early 1960s Shell International Petroleum voluntarily implemented a new system of ballast handling on its crude carriers: the load-on-top system, or LOT. Other major oil companies followed Shell's example, and today LOT is a standard practice on tankers.

Fig. 11-3. This 70,000-dwt tanker, the *Wafra*, ran onto a reef after suffering engine failure near Cape Agulhas, South Africa, in 1971. Nearly half her 63,000-ton cargo of crude spilled into the sea. The ship was a total loss. U.S. Salvage Association.

Authorities estimate that use of LOT has reduced tanker discharges by over three million tons per year. This figure represents a substantial reduction in worldwide pollution, plus a savings in recovered oil to companies. LOT is particularly effective when combined with crude oil washing and multistage slop tanks (fig. 11-5).

Figure 11-4 shows how the LOT system works. At the discharging port the ship pumps water ballast into selected empty cargo tanks in the usual manner. (On crude carriers, these tanks would typically have been washed with crude oil during the discharge.) On the voyage to the loading port, other tanks are washed in preparation for clean ballast. (Each branch line is flushed first by pumping a few barrels of seawater into tanks that are to be cleaned.)

Tank-cleaning slops are pumped into the aftermost center tank and retained on board. The newly cleaned tanks are then filled with ballast which, if the tanks have been washed properly, should be clean enough to pump overboard. In the meantime the initial dirty ballast has had time to settle out; that is, free oil in the ballast has had time to float to the surface. Most of the clean bottom water can therefore be pumped overboard

# 'Load on top' system of controlling pollution at sea

After discharging cargo, a tanker requires quantities of sea-water in some of its tanks to serve as ballast. When the water is loaded it mixes with oil residues in the tanks and becomes 'dirty'. During the voyage this dirty ballast water has to be replaced by clean ballast which can be pumped back to the sea without risk of pollution when the tanker reaches the loading port. Some empty tanks must therefore be cleaned at sea to ensure that the sea-water pumped into them as ballast remains clean and free of oil.

**1** During the voyage tanks to be filled with clean ballast water are washed and the oily washings are collected into one slop tank.

The oil in the neighbouring 'dirty ballast' tanks floats to the top.

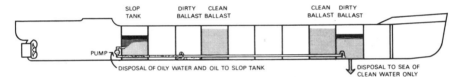

**2** The now clean tanks are filled with ballast water which will remain clean and suitable for discharge at the loading port.

In the 'dirty ballast' tanks, the clean water under the oil is discharged to the sea and the oily layer on top is transferred to the slop tank.

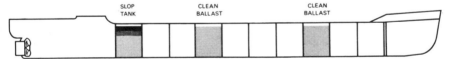

**3** In the slop tank, the dirty washings and the oil from the dirty ballast settle into a layer of oil floating on clean sea-water.

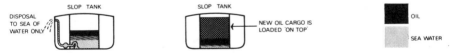

**4** This clean water under the oil is carefully pumped back into the sea and the oily waste left on board. The next cargo is loaded on top of the remaining oil and all of it is discharged when the tanker berths at the refinery.

Fig. 11-4. The load-on-top system decreases the amount of slops accumulated during the ballast passage. It is particularly effective when combined with crude oil washing and multistage slop tanks. Shell International Petroleum.

(to within perhaps two meters of the bottom). The remaining water and oil are then stripped to the slop tank.

The slop tank is allowed to settle in the same manner before pumping out the clean bottom water. As discussed in chapter 9, the separating process can be enhanced by using two or three slop tanks in stages. Slops are first pumped to a *dirty* slop tank. The bottom water is gravitated to one or more *clean* slop tanks. After adequate settling, it is carefully decanted to sea (fig. 11-5). The use of an electronic ullage/interface detector (fig. 11-6) is helpful in finding the exact location of the oil interface.

After following the procedure just described, a tanker is, for all practical purposes, in clean ballast. Before any of this ballast is pumped overboard, however, it may be necessary to flush the pumps and bottom piping into the slop tank as discussed in chapter 9. This is done before draining the bottom water from the slop tank, so that additional water introduced while flushing can also be settled out and discharged.

If upon arrival at the loading port a small amount of emulsified oil and water remains in the slop tank, the new cargo can be commingled with this mixture ("loaded-on-top") or—as is often the case—the residues can be disposed of by pumping to a shore slop tank.

**Discharging slops and dirty ballast to shore facilities.** The load-on-top technique works well on crude carriers making long ballast passages, but it cannot be used by all tankers. For example, on ships carrying refined products, loading on top would produce serious contamination in most cargoes.

Vessels making short hauls along the coast are also unable to use load-on-top, for two reasons:

1. Slops and ballast must have sufficient time to settle before draining off bottom water. A short voyage does not permit adequate settling.

2. It is illegal to pump *any* oil overboard within the *prohibited zone* (that is, within 50 miles of the coast—farther in some areas). The load-on-top system, no matter how effective, involves the release of some oil.

Product carriers and tankers making short hauls along the coast must therefore deal with slops and dirty ballast in another manner. One obvious answer is to pump slops ashore at the loading terminal, where they can be processed in shore separators. Because product carriers load nearly all of their cargoes at refineries, where facilities for handling slops and dirty ballast are available, this has become the logical solution to their dirty ballast problem.

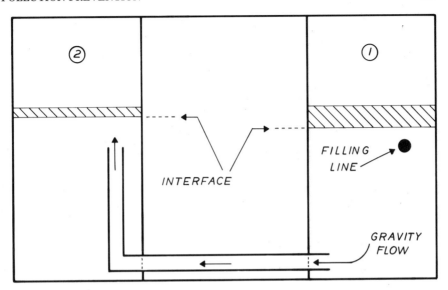

Fig. 11-5. A two-stage slop separating system, using a pair of wing tanks. The tanks are first filled partially with clean seawater. Slops are pumped into the *dirty* slop tank (1) at about midlevel. Bottom water gravitates from the dirty slop tank to the midlevel of the *clean* slop tank (2). The bottom water from the clean slop tank can be recirculated to the tank-cleaning machines or pumped overboard after adequate settling.

Tankers entering dry dock for repairs also face a problem of slop disposal. Luckily, nearly all major repair yards in the world are now provided with facilities capable of handling a substantial volume of dirty ballast and slops.

Vessels cleaning tanks for the shipyard therefore use a modified form of the load-on-top system. On the sea passage to the yard, tanks are cleaned and ballast transferred in the usual manner. Upon arrival, instead of "loading on top" as would normally occur at a loading terminal, slops are stripped ashore.

**Crude oil washing (COW)** greatly reduces the amount of slop water accumulated and thus lessens the problem of slop disposal. Crude oil, drawn from the ship's cargo, is sprayed onto tank surfaces with the regular fixed machines. If necessary the crude oil wash is followed by a water rinse. See chapter 9 for a more detailed discussion of COW.

**Vapor control systems.** A significant source of pollution is the vapor given off by petroleum cargoes. In fact, many tons of petroleum are re-

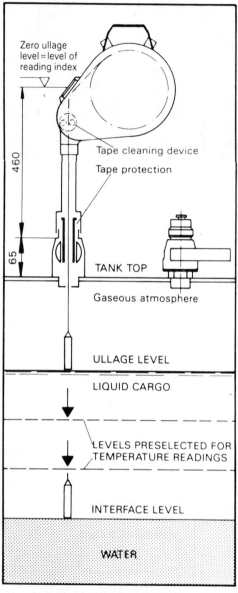

Fig. 11-6. An interface detector is helpful in finding the exact location of the oil/water interface. The installation shown here employs a specially designed ball valve, through which the ullage tape and sensor are inserted. Ullage, temperature, and oil/water interface can therefore be measured under completely closed conditions. American United Marine Corporation.

leased into the atmosphere each year through evaporation. A number of ports now prohibit the venting of hydrocarbon vapors, and ships calling at such ports must be specially fitted for vapor control. (See chapter 14 for a discussion of vapor control systems.)

## COLLISIONS AND GROUNDINGS

The waterways of the world are crowded. Ships of all types, not just tankers, run the risk of collision every day. Whether navigating from Indonesia to Japan or from Saudi Arabia to the Netherlands, every trip on a tanker seems to involve at least a few watches in heavy traffic. Of course, this situation is not entirely new. In some areas, such as the English Channel and the South China Sea, maritime traffic has been congested for many years. But ships are bigger than they used to be, and the consequences of a collision, especially one involving a tanker, are much greater. The old hit-or-miss methods of dodging other ships are no longer acceptable.

In recent years, maritime nations have taken steps to control ship movements more precisely. One example has been the introduction of traffic lanes in congested waterways such as the English Channel, the Strait of Malacca, and the Cape of Good Hope (and on approaches to major harbors such as New York).

Radar monitoring of ship movements has also been used effectively in some ports and in such areas as the Strait of Dover—through which a large portion of Europe's tanker traffic must pass. (Unfortunately, at this writing there are many ports worldwide where radar monitoring is either nonexistent or ineffective. Most ship's masters would probably agree that this is an area where improvement is needed.)

Improvements continue to be made in shipboard navigation equipment. Tankers are now equipped with accurate and reliable radar, collision avoidance systems, and satellite navigation systems. The global positioning system, or GPS, provides continuous satellite fixes of high accuracy and reliability. *Differential GPS*—in which a fixed shore station "corrects" the satellite signal—produces a remarkably precise position (within about 5 meters). Another breakthrough is *ECDIS* (electronic chart display and information systems), in which a ship is navigated on an "electronic chart." By using such a system, a navigator can virtually pinpoint the ship's position continuously in real time.

With the advent of VLCCs, groundings have become a more serious risk than in previous years. Many nautical charts in use today were made for ships drawing about 30 feet; some are based on surveys from the nineteenth century. Today hundreds of ships drawing 60, 70, 80 feet, and over

Fig. 11-7. Automated bridge of a modern tanker. Improved navigation equipment helps to minimize chances of collision and grounding. Kockumation.

are plying "shallow" waters, previously deep enough for any ship, with no real assurance that they won't strike bottom. In fact, a few have struck bottom, most notably in the Strait of Malacca near Singapore, where the bottom is granite. It is hoped that improved surveys, combined with precise depth-finding equipment and careful navigation, will be the ultimate solution to this problem. Another solution is to keep VLCCs out of shallow water. Because these vessels draw too much water to enter major harbors anyway, they often call at offshore terminals where they load and discharge through submerged pipelines. Many of these terminals now use single-point moorings, or SPMs (fig. 11-9). An underwater pipeline carries cargo along the ocean floor to the shore terminal, often miles away. Deep-draft tankers thus avoid the uncomfortable task of feeling their way into shallow harbors.

The job of piloting a VLCC, whether in a harbor or along the coast, is a tricky one. A variety of sophisticated equipment has been developed to make the job easier—bow and stern thrusters, Doppler speed indicators, etc. However, different ships use different equipment and this sometimes

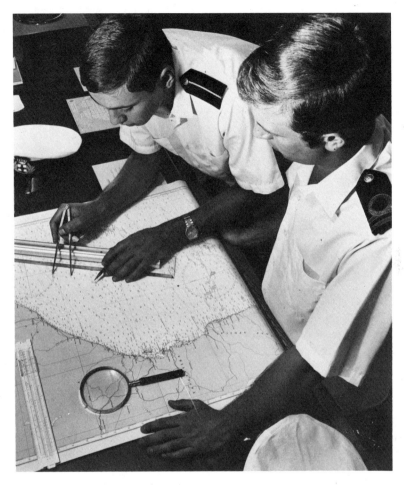

Fig. 11-8. Outbound from the Persian Gulf, the watch officer and cadet navigate a VLCC down the east coast of Africa. Destination: Western Europe via the Cape of Good Hope. British Petroleum.

confuses pilots. For this reason, it is extremely important for the master and other officers to assist pilots in every way possible and to advise them about the ship's maneuvering characteristics. Some companies use a form (fig. 11-10) to make sure important information is exchanged between pilot and ship's master.

**Changes in tanker design.** After the grounding of the *Exxon Valdez,* Congress passed a piece of legislation with far-reaching implications for

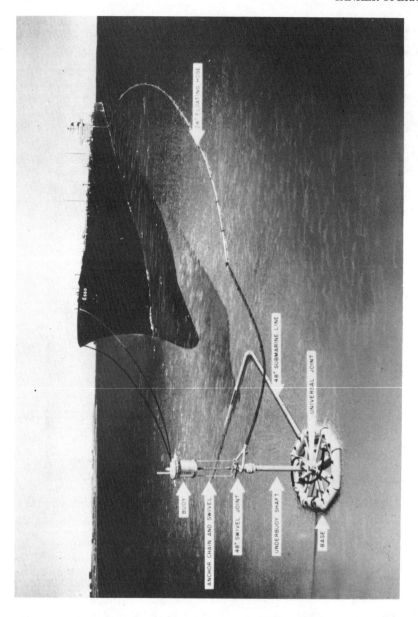

Fig. 11-9. Schematic diagram of a single-point mooring off the north coast of Africa. Exxon.

the tanker industry. The Oil Pollution Act of 1990 (OPA-90) requires, among other things, that most new tankers be of double-hulled construction. The idea of double hulls is to reduce the number of oil spills caused by collisions and groundings, and it is generally agreed that the double-hull design will, indeed, prevent many such spills from occurring.

**Before proceeding on pilotage, please give the following information to the vessel Master:**

1.  What is your intended plan of navigation and approach to the berth?

2.  How many tugs will be used?

3.  When and where will tugs make fast?

4.  Will ship's lines be used for tugs?

5.  What are the tide and current conditions along the route?

6.  What is the force and direction of wind expected along the route?

7.  What visibility conditions do you anticipate?

8.  Available anchorage en route?

During pilotage, develop a specific berthing plan with the Master. Pay particular attention to angle and velocity of approach to the jetty, line running sequence, and the tug/mooring boat control system. Develop this plan in sufficient time for it to be explained to the ship's officers. If necessary, develop an alternative plan to use if things should go wrong.

Take your time. Slow down, if necessary, to ensure that all parties agree to proposed action.

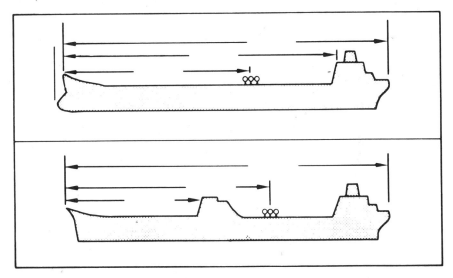

Prepared by _____ . Master

Read and understood _____ . Pilot

Fig. 11-10. Vessel/Pilot Information Exchange form. ARCO.

## PREVENTING SPILLS

Accidental spills while loading and discharging account for only a small portion of total pollution. They are nevertheless a constant worry—perhaps the greatest worry of all—for the ship's officers. If you have a spill, even a small one, the consequences to you personally may be devastating, involving huge fines and possible loss of your license. Prevention of such spills is therefore vital, not only for the protection of harbors and coastlines, but for your own well-being. Some common sources of spills are described in the following paragraphs.

**Hoses and loading arms.** These form at best a delicate bond, easily broken, between ship's manifold and shore pipeline. Flexible hoses with flanged couplings are connected by inserting a fiber gasket (used once only) between flanges, which are then bolted together. This is an important operation and must be done carefully. In ports where loading arms take the place of hoses, a special hydraulic clamp is sometimes used in lieu of the conventional hookup with bolts. Quick connect/disconnect hoses are also used on some ships. Whichever method is used, the connection should be made with deliberate attention and care.

Flexible hoses should be supported by belt slings, saddles, or bridles, *not a single rope sling* (fig. 11-11). These are hung from hose booms provided in the manifold area. They should be placed approximately every 10 feet along the length of the hose. Topping lifts and runners supporting hoses should be *made fast to cleats,* never left on capstans or gypsyheads.

Loading arms are in some ways superior to hoses, but they can tolerate little fore-and-aft movement. A strong surge forward or aft can snap loading arms like so many matchsticks. The result is not just a spill, but a deluge. The way to prevent this problem is to tend mooring lines carefully and to keep manifold and loading arms aligned as closely as possible.

Small spills frequently occur when hoses and loading arms are drained before disconnecting. Hoses are normally drained into ship's tanks, blown clear with compressed air, sucked out with shore pumps, or simply drained into drip pans. Whichever method is used, make sure it is done carefully. After disconnecting, have crew members attach blank flanges to hoses, loading arms, and manifold connections (fig. 11-13). A common mistake occurs when crew members forget to bleed air into the line as hoses are being sucked out by shore pumps. This creates a vacuum that holds oil in the hose. As a result, oil sometimes floods out on deck when the hose connection is broken. In the event that some oil does leak out for any reason, never allow the sailors to drain it overboard by pulling scupper

Fig. 11-11. Flexible hoses should be supported by belt slings, saddles, or bridles. Chevron Shipping.

plugs. It is amazing how many veteran seamen still try to get away with this. It may save them a messy cleanup job, but it is also a crime.

**Communication.** Language differences can cause plenty of trouble in foreign countries. Be sure to reach a clear understanding with the shore as to which language will be used, and make sure everyone involved understands signals for starting and stopping cargo.

Communication is sometimes a source of difficulty at offshore terminals. Be sure to know which radio frequency the shore is using. In addition, specify an emergency shutdown signal (usually a long blast of the ship's whistle) in case the radio malfunctions.

**Equipment failure.** Many spills have been caused by jammed valves and broken ullage tapes. These spills are difficult to prevent, since the equipment may seem to be working fine. For example, a gate valve may "feel" closed after turning down 25 turns when in reality it has jammed with 5 turns to go. Such spills can, however, be minimized and contained by alert watchstanding. Be on guard for malfunctions and never assume your equipment is flawless; it isn't.

Fig. 11-12. Loading arms can tolerate little fore-and-aft movement. Mooring lines must be tended carefully to maintain alignment with the manifold and to prevent surges forward or aft. Shell International Petroleum.

**Sea valves.** Improperly set sea valves have been the source of some disastrous spills. The following is an example of how this could happen.

A tanker on the final leg of her ballast passage approaches the loading port. Sea valves are opened and ballast is discharged to sea. For one rea-

Fig. 11-13. Cargo hoses must be blanked off after disconnecting. Exxon.

son or another, the pumpman forgets to close the sea valves afterwards. The ship arrives at the dock and the officers complete the preloading checkoff—neglecting, however, to check the sea valves.

Fig. 11-14. Proper communication between ship and terminal is essential. Chevron Shipping.

Loading commences. It is nighttime and a strong tide is running. Hundreds of barrels of oil flow silently into the harbor via the open sea valves. Unnoticed by crew members, it drifts into the darkness with the tide.

To avoid this type of spill, always check sea valves carefully before loading starts. In fact, it is wise for two officers to do so independently. *This inspection is essential; don't neglect it.* It is also important to make regular checks of the water around your vessel during cargo watches, day and night. If you see anything that looks like oil, shut down until you find out where it's coming from.

### WHAT TO DO IF A SPILL OCCURS

Quick and intelligent action can minimize the effects of a spill. Should a spill occur while you are in charge, resulting in the leaking of oil to harbor waters, take the following steps immediately:

1. Shut down and close valves from which oil is escaping.
2. Call the master and chief mate and tell them what has happened.
3. Alert the engine room and have them pressurize the fire main, if necessary. Have crew members break out fire-fighting gear.
4. Notify the terminal.

5. In an American port, call the Coast Guard by radio or telephone and report the spill. Give your name and title, vessel name, company name, location of spill, and approximate quantity of oil involved. The law requires you to make this report as soon as possible after discovering a spill.

## LAWS RELATING TO POLLUTION

There are numerous national, regional, and local laws relating to pollution, all of which must be obeyed by tanker operators. Essentially, no oil whatsoever may be discharged in harbors or along coastlines. On the high seas the amount of oil that may be discharged is strictly limited by the MARPOL convention, as described in the following section.

**MARPOL.** In the fall of 1973, representatives of the maritime nations met in London and drafted the International Convention for the Prevention of Pollution from Ships, 1973. In 1978 a protocol containing additional requirements was added. The 1973 Convention and subsequent protocol are often referred to simply as MARPOL.

MARPOL prohibits the discharge of oil and oily mixtures within 50 miles of nearest land. Discharges are also prohibited within certain "special areas" (Mediterranean, Baltic, Black, and Red seas, and the Persian Gulf). Ballast water discharged in the prohibited zones may contain no more than 15 parts per million of oil—a miniscule amount.

Unlike regulations passed by individual nations, MARPOL's scope is international, including the high seas. It is administered by the International Maritime Organization (IMO), an agency of the United Nations.

Besides establishing prohibited zones, MARPOL limits the amount of oil discharged outside these zones (that is, on the high seas). The total oil discharged, per voyage, may not exceed 1/30,000 of the total tonnage of cargo last carried (1/15,000 on some older tankers). The instantaneous flow rate may not exceed 30 liters per mile. This is a very small quantity of oil considering what tankers used to dump into the ocean. Future conventions will, in all likelihood, completely prohibit the discharge of oil on the high seas.

MARPOL also limits the size of tanks on new ships and requires most new tankers to be fitted with segregated ballast tanks (SBT). Existing crude carriers not fitted with SBT are required to have crude oil washing systems.

More recent supplements, or annexes, to MARPOL have made additional requirements. For example, Annex II sets standards for the operation of chemical tankers; in general the main focus has been shifted from waste management to improved recovery of cargo. Annex V is designed to reduce the amount of garbage dumped into the oceans by ships. An important aspect of Annex V is that it completely prohibits the discharge of plastics at sea.

**OPA-90.** As discussed earlier, the passage of the Oil Pollution Act of 1990 was a consequence of the *Exxon Valdez* grounding. Although a U.S. law, OPA-90 has worldwide implications. The increasingly international nature of the tanker industry makes it impossible for any nation to operate in a vacuum, and the passage of this historic law has already drawn reactions from tanker owners and operators throughout the world. At this writing, it is not yet clear what the long-term effects of OPA-90 will be. (For an in-depth discussion of the ramifications of OPA-90, see chapter 12.)

### KEEP IT IN THE TANKS

Thor Heyerdahl, the Norwegian explorer, made an epic crossing of the North Atlantic on his raft, *Ra,* in 1969. His 57-day voyage started in Morocco and ended in Barbados in the Caribbean. Heyerdahl made the following statement about his passage: ". . . at least a continuous stretch of 1,400 miles of the open Atlantic is polluted by floating lumps of solidified, asphalt-like oil."

Many people still think the seas, in their vastness, will remain forever immune to danger from human influence. This is a naive belief. The seas are vast but not infinite; they can absorb just so much oil. Spilled oil is the potential enemy of all living creatures, human beings included. It destroys or limits the growth of marine life, ruins wildlife nesting areas along shores, spoils beaches and recreation areas, kills birds, contaminates drinking water, causes fire hazards, and releases noxious vapors. In plain words, the most important duty of every member of a tanker's crew is to keep the oil where it belongs—in the tanks.

# CHAPTER 12

# THE TANKER AND THE LAW
## BY NICHOLAS BLENKEY

A MISINTERPRETATION of a radar echo. A valve closed a little late. Both are simple human errors that can initiate chains of events with disastrous consequences—especially where tankships are involved. What does all this have to do with the law?

So far as tanker operations in U.S. waters are concerned, the law has recently been changed, and changed dramatically. Everyone involved with tanker operations should be aware that, with passage of OPA-90 (the U.S. Oil Pollution Act of 1990), there is a very real possibility that simple human errors can bring the possibility of criminal prosecution, should a local prosecutor feel that negligence or misconduct is involved.

OPA-90 also ushers in an era of unlimited liability for pollution damage that could see a financially sound, responsible shipping company bankrupted by a single major pollution incident.

In many ways, too, OPA-90 marks a breach between the United States and the rest of the international maritime community.

The law that prevails on board a tanker—or any other ship—is that of the flag state (the country of registration). But when a ship enters the waters of another country, it becomes subject to the laws of that country (the port state).

Obviously, there is great potential for conflicts between the shipping laws of the various countries that a ship may visit on a single voyage. Different countries have very different ideas about how ships should be operated.

Until passage of OPA-90, however, the international maritime community had achieved a workable mode of overcoming those differences. That mode still prevails outside of U.S. waters and, indeed, within U.S. waters so far as many aspects of shipping operations that are unaffected by OPA are concerned.

## INTERNATIONAL CONVENTIONS

The way in which the international community insures uniformity of treatment of ships trading internationally is through a variety of international conventions. The most significant of these have been drawn up under the auspices of IMO (the International Maritime Organization). Based in London, IMO is a United Nations Agency that was originally entitled IMCO (the Intergovermental Maritime Consultative Organization).

Over the years, the agency has developed international conventions covering most aspects of ship design and operation. Among them are the MARPOL and SOLAS conventions, covering respectively marine pollution and safety of life at sea, and the STCW convention covering safety, training and certification of watchkeepers. (For a discussion of the MARPOL convention, see chapter 11).

It is important to realize that the conventions themselves are *not* laws or regulations. They are agreements between nations. The nations that are signatories to the conventions then write national laws that give effect to the detail of the convention. They then impose these national laws on their own ships and, equally importantly, on ships visiting their waters. There can be minor differences in how nations interpret the conventions, but generally a port state will be satisfied if a ship meets its own nation's interpretation of the convention.

The slight discrepancies in interpretation may mean, for example, that different versions of certain items of equipment have to be sold in different markets, but overall a reasonable uniformity prevails.

For many years, the system of international conventions has worked well. One reason for this is that IMO has served not as a political forum so much as an international technical workshop. The details of the conventions are framed by technical and other experts who know ships and shipping well. The agency that represents the United States at IMO is the U.S. Coast Guard.

**IMO committees.** Space here does not permit a lengthy treatise on "how IMO works," but, very basically, problems that need addressing are referred by member nations to the agency and then considered by key IMO committees. The two most significant are the Maritime Safety Committee and the Marine Environmental Protection Committee.

The committees then enlist the necessary technical expertise to develop draft conventions. Should the draft conventions be accepted by the committees, they are then referred to the IMO assembly for a vote.

**The ratification process.** Once a convention (or a modification or supplementation of an existing convention) is accepted by the assembly, national governments must decide whether they will sign it. Nations always have the right not to accept a convention, but there are many advantages for the free flow of world trade when nations treat each others' ships with a degree of reciprocity.

Conventions come into effect after a predetermined interval following their acceptance by a sufficient number of nations to make them viable. They contain a formula that requires acceptance by a minimum number of nations representing a minimum percentage of the world merchant fleet before they can come into effect. Once in effect, they are binding on all nations that have signed acceptance.

## OPA-90

Essentially, IMO works by consensus. The problem with this is that consensus takes time to achieve. To its critics, including some in the U.S. Congress and in environmental protection circles, the IMO process can seem agonizingly slow. Which brings us back to OPA-90.

The legislation was passed by the United States in response to public reaction to the *Exxon Valdez* spill and other tanker accidents that followed it.

Congress decided that the United States must take unilateral action to protect its waters, and OPA-90 makes far more stringent demands than those contained in any of the IMO-sponsored conventions in force at the time of its enactment.

Very significantly, Congress also decided that OPA would *not* preempt individual state legislation on tanker pollution liability. Though OPA does limit liability for pollution damage, in certain circumstances, some coastal states, in fact, do not. Tanker operators therefore not only have to acquaint themselves with the federal requirements, but also those of all the coastal states whose waters they will transit.

As this was written, the regulations implementing OPA were still in process of being written. But elements of the act include the fact that it takes the United States out of the internationally agreed framework of liability limitation and pollution cleanup compensation. It also requires tankers trading to the United States to have Certificates of Financial Responsibility (COFRs) that, at this time, appear to be impossible for the insurance community to underwrite.

**Double hulls and alternative designs.** A well-publicized provision of the act is a requirement that, after a fairly generous phase-out period for existing tonnage, tankers trading in U.S. waters have double hulls—or some equally effective means of protecting the environment in the event of a spill (see figure 12-2). This puts the United States at odds with the

Fig. 12-1. With a gigantic piece of Bligh Reef still stuck in her hull, the *Exxon Valdez* sits in dry dock after her 1989 grounding. The Oil Pollution Act of 1990 (OPA-90) was passed by the United States in response to the *Exxon Valdez* spill and other tanker accidents that followed it. National Steel and Shipbuilding.

tanker construction requirements of the MARPOL convention though, at the time of writing, efforts were being made within IMO to write a double-hull-or-equivalent requirement into MARPOL.

The issue of alternatives to double hulls is already provoking controversy. Many experts are endorsing a design called the mid-deck tanker (fig. 12-3) as actually superior to the double hull in some types of collision or grounding incidents. As this was written, however, it looked very much as though the mid-deck design might be endorsed by IMO and the international maritime community long before proving acceptable to the U.S. Congress.

**Existing tankers.** OPA also requires that the U.S. Coast Guard regulate existing tankers so that they operate more safely until such time as they are replaced by double-hulled ships. This is yet another area that had still

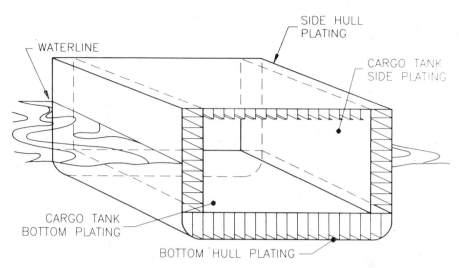

Fig. 12-2. A well-publicized provision of OPA-90 is a requirement that, after a fairly generous phase-out period for existing tonnage, tankers trading in U.S. waters have double hulls—or some equally effective means of protecting the environment in the event of a spill. (A double hull incorporates a void formed between the ship's outer side and bottom hull plating and the cargo tank plating both at the sides and bottom.) Reprinted with permission from *Tanker Spills, Prevention by Design,* © 1991 by the National Academy of Sciences. Published by National Academy Press, Washington, D.C.

to be resolved at the time of writing but this issue also offers the potential for ongoing differences with the rest of the international community. Some countries are asking IMO to reconsider regulations for existing tankers, but it is a basic principle of IMO conventions that ships need comply only with those structural requirements in force at the time of newbuilding or conversion, unless a compelling case for change can be made.

The U.S. regulations for existing ships could well require some structural changes, carriage of additional navigational equipment, stricter compliance with vessel traffic systems, and changes in operating procedures. However, all this must be determined through a fairly lengthy rulemaking process.

**Spill-response contingency plans.** Yet another onerous provision of OPA is that it requires ships trading in U.S. waters to have approved spill-response contingency plans. These must be tailored to the specific ports the vessel will serve. The plan must designate which local contractors and equipment a ship will use in the event of a spill.

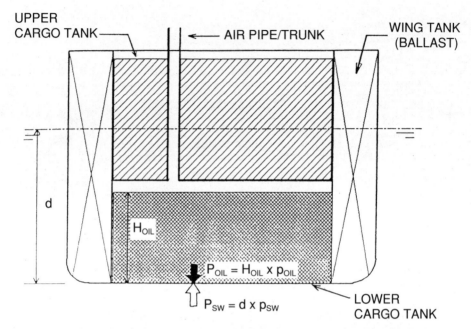

Fig. 12-3. Many experts are endorsing a design called the mid-deck tanker as actually superior to the double hull in some types of collision or grounding incidents. As shown in this diagram, the height of the mid-deck is arranged so that the outside seawater pressure is greater than the oil pressure within the lower cargo tank. *Marine Log.*

### LAWS IN TRANSITION

To sum up, the law concerning tanker operations is in transition, particularly where U.S. waters are concerned. About all that seems certain is that, once OPA-90 regulations have been framed it is those regulations that the U.S. Coast Guard will enforce, regardless of a ship's flag, and even when those regulations are in conflict with the requirements of international treaties to which the United States is a signatory. Furthermore, because OPA does not preempt state laws, tanker personnel will have to bear in mind, at all times, that they may one day have to defend their actions before a state prosecutor and a local jury in a state court.

Meantime, the OPA-90 rulemaking process continues. The procedures give the shipowning community and others ample opportunities to have their views heard so that the rules will ultimately be workable. The Coast Guard has some flexibility in drawing up the rules, but it cannot subvert the basic purposes of the act. To many observers, some aspects of the act

Fig. 12-4. The law concerning tanker operations is in transition, particularly where U.S. waters are concerned. About all that seems certain is that, once OPA-90 regulations have been framed, it is those regulations that the U.S. Coast Guard will enforce, regardless of a ship's flag, and even when those regulations are in conflict with the requirements of international treaties to which the U.S. is a signatory. Cyprus Shipping Council.

seem impossible to fulfill, in particular the requirements for Certificates of Financial Responsibility. There seems every possibility that Congress may have to look at OPA once again in order to amend those requirements. If it does so, other aspects of the legislation may also be reconsidered—and there is no guarantee that any changes made will be to the liking of the maritime community.

CHAPTER 13

# INERT GAS SYSTEMS

In this chapter we will discuss inert gas (IG) system components and general operating procedures. Any tanker fitted with an IG system must also be provided with a detailed operating manual. All officers and other crew members involved with the operation of the IG system should study the ship's manual thoroughly. Inert gas systems are now required on many tankers. Generally speaking, most tankers of 20,000 dwt and above must have inert gas systems.

## A "CLOSED" SYSTEM

As discussed in chapter 9, tankers operated for many years without IG systems; this meant, of course, that tanks were vented directly to the atmosphere. As a result, air was drawn into the tanks and allowed to mix with cargo vapors. The obvious problem is that air contains 21 percent oxygen. When oxygen is mixed with hydrocarbon vapors in the right proportions, the result is a very dangerous mixture indeed.

Inert gas systems remedy this situation by forming a *closed* system from which air is entirely excluded. Instead of air, a different mixture of gases is introduced into the tanks. This mixture must be effectively *inert*—it must not promote combustion. On most tankers, the boiler flue gases are used for this purpose. These gases generally contain less than 5 percent oxygen. Some tankers use a special inert gas generator instead of the flue gases (see figures 13-2, 13-14, and 13-15). This might be the case where gas of high purity is needed, or if the ship's engine alone produces insufficient gas for cargo tank inerting.

## BASIC IG SYSTEM

To get a general idea of how a typical system works, let's follow the route of the inert gas from the ship's boiler to the cargo tanks. Flue gas is drawn from the uptake via an *uptake valve.* It passes through a *scrubber* where it is cooled and cleansed of impurities such as soot and sulphur oxides. It is next drawn through a *demister,* where excess water is removed. It then passes through a *fan,* which is situated on the "clean" side of the scrubber

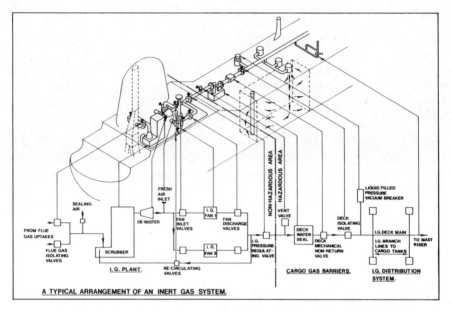

Fig. 13-1. Typical inert gas system arrangement. Howden Engineering.

and demister. This fan provides the positive pressure that makes the system work. From the fan, the gas passes through a gas regulating valve which, as the name implies, is used to regulate the pressure of inert gas entering the tanks.

From the gas regulating valve the gas leaves the *nonhazardous* area and enters the *hazardous* area—that part of the system where hydrocarbon gas is encountered. Separating these two areas is a *deck water seal,* which is designed to prevent the backflow of hydrocarbon vapors into the nonhazardous area. From the deck seal the gas passes through a *nonreturn valve* which serves as a backup to the deck seal. From here the gas passes through the *deck isolating valve.* This valve is used to isolate the main line to the tanks when the IG system is secured. From the main line the gas enters the tanks via the various branch lines.

We will discuss the major components of IG systems in the following pages. But first we should take a look at the actual operation of an inert gas system in various situations.

## PURGING

When starting with an empty tank containing 21 percent oxygen, it is not enough merely to pump inert gas into the tank. In order to achieve a

**TYPICAL FLOW DIAGRAM**

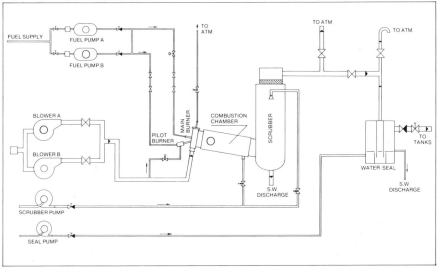

Fig. 13-2. Typical flow diagram for an inert gas system using an IG generator. Systems with an IG generator are used when gas of high purity is needed, or if the ship's engine alone produces insufficient gas for cargo tank inerting. Permea Maritime Protection.

properly inerted mixture, it is necessary to remove air (and thus oxygen) from the tank. This is done either by *dilution* or *displacement.*

The dilution method is used on most ships. Inert gas is introduced at high velocity into the tanks, and it is usually necessary to change the tank atmosphere three to five times before the tank is fully inert. A high velocity is required so that the gas stream can reach the tank bottom and eliminate the formation of dangerous vapor pockets.

The displacement method, on the other hand, is quite different. Gas is introduced at *low* velocity (3 to 5 meters per second). An *interface* is formed between incoming inert gas and outgoing air. As inert gas settles into the tank, the outgoing air is forced out of the tank through a purge pipe. This method normally requires about 1½ atmosphere changes.

It is important to emphasize that the method used must suit the ship. Depending on the particular equipment and piping, only one or the other is suitable. (Read your ship's IG system manual.)

Regardless of the method used, oxygen readings must be taken at various levels in the tank to ensure that the atmosphere has been properly inerted. These readings must fall consistently below 8 percent before the tank can be considered inerted. In some cases, company or government guidelines may require even lower readings.

After discharging cargo or cleaning tanks, the tanks are often *purged* with inert gas in order to remove hydrocarbon vapors. Purging is necessary because in the event of a collision hydrocarbon vapors would rapidly form an explosive mixture with oxygen introduced through damaged bulkheads, decks, etc.

In order to *gas-free* a tank, the same procedure is used as when purging with inert gas. However, in this case *air* is blown into the tanks and inert gas is vented from the purge pipes. We will discuss this procedure later in this chapter.

It is important to note that only a limited number of tanks can be purged at one time. If the velocity of inert gas (or air) entering the tanks is too low, pockets of vapor may be left in the tanks. Also, the vapors leaving the purge pipes must do so at high velocity in order to carry well clear of the ship for safe dispersal in the atmosphere. When too many tanks are purged at once, the pressure drops—and so does the exit velocity. As a result hydrocarbon vapors can accumulate around the main deck.

## LOADING

Prior to loading, the cargo tanks should, if necessary, be purged until the oxygen level is below 8 percent in each tank. At this point, unless the ship will be loading and deballasting simultaneously, the deck isolating valve is closed and the IG system is secured.

As cargo is loaded, the inert gas is vented to the atmosphere (unless prohibited by local regulations—see below). Depending on vessel design, the gas will follow one of two routes: 1) up the *mast riser* or 2) directly to atmosphere via *high velocity PV valves* at each tank (see figure 13-13). In either case the idea is to allow the gas to disperse well above the main deck.

If the ship is loading and deballasting at the same time, the situation becomes more complicated. For example, if the deballasting rate exceeds the loading rate, a vacuum will develop in the tanks. As a result, air will be drawn into the system through the PV valves. Therefore, in this situation inert gas must be supplied to the tanks, and pressure must be maintained on the IG system until deballasting is finished. The deck isolating valve can then be closed and the IG system secured until loading is completed.

**Vapor control systems.** If operating in a port where vapor emissions are prohibited, the mast riser bypass valve must not be opened during loading. (In some ports, controls to the mast riser bypass valve are actually

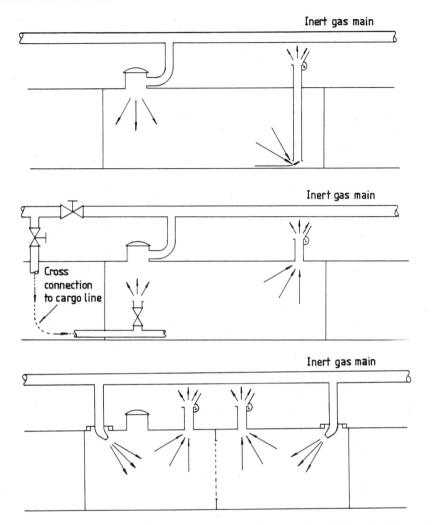

Fig. 13-3. A: Purging by purge pipe. B: Purging via cargo line. C: Purging by nozzle (tank with swash bulkhead). Howden Engineering.

sealed, so that officials will know if gas has been vented.) Displaced vapors and inert gas must therefore be sent back ashore via the vapor control system. (See chapter 14 for a complete discussion of vapor control systems.)

## THE LOADED PASSAGE

After loading is finished, the mast riser bypass valve and/or PV valves are closed. The IG system is started, and the deck isolating valve is opened slowly. After the tanks have been pressurized sufficiently, the system can in most cases be secured.

During the passage to the discharge port the inert gas pressure should be watched carefully. A low pressure alarm is also provided for this purpose. A vacuum must not be allowed to develop in the system; otherwise air will be drawn into the tanks. This situation might be expected to occur when passing into a region of colder sea temperatures, causing cargo to cool and contract. At any rate, the pressure should be watched carefully throughout the passage and, if necessary, the system should be restarted and brought back up to pressure.

## DISCHARGING

Upon arrival at the discharging port, the inert gas system is turned on. It is kept operating throughout the discharge. A steady supply of inert gas is needed to replace the cargo as it leaves the tanks. During the discharge, always watch the IG pressure carefully. Even when the system is running at full capacity, the pressure may start to drop—indicating that the cargo pumps are getting ahead of the inert gas system. When this happens, the pumping rate must be reduced until the IG system builds back up to a sufficient pressure.

Many crude carriers now wash their tanks with crude oil while discharging cargo. This does not particularly affect the operation of the inert gas system, but it offers an additional reason to operate the system carefully. By law, ships using COW must be properly inerted.

After discharging has been completed, it is a common practice to purge tanks of hydrocarbon vapors. But before doing so, check local regulations—it is prohibited in some ports. While purging with inert gas, readings are taken with a combustible gas indicator. This instrument must be of a design that works in oxygen-deficient atmospheres, such as the *Tankscope* or *Gascope*. Tanks are purged until an acceptable reading is obtained (generally 2 percent hydrocarbon vapors or less).

## TANK CLEANING

Prior to cleaning tanks, an oxygen reading is obtained at several levels in each tank. If necessary, tanks must be purged with inert gas to bring the reading below 8 percent.

Pressure is maintained continuously while tanks are being cleaned. Unless the ship is simultaneously discharging—as when using COW—very little gas will actually move through the lines. The inert gas fans are fitted with recirculating lines to prevent overheating in this situation. The practice on some ships is to crack the mast riser bypass valve a few turns to allow a continuous flow of gas through the line. This increases the efficiency of the system and decreases the absorption of oxygen from the scrubber cooling water. (This can be a factor when gas is recirculated for prolonged periods.)

After tanks have been cleaned—and especially after COW—they should be purged of hydrocarbon vapors in the usual manner.

### GAS-FREEING

Before a tank is gas-freed it should first be purged of hydrocarbon vapors. There is a good reason for this precaution. If air is introduced into a tank containing a mixture of hydrocarbon vapors and inert gas, there is a good chance that at some point in the process the vapors and air will form an explosive mixture. At this point, the percentage of hydrocarbon vapors and oxygen will both be right to promote an explosion. Only one more element will be required—a spark. So by all means purge tanks with inert gas before gas-freeing. (And, once again, check local regulations before venting inert gas or hydrocarbon vapors to the atmosphere.)

**Gas-freeing the entire ship** is very similar to purging. The only difference is that fresh air is supplied instead of inert gas. The regular IG fans and deck lines are used. The inert gas is allowed to vent from the purge pipes, stand pipes, or high velocity PV valves in the usual manner.

**Gas-freeing an individual tank.** This operation must normally be carried out with portable blowers mounted in openings on the main deck (see chapter 9). Before the deck plates are removed, the tank is isolated from the rest of the IG system and the pressure is carefully vented. The blowers should supply as high a volume of air as possible. This will ensure a thorough purging of all parts of the tank, and it will also eject the inert gas from the purge pipes at high velocity. In this manner the gas and any remaining hydrocarbon vapors will disperse well above the main deck.

*Before gas-freeing a tank in this manner be sure to consult your ship's inert gas manual for any special precautions.*

**Entering the tanks.** It is important to be patient when gas-freeing. The process must be thorough, and thoroughness takes time. Periodic readings should be taken at the purge pipes and at several tank levels to determine oxygen content. When a consistent reading of 21 percent is

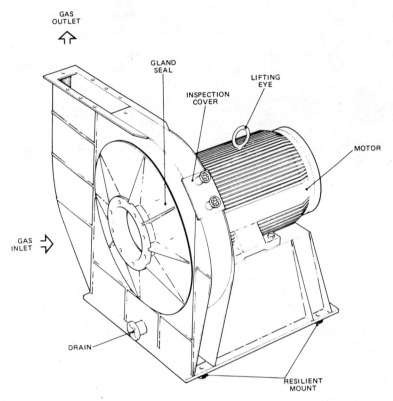

Fig. 13-4. Inert gas fan. Permea Maritime Protection.

achieved, it is *probably* safe to enter the tank. Any reading under 21 percent is unsafe. A continuous flow of fresh air to the tank must be maintained as long as personnel are inside.

*Entering tanks is dangerous.* The process must always be careful,
deliberate, and methodical.

### IG SYSTEM COMPONENTS

At this point we will take a closer look at some of the components of an IG
system and briefly discuss their operation. But first we should stress that
the operation of any IG system is largely a cooperative effort between deck
and engine departments. Before starting the system, the chief mate or
officer in charge must call the engine room and ask the engineers to set it
up. After being informed by the engine room that the system is ready to
go, the deck department assumes control.

## CONTROLS, INDICATORS, AND ALARMS

The following controls are located in the cargo control room (on older, retrofitted ships they may be located in the engine room):

**The start/stop button** is used to start the system after getting the OK from the the engine room.

**The pressure controller** is used to regulate the pressure of the inert gas entering the system. In some situations—such as purging—the controller might typically be set at maximum. In other situations—such as stripping or tank cleaning—the controller might be set much lower.

In addition to controls, certain indicators are also installed in the control room:

**Pressure indicator/recorder.** It is important to keep an eye on this indicator because a drop in pressure could result in air being drawn into the tanks. An additional pressure indicator is normally installed in the wheelhouse, enabling the mate on watch to monitor the pressure while on sea passage.

Pressure indicators are generally calibrated in millimeters or inches of water, expressed as *water gauge (WG)*. A typical pressure might be 700 millimeters WG—about 1.0 psi (0.07 kg/cm$^2$).

**Oxygen indicator/recorder.** This instrument receives information from an *oxygen analyzer* which is normally installed between the fan discharge and the gas regulating valve. In other words, it samples the gas *before it is piped to the tanks.* In order to keep the oxygen content in the tanks below 8 percent, the oxygen content of the supply gas must be somewhat lower (below 5 percent). Like the pressure indicator, the oxygen indicator is used in conjunction with a recorder, to provide a graphic record of oxygen content.

Alarms are also provided in the cargo control room, and these form an important part of the system:

**High oxygen alarm.** Whenever the IG oxygen content exceeds permissible limits, an alarm sounds in the control room and also in the engine room.

**Low pressure alarm.** Whenever the inert gas pressure falls below permissible limits, an alarm sounds in the control room. A *high pressure alarm* is also provided.

**The deck seal low water alarm** gives early warning of any problem with the deck water seal.

**Scrubber alarms** consist of a high water level alarm and a low water supply pressure alarm, as well as a high gas temperature alarm.

### AUTOMATIC "TRIPS"

As a backup to the various alarms and indicators, the typical system is designed to "trip" automatically in certain situations. For example, the inert gas fan will automatically shut down when any of the following conditions occur: 1) inadequate water supply to the scrubber, 2) high water level in the scrubber, 3) high inert gas temperature, and 4) high inert gas pressure.

The gas regulating valve closes automatically in any of the above situations. It also closes whenever the IG fan is stopped for any reason, or if there is a power failure. This part of the gas regulating valve's operation is an important safety feature, because it helps to prevent backflow of hydrocarbon vapors into the nonhazardous area.

### OTHER MAJOR COMPONENTS

**The scrubber** (fig. 13-5) serves three basic purposes: 1) to cool the inert gas, 2) to remove particulate matter such as soot, and 3) to remove chemical impurities such as sulphur oxides.

The scrubber consists of three sections: the precooler, the venturi, and the scrubbing tower. In the precooler, hot gas drawn from the boiler uptakes is cooled rapidly. The gas then passes through the venturi, where most of the soot removal takes place. The gas then enters the bottom of the scrubbing tower, where it is sprayed with water and filtered by passing through water-soaked banks of plastic chips or similar material. Most of the sulphur oxides are removed in the scrubbing tower.

To operate properly, the scrubber requires a continuous high volume of water. If the water supply fails at any time, the temperature of the gas will rise quickly. As previously mentioned, alarms give early warning of any problem in the scrubber—such as high gas temperature, low water supply pressure, or high water level.

**The demister** is mounted on the outlet side of the scrubber. Its job is to remove water and leftover soot particles from the gas before it passes on to the fans. A typical demister might consist of polypropylene mesh pads.

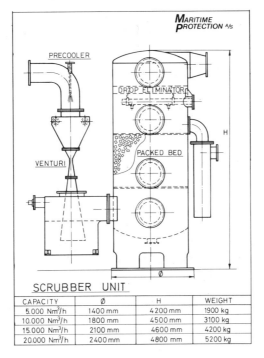

Fig. 13-5. The IG scrubber cools the gas and removes impurities such as soot and sulphur oxides. Permea Maritime Protection.

As inert gas passes through, water droplets form on the pads and fall back into the scrubber by gravity. (Although the demister removes the water droplets, the relative humidity of exiting gas is still 100 percent.)

**Fans.** Two independent IG fans are provided, but typically only one is operated at a time. Because the highest demand for IG occurs during the discharge, the combined fan capacity is required to be set at 125 percent of the maximum rated capacity of the cargo pumps. This required capacity can be met by two fans of equal size, or by one large and one small fan. (Most systems now in use can meet the 125 percent requirement with either fan operating alone.)

To prevent overheating of the fans when IG flow is minimal, a *bypass line* or *recirculation line* is provided. Excess inert gas can either be recirculated within the system or, in the case of some IG generator systems, it can be vented directly to the atmosphere (that is, back to the ship's stack). The *bypass valve* works in conjunction with the gas regulating valve (both valves receive a signal from the pressure controller in the control room), and it opens automatically at a given back pressure.

A *fresh air intake,* located near the fans, makes it possible to gas-free the tanks through the inert gas piping. *The fresh air intake must be blanked off when not in use.* Otherwise, air might be drawn into the system during the inerting process.

**Gas regulating valve (GRV).** This valve is located just inside the forward bulkhead of the deck house; it marks the boundary between hazardous and nonhazardous areas. The gas regulating valve operates on a signal from the pressure controller in the control room. It forms an important part of the fail-safe design of the IG system—it closes automatically whenever the system shuts down. This valve is also referred to as the pressure control valve or primary control valve.

**Deck water seal.** As we discussed earlier, the purpose of the deck water seal is to prevent the backflow of hydrocarbon vapors into the nonhazardous area. To demonstrate the basic principle of the deck water seal, take a straw, place it in a glass of water, and blow bubbles through it. (Inert gas flows through the water seal, on its way to the tanks, in essentially the same manner.) Next take your mouth away from the straw and try blowing air onto the surface of the water. Naturally, the air cannot penetrate the surface of the water, and there is no backflow of air through the straw.

The actual design of deck water seals is a bit more sophisticated than a straw in a glass of water, and there are several different types. The "wet" type (fig. 13-7) is the simplest. When back pressure develops on the discharge side of the seal, a *water plug* is forced back into the line. This plug effectively blocks vapor backflow.

Deck water seals can also be of the "semidry" and "dry" types. The semidry type (fig. 13-8) is designed so that, during normal operation, the inert gas flow creates a vacuum by means of venturi action, thus drawing the sealing water into a holding chamber. In this manner, the carryover of water droplets to the cargo tanks is greatly reduced. During shutdown, the sealing water flows back into the seal.

The dry type of deck water seal (fig. 13-9) is equipped with a drop tank for the sealing water. During normal operation, the system thus remains "dry." If the IG system is shut down, or if the cargo tank pressure exceeds the discharge pressure of the IG fans, the drop tank opens and fills the seal. The advantage of this type of seal is that it eliminates water carryover completely. The disadvantage is that the seal depends on the reliable operation of automatic valves. If the valves fail, the seal could also fail.

An important thing to remember about any deck water seal, regardless of design, is that it needs water to function properly. One of the things

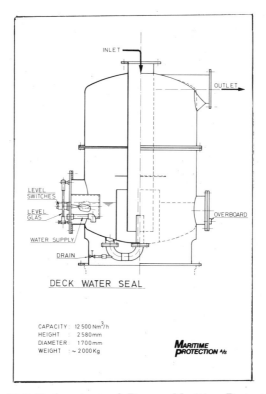

Fig. 13-6. Deck water seal. Permea Maritime Protection.

to check before starting the IG system is the water level and supply to the deck seal. Also, the deck seal low water alarm should be tested at this time.

On the main line forward of the deck water seal, two important valves are fitted. The first, a *nonreturn valve,* is designed to prevent backflow of hydrocarbon vapors. The second, a *deck isolating valve,* is closed whenever the IG system is secured. It thus provides a positive means of separating hazardous and nonhazardous areas.

**Liquid-filled PV breaker.** If a sudden, large overpressure occurs in the IG system, it is conceivable that the mechanical PV valves may be unable to relieve it quickly enough. Such a scenario could result in a "blown" deck water seal and resultant backflow of hydrocarbon vapors—and possible disaster. To prevent such an occurrence, a high capacity PV breaker (fig. 13-10) is needed.

Figure 13-11 shows the operating principle of a liquid-filled PV breaker. The liquid used is generally a water-antifreeze mixture. In the *high pressure* mode the liquid is literally blown onto the main deck, leaving a clear

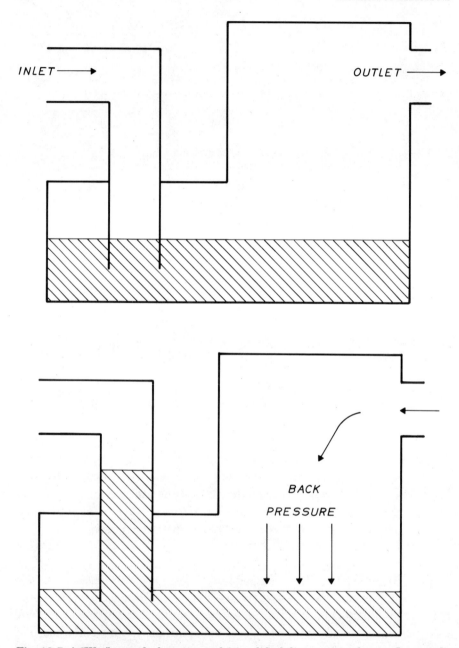

Fig. 13-7. A:"Wet" type deck water seal (simplified diagram) in the nonflow condition. B: The deck water seal prevents vapor backflow into the "nonhazardous" area
of the engine room. In the situation shown here, back pressure from the IG deck
main has forced a *water plug* into the inlet piping; this plug effectively blocks
vapor backflow.

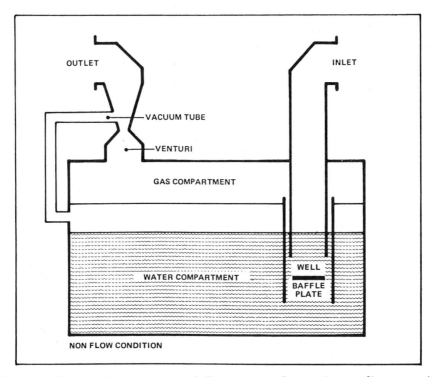

**OUTLET**   **INLET**

VACUUM TUBE

VENTURI

GAS COMPARTMENT

WATER COMPARTMENT   WELL

BAFFLE PLATE

NON FLOW CONDITION

Fig. 13-8. "Semidry" deck water seal. During normal operation, sealing water is drawn into a holding chamber by venturi action—thus reducing water carryover. Wilson Walton International.

pathway for relief of pressure. In the *vacuum* mode the liquid is sucked into the line, along with atmospheric air.

The PV breaker is set to blow at a pressure slightly greater than the mechanical PV valve settings. On a typical system, this might translate to a PV breaker setting of approximately 2,300 millimeters WG (3.5 psi) for pressure and −700 millimeters WG (−1.0 psi) for vacuum.

Of course, whenever a PV breaker blows, it must be refilled. When doing so, *always use the recommended liquid.* Chief mates have occasionally made the mistake of refilling with water, only to remember (too late) that many tanker ports get cold in winter, and water freezes.

**Mast riser and bypass valve.** Figure 13-13 (A, B, and C) shows some of the tank venting arrangements typically used on tankers with inert gas systems. On many ships the vent lines lead to a mast riser which is designed to vent the vapors and inert gas a certain distance above the main deck. Although the mast riser itself may only project a few meters above

GAS FLOW TOWARDS CARGO TANKS                    BACK PRESSURE IN CARGO TANKS

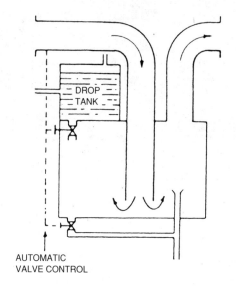

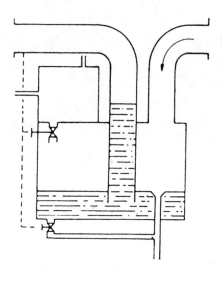

AUTOMATIC
VALVE CONTROL

Fig. 13-9. "Dry" deck water seal. Sealing water is held in a drop tank during normal operation, thus eliminating water carryover completely. International Maritime Organization.

the main deck, the velocity of gases leaving the line is usually sufficient to carry it to a considerable height.

When loading in a locality with no vapor emission restrictions, the mast riser bypass valve is normally opened—allowing inert gas to vent to the atmosphere as it is displaced by incoming cargo. When discharging, the bypass valve must remain closed to keep the system pressurized and to prevent air from entering the tanks.

**Tank isolating valves.** Each branch line is fitted with a valve, making it possible to isolate each tank from the system. This is normally done only when an individual tank must be gas-freed, or to relieve pressure in a tank before manual gauging and sampling. In any event, when a tank isolating valve is closed, the isolated tank must have some other means of venting to atmosphere (an open purge pipe, tank lid, etc.) to prevent the buildup of pressure or vacuum within the tank.

### SPECIALIZED SYSTEMS

Sometimes the supply of flue gas is insufficient or too poor in quality to meet the demands of a particular vessel. (For example, liquefied gas car-

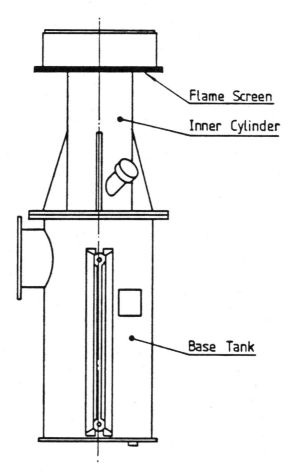

Fig. 13-10. Liquid-filled pressure-vacuum breaker. Howden Engineering.

riers and many chemical carriers require IG of high purity and low moisture content to prevent cargo contamination.) In such situations, various types of inert gas generating or separator systems may be used.

**Inert gas generator.** Figure 13-14 shows an elevation view of an inert gas generator. Such systems function very much like a standard flue-gas system, except that inert gas is generated by the unit itself rather than the ship's engine exhaust. Most units in service today burn marine diesel or heavy fuel oil, although a number of newer units now burn methane.

**Flue gas system with integrated topping up generator.** This type of system is often preferred for OBOs and VLCCs. The flue gas system pro-

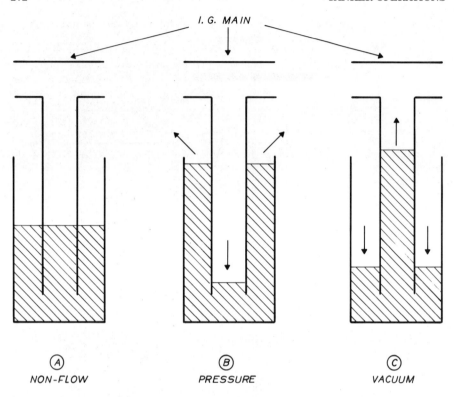

Fig. 13-11. The liquid-filled PV breaker is designed to relieve sudden excessive pressure or vacuum which cannot be accommodated by the mechanical PV valves. In the *high pressure* mode (B) the liquid is literally blown out on deck, leaving a clear pathway for relief of pressure. In the *vacuum* mode (C) the liquid is sucked into the line, along with atmospheric air.

vides all or most of the inert gas during cargo discharging. A small topping up generator maintains the required inert gas pressure during the sea passage.

Other combined flue gas/generator systems are also used, depending on the needs of the vessel. For example, a system installed on a number of ships can act as an independent inert gas generator or in concert with the flue gas system, and can even be used to burn off excess oxygen in flue gas.

**Inert gas generator with cooler/dryer.** This highly specialized variant (fig. 13-15) is used primarily on LNG/LPG carriers or chemical carriers, where "wet" inert gas might condense and contaminate the cargo.

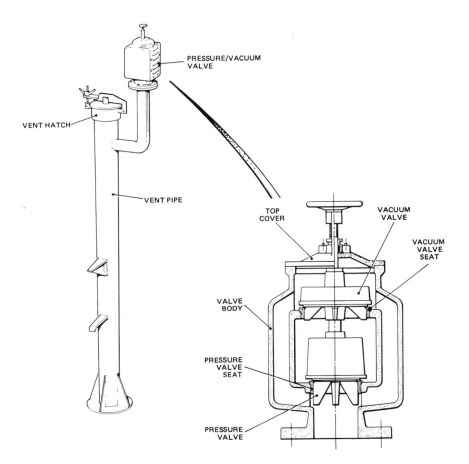

Fig. 13-12. This illustration represents one of several possible PV valve arrangements. In this case, each cargo tank is fitted with its own PV valve, which is mounted on the vent pipe at the forward end of the tank. With the vent hatch in the open position (for example, when gas-freeing), displaced gases bypass the PV valve and vent directly to the atmosphere. Permea Maritime Protection.

**Membrane nitrogen system.** A relatively new development on specialized chemical and LNG/LPG carriers is the nitrogen membrane separator. Nitrogen supplied by such systems is highly pure (95-99% $N_2$ purity) and dry. When used to inert tanks, nitrogen of such purity and dryness not only protects against explosion, but also preserves water- and oxygen-sensitive cargoes, which might otherwise deteriorate.

Figure 13-16 illustrates the process by which nitrogen is separated. Each separator consists of a cylindrical shell filled with tiny, hollow fibers.

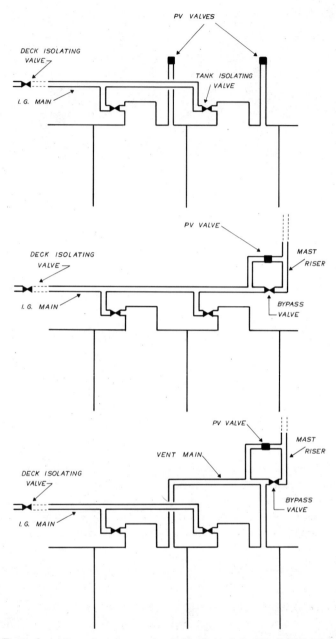

Fig. 13-13. Typical venting arrangements. A: Each tank is fitted with a high velocity vent and PV valve; no common vent line is used. B: Common venting through the IG piping. A single PV valve and mast riser serve a number of tanks. C: Common venting through a vent main, separate from the IG main.

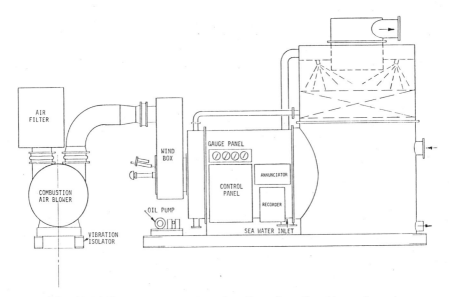

Fig. 13-14. Inert gas generator, elevation view. Gas Atmospheres.

As compressed air is fed into the separator, oxygen, water vapor, and other gases permeate through the walls of the fibers faster than nitrogen. The secondary oxygen-rich mixture is vented to atmosphere, and a stream of relatively pure, dry nitrogen emerges at the outlet.

### PRECAUTIONS AND REMINDERS

Before ending our discussion of IG systems, we should consider a few special points as noted in the following paragraphs.

**Opening a "closed" system.** Ideally a ship fitted with an inert gas system should keep her tanks closed and fully inerted at all times. However, what should be done in theory and what is actually done in practice are not always the same thing—as anyone with experience on tankers can tell you. At this writing, the practice on many ships fitted with IG systems falls far short of what might be called ideal.

First of all, cargo surveyors and consignees distrust closed ullaging systems. They often insist on a visual ullage with hand tapes. The IG pressure must therefore be vented and ullage covers lifted in order to gauge the cargo.

Another example is the use of portable tank-cleaning machines. Ideally, any ship fitted with an inert gas system should also have fixed tank-

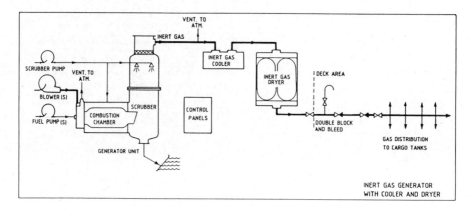

Fig. 13-15. Inert gas generator with cooler and dryer. Such a system is useful on chemical carriers or LNG/LPG carriers where "wet" inert gas might condense and contaminate the cargo. Permea Maritime Protection.

cleaning machines. However, at this writing some ships in the 20,000 dwt to 40,000 dwt range are still using portable machines. Of course, this type of operation involves removing deck plates for tank-cleaning machines—which largely defeats the purpose of an IG system.

Undoubtedly these examples are just temporary "bugs" that will disappear as equipment, procedures, and attitudes adjust with time. But for now, tankermen must work with the equipment they have on hand, and this requires caution. *Crew members should be particularly careful when opening purge pipes, ullage covers, deck plates, etc., on any tank that may be pressurized.*

**Cargo separation.** As mentioned earlier, some petroleum products—such as petrochemicals—may become contaminated by inert gas from the ship's boilers. Tankers carrying these products are normally fitted with a special inert gas generator burning a high grade of fuel oil or with a nitrogen membrane separator.

Another potential problem for product carriers is cross contamination. Different parcels of cargo—although carefully separated in the cargo system—may be "common" in the IG system. Contamination through vapor mixing is a very real problem and should be guarded against.

Remember that inert gas systems add complexity to a tanker's operation and introduce pitfalls—sometimes unforeseen—which can make the IG system more of a liability than an asset. Therefore, the possibility of cross contamination through the IG system should always be kept in mind.

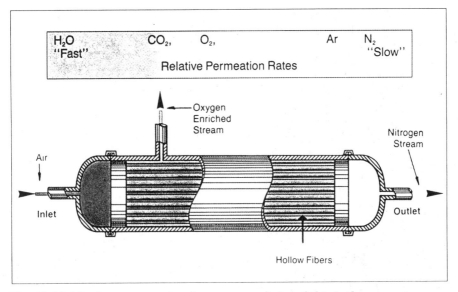

| H₂O "Fast" | CO₂, | O₂, | | Ar | N₂ "Slow" |
|---|---|---|---|---|---|

Relative Permeation Rates

Fig. 13-16. Membrane separator. As compressed air is fed into the separator, oxygen, water vapor, and other gases permeate through the walls of the fibers faster than nitrogen. The secondary oxygen-rich mixture is vented to atmosphere, and a stream of relatively pure, dry nitrogen emerges at the outlet. Permea Maritime Protection.

**Quantity and quality.** The efficient operation of an IG system depends on high quality inert gas at the source. Efficient combustion in the boilers is vital.

This condition can be evaluated in two ways: 1) by watching the oxygen indicator in the control room and 2) by watching the stack gas as it leaves the stack. Large quantities of smoke, either black or white, indicate inefficient combustion. *Light haze* is the best indication of good combustion.

When boiler load is exceptionally light—for example, in port and no cargo pumps running—it may be difficult to produce inert gas in the quantity and quality necessary to purge the tanks. In such a situation it may be necessary to create an artificial load on the boiler by recirculating cargo or ballast with the pumps.

**Blowing tubes.** Boiler sootblowers must never be used when an IG system is operating, and interlocks are fitted to prevent it. The best practice is to blow tubes soon before starting an IG operation. This will ensure higher quality inert gas for the system, and it will also eliminate the necessity for blowing tubes in the middle of the operation (which would of course involve securing the IG system).

**Crude oil washing.** The use of crude oil as a washing medium can generate large static charges in the tanks, especially if water is present in the crude. Using COW in noninerted tanks is very dangerous indeed—and illegal.

Whenever COW is being used, the IG system must be operating, and the oxygen content in the tanks must remain below 8 percent.

**Pyrophoric oxidation.** Ships carrying *sour* crudes, such as Mexican and Arabian crudes, face a special hazard. These types of crude give off *hydrogen sulfide* which, besides being very poisonous, undergoes a chemical change when stored in oxygen-deficient atmospheres.

Rust (iron oxide) combines with hydrogen sulfide to form iron sulfide. Later, when oxygen is introduced into the tanks, the process is reversed. Iron sulfide combines with oxygen to form iron oxide, sulphur dioxide, and *heat*. So much heat is generated that individual particles may become incandescent. If hydrocarbon vapors are in the tank along with oxygen, all of the elements for an explosion are present.

Three things are needed to start the pyrophoric process: 1) rust, 2) hydrogen sulfide, and 3) lack of oxygen. All three elements can be found on inerted crude carriers hauling sour crudes.

This all suggests that special attention must be paid to the IG operation on the ships in question. No air must be allowed to enter the tanks when hydrocarbon vapors are present. Before gas-freeing any tank, *purge thoroughly* with inert gas.

### KNOW YOUR SHIP

At this point an important bit of advice is in order: *You can't learn tankers from a book; don't try to do so.* Ships are designed and equipped differently, and no two are exactly alike. In the end, there is no substitute for seeing the actual equipment and operating it yourself. With inert gas systems, as with all shipboard operations, the best advice is to learn everything you can about your own ship and her eccentricities.

CHAPTER 14

# MARINE VAPOR CONTROL SYSTEMS
## BY MARK HUBER

T HE introduction of marine vapor control systems is an outgrowth of the Clean Air Act of 1970. The goal of this act and the amendments that followed is to improve air quality by specifying *national ambient air quality standards (NAAQS)* for the following primary pollutants: 1) carbon monoxide, 2) particulates, 3) sulphur oxides, 4) nitrogen oxides, and 5) hydrocarbons.

Under the authority of the act, the federal government directed states to establish a *state implementation plan (SIP)* designed to meet the standards. Unfortunately, many of our nation's metropolitan areas are unable to meet the standards and are thus classified as "nonattainment areas." As part of the effort to remedy this problem, a number of states have enacted legislation limiting the release of hydrocarbon vapors from tankers. Such vapors are typically released during loading, ballasting, purging, and gas-freeing of cargo tanks.

The installation and use of marine vapor control systems are expected to achieve the following:

1. To reduce the quantity of *volatile organic compounds* emitted to the atmosphere. VOCs are an essential ingredient in the formation of secondary pollutants such as ozone.

2. To provide industry with a means of meeting new, more stringent limits of occupational exposure to benzene and other health-threatening substances.

At the present time, vapor control regulations only address vessels collecting vapors of crude oil, gasoline blends, and benzene cargoes. It is likely that the list of "regulated" cargoes will expand as more detailed information becomes available about these substances.

For many years the maritime industry has wrestled with the problem of venting vessel cargo tanks to atmosphere while loading. The primary industry concerns were related to:

1. Risk of fire and explosion resulting from flammable concentrations of hydrocarbon vapors at the deck line and around the superstructure.

2. Health hazards caused by breathing toxic vapors.

As a result of these concerns, cargo tank venting has evolved over the years from traditional open venting at the deck line to controlled venting systems. Figure 13-13 in the previous chapter illustrates typical controlled venting arrangements. Controlled venting ensures adequate dilution of exiting vapors well above the vessel where they are further dispersed by prevailing winds.

Vapor control systems represent the next stage in the evolution of cargo tank venting arrangements. The basis of the system is a closed loading operation. All deck openings to the cargo tanks are secured and remain so for the entire transfer. By means of a network of vapor collection piping and manifold on deck, the vapors from each cargo tank are directed ashore for processing. The facility has the option of destroying, recovering, or returning the vapors to the shore tank. Typically, the vapors involved are those displaced by the incoming liquid during loading operations as well as those released due to cargo vaporization.

The quantity of VOCs emitted during loading and ballasting was documented by the U.S. Environmental Protection Agency in 1985 (table 14-1).

Table 14-1

EPA EMISSION FACTORS IN POUNDS PER 1,000 GALLONS OF LIQUID

| Emission Source | Loading Operations | | Tanker Ballasting |
|---|---|---|---|
| | Ships | Barges | |
| Gasoline | 1.8 | 3.4 | 0.8 |
| Crude oil | 0.61 | 1.0 | 1.2 |
| JP-4 | 0.5 | 1.2 | unknown |
| Kerosene | 0.005 | 0.013 | unknown |
| Distillate oil No. 2 | 0.005 | 0.012 | unknown |
| Residual oil No. 6 | 0.00004 | 0.00009 | unknown |

Courtesy U.S. Environmental Protection Agency

## VAPOR CONTROL SYSTEM COMPONENTS

The U.S. Coast Guard developed and published regulations (46 CFR Part 39) governing the design, construction, and operation of vapor control systems on tankers operating in U.S. waters. However, it is the individual states, not the Coast Guard, that enact regulations requiring the installation of these systems.

**Vapor control piping.** The collection of vapors is accomplished through permanently installed deck piping consisting of a common main, branch lines, and vapor manifold. On tankers fitted with an inert gas (IG) system, modification of the IG distribution piping will permit its use for vapor control while loading (fig. 14-1). When a tanker is equipped with an IG/vapor control main, there must be a means of isolating the IG supply. The deck isolating valve required under existing IG regulations satisfies this requirement.

The vapor control piping terminates in a vapor manifold located as close as practical to the cargo manifold. To clearly distinguish the vessel vapor connections the last meter of piping must be painted with red/yellow/red bands labelled with the word "VAPOR."

As an additional safeguard against possible cross connection of a cargo hose to the vapor manifold, a special flange is employed. The vessel vapor connection flange must have a 0.5-inch stud at least one inch long projecting outward from top dead center on the flange face. Finally, the vapor manifold must be fitted with a manually operated isolation valve that gives clear indication of the valve's status (fig. 14-2).

If a ship is carrying incompatible cargoes, it is important that vapors from each type of cargo be segregated from each other. On a tanker with a common vapor control main, this can be accomplished by closing valves on the appropriate branch lines. Other tankers (such as chemical or other product carriers) are fitted with "dedicated" vapor control systems for individual cargo tanks or tank groups.

To further guard against contamination of dissimilar cargoes, drains must be provided for removal of liquid condensate from the vapor control piping resulting from: 1) liquid carryover while loading due to mists in the vapor stream, 2) condensation in the piping due to temperature changes, 3) cargo tank overfill, or 4) cargo sloshing at sea.

**Vapor control hose.** The hose used for transferring vapors must be electrically continuous and constructed of material that is resistant to kinking and abrasion. The hose assembly should be provided with proper support to prevent excessive strain, kinking, or collapse of the hose.

The vapor hose must also meet the following *minimum* strength criteria:

| | |
|---|---|
| Design bursting pressure | 25 psi |
| Maximum allowable working pressure | 5 psi |
| Vacuum (without collapsing/constricting) | −2 psi |

The color and marking at each end of the hose should be similar in all respects to the vessel vapor manifold (fig. 14-2). As part of the Declaration

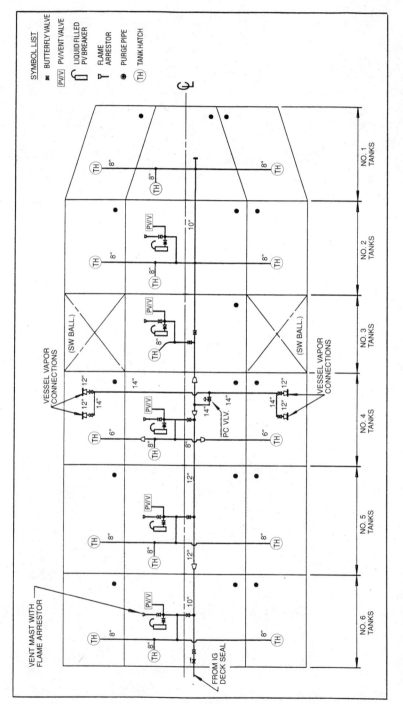

Fig. 14-1. Diagram of the inert gas distribution piping on the deck of a typical tanker. Note the modifications that have been made to permit the use of IG piping for vapor control.

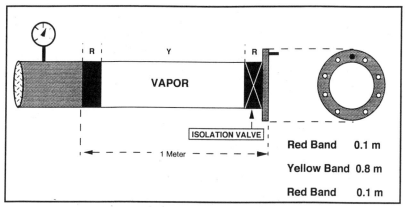

**DETAIL AT VESSEL MANIFOLD END OF VAPOR CONTROL PIPING**

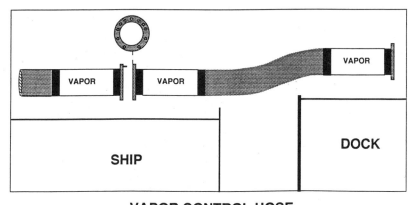

**VAPOR CONTROL HOSE**

Fig. 14-2. The vapor manifold must be fitted with a manually operated isolation valve that gives clear indication of the valve's status. The color and marking at each end of the vapor hose should be similar in all respects to the vessel's vapor manifold. Richard Beadon, Mark Huber.

of Inspection the hose should be inspected for cuts, tears, or defects that may render it ineffective.

## CLOSED GAUGING

In an effort to achieve a vapor-tight deck and leak-free transfer, all tankers engaged in vapor control must be equipped with a closed gauging system designed to operate over the entire tank depth. Closed gauging has been widely used for a number of years as part of the IG regulations. It originated as a result of the need to maintain atmosphere control and a positive deck pressure during cargo operations. Consequently, there are a number of closed gauging systems on the market, details of which can be found in chapter 3.

**High level/overfill alarms.** One of many concerns associated with a closed loading operation is the risk of cargo tank overfill. Pressing up a cargo tank while topping off can result in structural damage to the vessel and cargo in the vapor control system. The most common causes of spills while loading are:

1. Human error: poor judgment, fatigue, inattentiveness, inexperience, lack of communication.
2. Mechanical failure.
3. Malfunctioning tank valves.
4. Faulty gauging system.
5. Improper lineup.
6. Cargo gravitation.
7. Faulty alarms.

To protect against such an occurrence, alarms for both high level and overfill conditions must be fitted on vessels equipped for vapor control. Each alarm is designed to provide both audible and visual warning when the cargo reaches predetermined settings.

The alarms are required to be intrinsically safe and totally independent of each other. The alarm system must be equipped to permit testing prior to cargo transfer. It must also give warning in the event of power or circuit failure.

The high level alarm is set to activate when the liquid level rises above 95 percent of tank capacity and before the overfill alarm sounds. The secondary overfill alarm must be set to provide ample warning for the officer in charge to shut down before the cargo tank overflows.

Both alarms should be clearly indicated by the following black lettering on white background:

"HIGH LEVEL ALARM"

"TANK OVERFILL ALARM"

Additional options are available to protect the vessel structure against damage from tank overfill. One option is the use of a spill valve or rupture disc on each cargo tank. These devices generally are set to relieve at a higher pressure than the tank PV valve but certainly less than the maximum design working pressure of the tank. For vessels in ocean/coastwise service, provision must be made to prevent accidental opening due to cargo sloshing.

A second option is to install an overfill control system. In this system, which is generally used on tank barges, the overfill sensors on the vessel are connected to the shore facility. In an overfill condition, the system shuts down the operation automatically at least 60 seconds before the tank is "pressed up" to capacity.

**Vessel pressure-vacuum (PV) protection.** Another consequence of closed loading operations is the possibility of over or under pressurization of a cargo tank. Since the advent of inert gas on tankers, numerous cases of cargo tank rupture and collapse have been attributed to closed operations (see figure 14-4). As a result, the need for safe operating procedures and attention to detail during cargo operations cannot be overstated. Some of the potential causes of cargo tank over/under pressurization are: 1) excessively high loading rates, 2) malfunctioning/undersized PV devices, 3) vapor line constriction, 4) improper vapor system lineup, 5) excessive withdrawal of vapors or cargo, 6) expansion/contraction of cargo, and 7) cargo sloshing.

To protect against the foregoing, the regulations stipulate that the system should be capable of handling vapors at 1.25 times the maximum loading rate of the vessel. Additionally, an inerted tanker is provided with the following pressure-vacuum relief devices: 1) individual tank PV valves, 2) mast riser PV valve (if fitted), and 3) liquid-filled PV breaker.

The set points at which these devices relieve excess pressure or vacuum should fall within the following ranges:

$$1.0 \text{ psi} < \text{pressure relief} < \begin{cases} \text{maximum design working pressure} \\ \text{or} \\ \text{setting of spill valve/rupture disc} \end{cases}$$

$$-0.5 \text{ psi} > \text{vacuum relief} > \text{maximum design vacuum}$$

The bar graph shown in figure 14-3 further illustrates the normal operating pressures and settings for PV relief devices in a vapor control system.

It is important to understand that PV valves are mechanical devices and, as such, are prone to failing when needed most. Therefore, routine inspection and maintenance are essential to ensure proper protection of the vessel. As part of the regulations, each new PV valve installation must

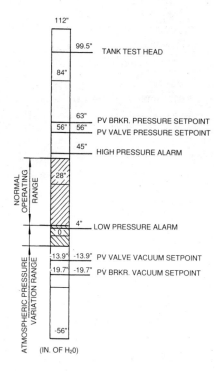

Fig. 14-3. Bar graph representing normal operating pressures and settings for pressure-vacuum relief devices in a vapor control system.

SYSTEM PRESSURE AND
SETPOINT BAR GRAPH

have a means of checking that the valve operates freely and does not remain in the open position.

## HIGH/LOW VAPOR PRESSURE PROTECTION

Every vapor control system must be equipped with a pressure sensing device that permits the officer in charge to monitor the pressure in the system. Also, high and low pressure alarms must provide both audible and visual warnings when a dangerous condition exists. The alarm settings are as follows:

High pressure alarm — not more than 90 percent of the lowest
                                      pressure relief valve setting

Low pressure alarm
                Inerted tanker    — Not less than 4 in. WG
                                      (0.144 psi)

                Noninerted tanker — lowest vacuum
                                      relief valve setting

## OPERATIONS

**Loading rates.** One critical element that affects the overall safety and success of vapor control operations is the determination of maximum allowable loading rates. The regulations specify that cargo loading rates take into account the pressure drop through the vapor piping system as well as the venting capacity of the pressure relief valves on the tank. A graph reflecting the cargo loading rate vs. pressure drop for a typical installation is shown in figure 14-5.

The maximum allowable loading rate must be determined and clearly understood by both vessel and terminal personnel prior to commencement of loading. While loading, ship's officers should closely monitor the loading rates and deck pressure to prevent damage to the system. When loading a "static accumulating" cargo the initial loading rate should be slow enough to minimize the development of a static electrical charge. Experience has shown that agitation, splashing, and pipeline friction contribute to charge separation in certain low conductivity cargoes. As a result, it is considered safe practice to limit the velocity to each tank to no more than one meter per second until a sufficient cushion is achieved. A table of flow rates corresponding to a linear velocity of one meter per second through various sizes of piping can be found in chapter 7 of the *International Safety Guide for Oil Tankers and Terminals* (ISGOTT).

**Final gauging.** Vapor control regulations prohibit the opening of a cargo tank to atmosphere during active cargo transfer. The intent of this requirement is to keep the system vapor-tight throughout the operation. In fact, it should be totally unnecessary to open a tank to atmosphere during loading if all required equipment is functioning properly.

Ship's officers are permitted to open tanks for the purpose of gauging, sampling, and taking temperatures provided the following criteria are met:

1. No active transfer to the tank.
2. In an inerted tank, a positive pressure is maintained.
3. In a noninerted tank, the vapor pressure is reduced to atmospheric.
4. The cargo is not required to be "closed gauged" by regulation.
5. If a static accumulating cargo, all metallic equipment introduced into the tank is bonded to the vessel and, if the tank is not inerted, a minimum 30-minute relaxation period has elapsed since loading ceased.

**Inerted tank vessels.** The vapor control regulations are designed to complement existing requirements for inerted vessels. Despite the nu-

Fig. 14-4. PV valves are mechanical devices that are prone to failing when needed most. On the ship shown here, a tank became over-pressurized when crew members forgot to open the inert gas branch line while loading. The PV valve, which was defective, failed to open. The main underdeck centerline girder fractured just forward of where it intersected with the tank's after bulkhead. In addition, the entire deck above the tank deformed upwards, and extensive repairs were required. LCDR Douglas B. Cameron/U.S. Coast Guard.

merous safeguards already in effect, the need to maintain atmosphere control for vessel safety has never been greater. Prior to engaging in vapor control operations, vessel personnel must test each cargo tank to verify that the oxygen content does not exceed 8 percent by volume. The oxygen measurements should be taken at one meter below the tank top and at the mid-point of the ullage space for each tank. Another concern involves facilities using a blower to assist in the transport of vapors. The use of such a blower could reduce the vessel deck pressure below the required minimum, which in turn could result in air being drawn into the system. Ship's officers must be mindful of this possibility and carefully monitor the deck pressure during closed operations to ensure the inert status of a tank is not compromised.

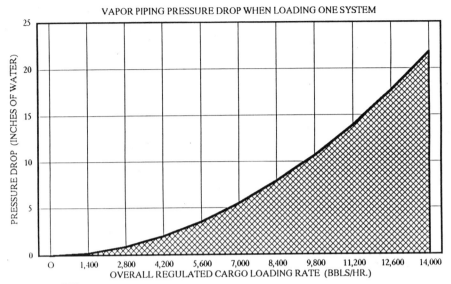

VAPOR PIPING PRESSURE DROP WHEN LOADING ONE SYSTEM

Pressure Drop is from No. 1 Center Tank (Most Remote Tank) to Aft Vapor Header

1) Pressure Drop is for a mixture of 45% Inert Gas and 55% Hydrocarbon Vapor.
2) Aft Port Vapor Header is furthest from the Vapor Main.

Fig. 14-5. This graph shows the relationship between cargo loading rate and pressure drop in the most remote tank. Regulations specify that cargo loading rates take into account the pressure drop through the vapor piping system as well as the venting capacity of the pressure relief valves of the tank.

**Declaration of Inspection.** For vessels intending to conduct vapor control, the Declaration of Inspection must include entries for critical aspects of the system. The Shell Oil addendum to the DOI in figure 14-6 illustrates the required entries for vapor control operations. Additionally, the use of a standard checklist (fig. 14-7) similar to those used in crude oil washing operations should help prevent unnecessary mishaps.

### CONCLUSION

As we have seen, there are many risks associated with vapor control operations. Sound operating practice and careful cooperation between ship and terminal are essential to reduce those dangers.

In the years ahead, the industry can expect changes in both the technology of vapor control and the regulations governing the use of that technology. One can only hope that these changes will result not only in protection of the environment, but also in greater safety for tanker crews.

S-13431 (6-91) 016241

# DECLARATION OF INSPECTION ADDENDUM
VAPOR CONTROL OPERATIONS

This addendum is to be used when collecting vapors associated with the loading of oil or chemicals in bulk.
The requirements are set forth in detail in 33 CFR 156.120 and 46 CFR 35.35-30 and therefore apply to both the facility and vessel unless otherwise indicated.

| VESSEL NAME ▶ | | INITIAL | |
|---|---|---|---|
| | | FACILITY | VESSEL |
| 1 | Vessel Certificate of Inspection has been endorsed as meeting the requirements of vapor control regulations. (39.30.1 (a)) | | |
| 2 | Initial loading rate and maximum transfer rate are determined. (156.120 (aa) 4; 35.35-30 (c) 4) _____ BPH | | |
| 3 | Maximum and minimum operating pressures at the facility vapor connection are determined. (156.120 (aa) 5; 35.35-30 (c) 5) | | |
| 4 | Cargo tank filling limits agreed. (39.30.1 (e)) | | |
| 5 | If inerted, oxygen content of the vessel cargo tanks is less than 8% oxygen by volume. (156.120 (aa) 9; 35.35-30 (c) 8) | | |
| 6 | Electrical insulating flange is fitted between vessel and facility vapor connections. (156.120 (aa) 3; 35.35-30 (c) 3) | | |
| 7 | All oxygen and hydrocarbon analyzers on the facility and vessel have been checked for calibration within the past 24 hours. (156.120 (aa) 7 ii) | | |
| 8 | Tank barge overfill control system is connected to the facility, tested and operating properly. (156.120 (aa) 6) | | |
| 9 | All cargo hatches and ullage openings are secured. | | |
| 10 | All facility and vessel alarms and shutdown systems have been tested within the past 24 hours. (156.120 (aa) 7 I; 35.35-30 (c) 6) | | |
| 11 | Manual valves properly aligned to collect cargo vapor. (156.120 (aa) 1; 35.35-30 (c) 1) | | |
| 12 | Vapor collection hose is in good condition. (156.120 (aa) 8; 35.35-30 (c) 7) | | |
| 13 | Facility vapor collection hose or articulated arm is connected to vessel vapor connection. (156.120 (aa) 2; 35.35-30 (c) 2) | | |

| FACILITY | VESSEL |
|---|---|
| SIGNATURE | SIGNATURE |
| TITLE | TITLE |
| TIME AND DATE | TIME AND DATE |

I certify that I have read the above declaration and detailed requirements and all conditions remain satisfactory

| UNIT | SUBSEQUENT PERSON-IN-CHARGE | TITLE | TIME AND DATE |
|---|---|---|---|
| VESSEL | | | |
| FACILITY | | | |
| VESSEL | | | |
| FACILITY | | | |
| VESSEL | | | |
| FACILITY | | | |

DATE AND TIME COMPLETED ▶

Fig. 14-6. This addendum to the Declaration of Inspection illustrates the required entries for vapor control operations. Shell Oil.

## CHECK LIST-MARINE VAPOR CONTROL OPERATING PROCEDURES

**PRE-ARRIVAL CHECKS**

- High level/overfill alarms tested within 24 hrs. before operation. ☐
- Deck pressure/tank oxygen readings checked and satisfactory. ☐
- Closed gauging systems checked and satisfactory. ☐
- Tanks to be loaded with regulated cargo identified. ☐
- Tanks identified which previously contained regulated cargo. ☐
- All cargo tank vents,P/V valves,tank hatches,tank cleaning openings tightly secured. ☐

**PRE-TRANSFER CHECKS**

- Vessel properly secured at loading berth. ☐
- Status of deck water seal satisfactory. ☐
- Low point drains on IG/Vapor control main secured. ☐
- Deck isolating valve secured. ☐
- Liquid P/V breaker at proper level ☐
- Atmospheric vent line open. ☐
- Power supply on to cargo tank alarms. ☐
- All alarms tested at each tank. ☐
- Oxygen level at each tank is below 8% by volume. ☐
- Vapor pressure alarm (audible/visual) tested. ☐
- Overfill control connected (vessel to vessel or vessel to shore). ☐
- All branch line valves to the vapor control main are at proper status (Consult compatability of cargoes). ☐
- Cargo system properly lined up. ☐
- Vapor collection system properly lined up. ☐
- Cargo hoses/Vapor hoses connected. ☐
- Insulating flange or non-conductive hose in use. ☐

Fig. 14-7. The use of a standard checklist should help to prevent unnecessary mishaps. Richard Beadon, Mark Huber.

## CHECK LIST-MARINE VAPOR CONTROL OPERATING PROCEDURES

- Pre-transfer conference required by DOI completed.
- Terminal consulted regarding dropping the deck pressure.
- If terminal operates a vapor line vacuum assist, have operating limits been determined?
- Certificate of Inspection or Certificate of Compliance endorsed.
- All oil transfer procedures complied with.
- Manifolds open - loading operations commenced.

### LOADING/TRANSFER OPERATIONS

- Initial loading rates observed.
- Cargo/Vapor connections checked and found satisfactory.
- Liquid/Vapor flow checked and found satisfactory.
- ISGOTT recommendations observed regarding static accumulator oils.
- Maximum allowable loading rates not exceeded.
- Vapor pressure on deck monitored.
- Loading rates adjusted as necessary for topping-off.
- All applicable regulations pertaining to Inert Gas systems complied with.

### POST TRANSFER CHECKS

- Finished loading and gauge out. (Note: IG vessel to maintain positive deck pressure.
- Cargo hoses drained, disconnected, and cargo system valves shut.
- Vapor manifold shut and vapor hose disconnected.
- Branch line valve status on IG vessel checked and satisfactory.
- IG plant run up and deck pressure topped up if necessary.

Fig. 14-7 *(cont.)*

## CHECK LIST-MARINE VAPOR CONTROL OPERATING PROCEDURES

**CRITICAL FAULTS INVOLVING VAPOR CONTROL SYSTEMS**

- Vapor hose constricts/collapses/kinks or damaged in any way which renders it ineffective.

- Tank overfill alarm is tripped.

- High level alarm/tank overfill alarm fault.

- Tank overfill control (auto-shutdown) inoperative.

- Inoperative gauging system.

- Mechanical failure of branch line/vapor manifold valve.

- High/Low vapor pressure condition.

- Inoperative P/V relief valves.

- Inability to maintain less than 8% oxygen by volume in cargo tanks.

- Inability to maintain a positive deck pressure throughout transfer.

- Faulty line-up of the vapor collection system.

**ALWAYS CONSULT COMPANY POLICIES AND OIL TRANSFER PROCEDURES FOR YOUR VESSEL.**

Fig. 14-7 *(cont.)*

# CONVERSION FACTORS

| To convert from: | To: | Multiply by: (Numbers in **boldface type** are exact values.) |
|---|---|---|
| barrels | cubic feet | 5.614583 |
| barrels | cubic meters | 0.15898729 |
| barrels | gallons (U.S.) | **42** |
| barrels | liters | 158.98284 |
| centimeters | inches | 0.39370079 |
| centimeters | meters | **0.01** |
| centimeters | millimeters | **10** |
| cubic feet | barrels | 0.1781076 |
| cubic feet | cubic inches | **1,728** |
| cubic feet | cubic meters | 0.028316847 |
| cubic feet | gallons (U.S.) | 7.4805195 |
| cubic inches | cubic centimeters | **16.387064** |
| cubic meters | barrels | 6.289811 |
| cubic meters | cubic centimeters | **1,000,000** |
| cubic meters | cubic feet | 35.314667 |
| cubic meters | cubic inches | 61,023.74 |
| cubic meters | gallons (U.S.) | 264.17205 |
| cubic meters | liters | 999.972 |
| fathoms | feet | **6** |
| fathoms | meters | **1.8288** |
| feet | centimeters | **30.48** |
| feet | fathoms | 0.166667 |
| feet | inches | **12** |
| feet | meters | **0.3048** |
| gallons (U.S.) | cubic inches | **231** |
| gallons (U.S.) | liters | 3.785306 |
| inches | centimeters | **2.54** |
| inches | millimeters | **25.4** |
| inches of water (4°C) | kg/cm$^2$ | 0.002539927 |
| inches of water | millimeters of water | **25.4** |
| inches of water (4°C) | psi | 0.03612625 |
| kilograms | pounds (avdp) | 2.2046226 |
| kilograms | tons (metric) | **0.001** |

| To convert from: | To: | Multiply by:<br>(Numbers in **boldface<br>type** are exact values.) |
|---|---|---|
| $kg/cm^2$ | inches of water (4°C) | 393.7122 |
| $kg/cm^2$ | millimeters of water (4°C) | 10,000.28 |
| $kg/cm^2$ | psi | 14.223343 |
| liters | cubic centimeters | 1,000.028 |
| liters | cubic inches | 61.02545 |
| liters | cubic meters | 0.001000028 |
| liters | gallons (U.S.) | 0.2641794 |
| meters | centimeters | **100** |
| meters | fathoms | 0.54680665 |
| meters | feet | 3.2808399 |
| meters | inches | 39.370079 |
| meters | millimeters | **1,000** |
| millimeters | inches | 0.039370079 |
| millimeters of water (4°C) | $kg/cm^2$ | 0.00009999709 |
| millimeters of water | inches of water | 0.039370079 |
| millimeters of water (4°C) | psi | 0.001422293 |
| pounds (avdp) | kilograms | **0.45359237** |
| psi | inches of water (4°C) | 27.6807 |
| psi | $kg/cm^2$ | 0.070306958 |
| psi | millimeters of water (4°C) | 703.089 |
| tons (long) | kilograms | 1,016.0469 |
| tons (long) | pounds (avdp) | **2,240** |
| tons (long) | tons (metric) | 1.1060469 |
| tons (metric) | kilograms | **1,000** |
| tons (metric) | pounds (avdp) | 2,204.6226 |
| tons (metric) | tons (long) | 0.98420653 |

# BIBLIOGRAPHY

Andersen, Steinar. "Inexpensive Bulk Nitrogen Production." *Shipbuilding Technology International,* 1989: 157-158.

Angelo, Joseph J. "A Status Report of Coast Guard Implementation of OPA Double Hull Related Requirements." Presented at *Marine Log's* Tanker Legislation 1991 Conference. Washington, D.C., September 24, 1991.

Baptist, C. *Tanker Handbook for Deck Officers.* Glasgow, Scotland: Brown, Son, & Ferguson Ltd., 1991.

Beaver, Earl R. "Permea Gas Separation Membranes Developed into a Commercial Reality. " Paper delivered to Seventh Annual Membrane Technology Planning Conference. Cambridge, Md., October 1989.

Berry, M. G. *Operation and Maintenance of Inert Gas and Crude Washing Systems.* Maidstone, England: Interlink Inert Gas Ltd., 1981.

Blenkey, Nicholas. "Living with the Law." *Marine Log,* February 1981: 34-37.

————. "Making Existing Tankers Safer." *Marine Log,* April 1991: 3.

Cameron, Douglas B. "Human Error Times Two." *Proceedings of the Marine Safety Council,* October-November-December 1989: 132-135.

*CG-174, A Manual for the Safe Handling of Inflammable and Combustible Liquids and Other Hazardous Products.* Washington, D.C.: U.S. Coast Guard, 1975.

*CG-329, Fire Fighting Manual for Tank Vessels.* Washington, D.C.: U.S. Coast Guard, 1974.

*CG-388, Chemical Data Guide for Bulk Shipment by Water.* Washington, D.C.: U.S. Coast Guard, 1982.

*CG-446, A Condensed Guide to Chemical Hazards.* Washington, D.C.: U.S. Coast Guard, 1985.

*CG-474, When You Enter That Cargo Tank . . . .* Washington, D.C.: U.S. Coast Guard, 1976.

"Congress Dictates Double Hulls." *Marine Log,* October 1990: 39.

*Controlling Hydrocarbon Emissions from Tank Vessel Loading.* (Prepared by the Marine Board of the National Research Council.) Washington, D.C.: National Academy Press, 1987.

"Crude Tanker Pollution Abatement" (Exxon Position Paper). Houston: Exxon Corporation, 1976.

*Crude Washing of Tankers.* Gothenburg, Sweden: Salen & Wicander AB, 1976.

*Double Hull Tank Vessels: A Review of Current Regulatory Efforts, Design Considerations, and Related Topics of Interest.* Paramus, N.J.: American Bureau of Shipping, 1991.

"Federal Oil Pollution Act of 1990." Summary of provisions prepared by Chevron Shipping Company, San Francisco, 1990.

*Fighting Pollution: Preventing Pollution at Sea.* London: Witherby & Co., 1991.

Fitch, Robert, and Gordon Marsh. "Coast Guard Requirements for Marine Vapor Control Systems." *Marine Technology,* September 1991: 270-275.

Flynn, Robert. "The Impact of OPA 90 and State Legislation on the Tanker Markets: What's Happened So Far?" Presented at *Marine Log*'s Tanker Legislation 1991 Conference. Washington, D.C., September 24, 1991.

*Fundamentals of Petroleum.* Austin: Petroleum Extension Service, University of Texas, 1982.

Gardner, A. Ward, and R. C Page. *Petroleum Tankship Safety.* Luton, England: Lorne & Maclean Marine Publishers, 1971.

Goudreau, J. "Developments in Shipboard Fire Suppression Systems." Synopsis of presentation to SNAME conference. May 11, 1990.

Grove, Noel. "Black Day for Brittany." *National Geographic,* July 1978: 125-34.

*Guide for Cargo Vapor Emission Control Systems on Board Tank Vessels.* Paramus, N.J.: American Bureau of Shipping, 1990.

"Guidelines for Marine Cargo Inspection." *Manual of Petroleum Measurement Standards* (Chapter 17, Section 1). Washington, D.C.: American Petroleum Institute, 1986.

Hodgson, Brian. "Alaska's Big Spill—Can the Wilderness Heal?" *National Geographic,* January 1990: 4-43.

Horrocks, J. C. S. "U.S. Oil Pollution Act of 1990." Letter to International Chamber of Shipping members. London: International Chamber of Shipping, 1991.

*Howden Inert Gas System Operating and Maintenance Manual.* Volume 1. Hounslow, England: Howden Engineering Ltd., 1983.

*Inert Flue Gas Safety Guide* (Prepared by the International Chamber of Shipping and the Oil Companies International Marine Forum). London: Witherby & Co., 1978.

*Inert Gas/Crude Oil Washing Syllabus.* Linthicum Heights, Md.: Maritime Institute of Technology and Graduate Studies, 1991.

*Inert Gas Systems.* London: International Maritime Organization, 1990.

"Inspection of Inert Gas Systems." *Marine Safety Manual* (Chapter 15). Washington, D.C.: U.S. Coast Guard, 1990.

*International Safety Guide for Oil Tankers and Terminals* (Prepared by the International Chamber of Shipping, Oil Companies Marine Forum, and the International Association of Ports and Harbors). London: Witherby & Co., 1990.

Jimenez, Richard. "The Evolution of the Load Line." *Surveyor,* May 1976: 7-11.

Ketchum, Donald E. *A Failure Modes and Effects Analysis of Vapor Collection Systems.* San Antonio, Tex.: Southwest Research Institute, 1988.

King, G. A. B. *Tanker Practice: The Construction, Operation, and Maintenance of Tankers.* London: Stanford Maritime Ltd., 1971.

"Marine Vapor Control Systems: Final Rule." *Federal Register,* June 21, 1990.

"Measurement of Cargoes on Board Tank Vessels." *Manual of Petroleum Measurement Standards* (Chapter 17, Section 2). Washington, D.C.: American Petroleum Institute, 1990.

"Mid-deck Tanker Can't Spill." *Marine Log,* January 1991: 40.

Mostert, Noel. *Supership.* New York: Knopf, 1975.

*Our Petroleum Industry.* London: British Petroleum, 1977.

Pendexter, L. A., and W. G. Coulter. *Classification Society Overview for Construction, Inspection, and Repair of OPA 90 Double Hull Tankers.* Paramus, N.J.: American Bureau of Shipping, 1991.

"Rebuilding the Exxon Valdez." *Marine Log,* October 1990: 36-38.

Rutherford, D. *Tanker Cargo Handling.* London: Charles Griffin & Company Ltd., 1980.

*Saab MaC/501 Tanker Monitoring and Control System, Technical Description.* Gothenburg, Sweden: Saab Marine Electronics, 1991.

*Tanker Cleaning Manual.* San Francisco: Gamlen Chemical Company, 1976.

*Tanker Spills: Prevention by Design* (Prepared by the Marine Board of the National Research Council). Washington, D.C.: National Academy Press, 1991.

*Technical Description, Saab TankRadar.* Gothenburg, Sweden: Saab Marine Electronics, 1991.

*The Unseen Menace: A Pocket Guide to the Atmospheric Hazards of Confined Spaces.* Pittsburgh: Bacharach, Inc., 1989.

Weller, G. Alex. "Learning to Live with OPA 1990." *Marine Log,* March 1991: 36-41.

# INDEX

ABS, 126-27
AFFF. *See* Foam
Air, compressed, clearing hoses with, 240
Air intake, IG system, 266
Alarms
    $CO_2$, 212, 217
    deck water seal, 264, 267
    fire, 218
    high level/overfill, 65, 284
    high oxygen (IG), 263
    IG pressure, 260, 263
    scrubber, 264
    vapor control system, 284, 286
Alaska pipeline, 26
Alkylation, 32
*Allegro,* collision involving, 202
Allowance
    dock water, 134-35
    fresh water, 126, 134
    zone, 128, 135-36
All-purpose extinguisher, 214, 219
All-purpose nozzle, 211
American Bureau of Shipping, 126-27
American Petroleum Institute, 26-27, 39,
    42, 49
Anchoring, at offshore mooring, 94-96
Angle valves, 68, 70
Annexes (MARPOL), 245-46
Anticline, oil-bearing, 21
API gravity. *See also* Specific gravity
    automatic readout, 54
    conversion to specific gravity, 50
    examples of, 53
    how determined, 50-51
    variation in final value, 100
Aqueous film forming foam. *See* Foam
Arabian crude, 188, 278
Aromatic hydrocarbons, 32
Arrival ballast tanks, 157
Asphalt-base crude oil, 26
Asphyxiation, 190-92
Aviation gasoline, flammability of, 35

Ballast
    arrival tanks, 157
    cargo tanks used for, 149, 157-58
    clean, defined, 152-153
    departure tanks, 157
    dirty, disposal of, 159, 227-33
    permissible oil content (MARPOL), 245
    plan, 152-54
    tanks, protectively located, 154-55
Baltic Sea ("special area"), 245
Barrel, U.S. petroleum
    defined, 39, 42
    gross, 42, 46
    importance in petroleum industry, 42
    net, 42, 46, 51, 55
    observed, 42
    standard, 42
Bell-mouth, 58, 115
Bending stress numerals, 138
Benzene
    API gravity, example of, 53
    flammable limits of, 201
    regulations for, 279
Black Sea ("special area"), 245
Bleeder valve (tank cleaning), 185
Blending (of petroleum products), 33
Blowing tubes, interlocks preventing, 277
Blowout, oil well, 21
Booster pumps, 103, 118
Bos'n, duties of, 180
Bottom flush, 178
Bottom wash. *See* Crude oil washing
"Bravo" flag, 78
Breathing apparatus
    compressed air type, 194-95
    crew member gassed while wearing, 190
    used by fire fighters, 221, 224
Bridge, location of, 3, 7
Buoyancy, center of, 132
Buoys
    hose, 94, 96
    mooring to, 94

Burnoff, bunker fuel, 100, 128, 135-36
Butterfly valves, 68-69
Butterworth tank-cleaning machines
    P-60, 164
    type "K," 162
Bypass valves
    IG recirculation line, 265
    mast riser. See Mast riser bypass valve

Calculator, loading, 138, 140-41, 143
Calibration
    of cargo tanks, 42
    tables, 42-43, 48
Carbon dioxide
    alarm, 212, 217
    automatic systems, 212, 216
    manual systems, 217, 221-24
    portable extinguishers, 212, 214, 218
    semiportable extinguishers, 212, 222, 223
    time delay mechanism, 217
Carbon monoxide, emission standards for,
    279
Carbon tetrachloride, 216
Cargo control room. See also Cargo control
        terminal
    console, 113, 118
    described, 65-66
    modern alternative to, 87
    operating pumps from, 110
    readouts for draft and trim, 118
Cargo control terminal. See also Cargo
        control room
    bridge location of, 51, 54, 65, 87
    mimic displays, 117, 119
    pump and valve operation from, 111
    readouts for draft, trim, and list, 118-19
    temperature and API readout, 51
Carryover, water, from deck seal, 266, 269-
    70
Casinghead gasoline, explosion involving,
    207
Catalyst (oil refining), 28, 32
Catalytic cracking, 28-32
Center of flotation, 130
Center tanks
    aftermost, used for slops, 172
    cross-section of, 176
    loading, 82-83, 98
Centrifugal pumps, 107-10, 112
Certificates of Financial Responsibility,
    249, 254
CG-388, 36-37

Chain reaction (element of fire), 201, 205
Charts, nautical, 235
Checklist, vapor control, 289-93
Checkoff, pretransfer, 78, 102-103
Check valves, 68-69, 102, 121
Chemical carriers
    IG systems used on, 186, 272-73, 276
    MARPOL standards for, 245-46
Chemical Data Guide for Bulk Shipment
        by Water, 36-37
Chemical Hazards Response Information
        System, 36, 38
Chief mate
    discharging orders, 116
    duties of, 124, 180
    loading orders, 83-86
CHRIS, 36
"Christmas tree," 24
Clean Air Act of 1970, 279
Clean ballast
    defined, 152-53
    segregated systems, 154-55
    tanks, in cargo system, 157
Cleaning charts, 170
$CO_2$. See Carbon dioxide
Coal, as cargo, 12
Coast Guard
    load lines enforced by, 125
    role as IMO representative, 248
Code, for voyage orders, 123
Cofferdams, 79
COFRs, 249, 254
Coils, heating, 91, 117
"Coker" unit, 31
Collisions, prevention of, 235-39
Combustible gas indicators
    Explosimeter, 190-91
    Gascope, 196, 260
    precautions when using, 188
    Tankscope, 196, 260
Combustible liquid, defined, 35
Combustion, spontaneous, 209-10
"Common" systems, 106, 274, 276
Communication
    at offshore terminals, 241
    by radio, 94, 241
    by satellite, 123
    voyage orders, 123
Compressed air
    breathing apparatus. See Breathing
        apparatus
    clearing hoses with, 240

Computers. *See also* Cargo control terminal
cargo data, automatic calculation of, 51, 54
integrated systems, 129, 140-41
software, 141
trim corrections, automatic, 48
types of, for load planning, 136, 140-41
various uses of, 10
Conduction, spread of fire by, 199
Console, engine room, 14
Contamination, cargo
through IG system, 276
through pumproom crossovers, 90
through vapor control piping, 281
Controlling zone, 128
Control room. *See* Cargo control room
Convection, spread of fire by, 199
Conventions, international. *See also* International Maritime Organization
general description of, 247-48
load line, 125
MARPOL. *See* MARPOL
ratification process, 248-49
SOLAS, 248
STCW, 248
Cooler/dryer, IG, 272, 276
COW. *See* Crude oil washing
Cracking (refining process), 28-32
Creosote, flammability of, 35
Crossovers
checking, before loading, 78
described, 61
diagram showing, 106
between main and stripper, 65, 178
manifold, 62, 64
between pumps, 106
to tank-cleaning system, 163
Crude carriers, described, 6. *See also* VLCCs; ULCCs
Crude oil. *See also* Crude oil washing
adaptability of, to COW, 177
classification of, 26
dewatering, 28
solvent properties of, 174
"sour," 27, 188, 278
Crude oil washing
arcs, washing, 164-65
benefits of, 174
bottom wash, 165-65, 173, 175
cargo recovery increased by, 174
combining with LOT, 230, 233
debottoming, 185
described, in general, 174-78

draining lines, 175
IG system required, 260, 278
IMO requirements for, 177
multistage, 181
"overlap," 173
prerequisites for, 175-77
pressure, typical, 174-75
purging (IG), importance of, 261
required on ships without SBT, 245
selective arc machines, 173, 175
of "shadow areas," 175
single-nozzle machines, 175
stripping, importance of, 175
top wash, 164-65, 175
twin-nozzle machines, 175, 177
two-stage, diagram of, 165
Curves, hydrostatic, 132-33
"Cuts," water, 43-45

Datum, ullaging, 42, 44
Deadweight. *See also* Tonnage
defined, 6, 128
scale, 130-31
Debottoming, 185. *See also* Crude oil washing
Deck isolating valve, IG, 256, 267, 274, 281
Deck water seal
alarm, low water, 264, 267
carryover from, 266, 269-70
diagrams of operation, 73-74, 267-70
"dry" type, 266
principle of, 266
purpose of, 256
"semidry" type, 266, 269
"wet" type, 266, 268
Declaration of Inspection, 80, 84-85, 289-90
"Dedicated" systems
ballast, 154-55
vapor control, 281
Deepwell pumps, 64, 110, 114
Demister, IG, 264-65
Departure ballast tanks, 157
Dewatering, of crude oil, 22, 28
Diesel engines, 6
Differential GPS, 235
Dilution method (IG purging), 257
Direct pipeline system
described, 58
diagrams of, 60, 149
used on T2, 10
Dirty ballast, disposal of, 159, 227-33
Displacement method (IG purging), 257

Displacement (tonnage)
 defined, 126, 128
 example of, 135-36
 relationship to draft, 139
Distillation tower, 28, 31
Dock water allowance, 134-35
DOI. *See* Declaration of Inspection
Double-hulled tankers
 drawings of, 18, 251
 endorsed by National Academy of
  Sciences, 17
 as OPA requirement, 16, 249-50
Draft
 change in, computing, 130, 133-34
 computer updates of, 129
 final, loading to, 99-100, 143
 formula for (MARPOL), 148
 readout, cargo control console, 118
 relationship to displacement, 139
 relationship to TPI, 130-31
 requirements when ballasted, 148-49
Drip pans, 63, 78
Drops
 checking before loading, 78
 described, 60-61, 104
 line, 61, 64, 178
 pumproom, 64, 104
 tank, 61
 valves, 60-61, 103-104
Drop tank (deck water seal), 266, 270
Dry chemical extinguishing agents
 all-purpose extinguishers, 214, 219
 applying on deck fire, 220
 theory behind, 205
Dry dock. *See* Shipyard
Duplex pumps, 106, 109
Dwt. *See* Deadweight

ECDIS, 235
Eductors, 65, 107, 111-12, 171
Electrical fire, extinguishing, 224
"Electronic chart," 235
Emission factors, table of, 280
*Energy Concentration,* 118
Engine room
 console, 14
 fighting fire in, 221-24
 IG operation, role in, 262-63
 location of, 3
 tank cleaning, role during, 163
Engines
 diesel, 6
 geared turbine (steam), 10

reciprocating steam, 6, 10
Epoxy coating of tanks, 165
Ethylene oxide, flammable limits of, 201
Explosimeter, 190-91
Explosion
 danger of, while tank cleaning, 182-85
 pyrophoric oxidation as cause of, 278
Explosive range. *See* Flammable limits
Explosive region, diagram showing, 203
Extinguishers, fire
 dry chemical, 214, 219
 portable $CO_2$, 212-14, 218
 semiportable $CO_2$, 212-14, 222-23
*Exxon Valdez,* 16, 227-28, 237, 249

Fans, IG, 260-61, 265
Fault, oil-bearing, 21
Fire
 classes of (table), 204
 extinguishers. *See* Extinguishers, fire
 point, defined, 34
Flame screen, 208
Flammable limits, 201-203. *See also* Lower
  explosive limit
Flammable liquid, defined, 35
Flammable region, diagram showing, 203
Flange, vapor connection, 281
Flash point, defined, 201
Float ullaging system, 43, 47-48, 117
Flue gas. *See also* Inert gas
 evaluating visually, 277
 oxygen content of, 255
Flushing
 bottom piping, 178
 branch lines, 178, 230
 discharge piping, 122
 pumps, 178
 submarine hose, 97
 tank bottoms, 178
Foam
 applying on deck fire, 220
 aqueous film forming (AFFF), 204,
  211
 aspirating discharge devices, 215
 monitor, 221
 nonaspirating discharge devices, 215
 types of, 211
 portable nozzle, 211, 214
 proportioners, 213
Fog (fire fighting), 211-12
Fractionation, 28, 31
Free flow systems, 71
Fresh water allowance, 126, 134

Gamajet II tank-cleaning machine, 172
Garbage, disposal at sea, 246
Gas carriers. *See* LNG carriers
Gascope, 196, 260
Gas-free certificate, 160
Gas-freeing
  entire ship, 261
  with IG fans, 167, 261
  isolated tank, 261
  with portable blowers, 167, 170, 261
Gasket, hose, 240
Gas oil, example of API gravity, 53
Gasoline
  aviation, flammability of, 35
  casinghead, explosion involving, 207
  classed as flammable liquid, 35
  dangers of cleaning with, 208
  example of API gravity, 53
  flammable limits of, 201
  sample page of *CG-388,* 37
Gas regulating valve, 264-66
Gassing
  pumproom, 115
  rescue, 192-95
  symptoms of, 188
  tank, 188-90
  while wearing breathing apparatus, 190
Gate valves, 66-67
Gauging. *See* Ullaging
Gear pumps, 107
Global positioning system, 235
Globe valves, 68
GPS, 235
Gravitation
  to adjust trim, 100
  caused by list, 81
  from slop tank, 233
  spill caused by, 122
  while loading, 88
Gravity. *See* API gravity
Gross barrel, 42, 46
Groundings, prevention of, 235-39
GRV, 264-66
Gunclean tank-cleaning machines, 166, 168

H2S. *See* Hydrogen sulfide
Halons, 205, 216-17
Hand taping, 42-43. *See also* Ullaging
Handy-size tanker
  defined, 6
  pipeline size, 58
  typical vent system on board, 75
Hazardous area (IG), 256, 267

Heating coils, cargo tank, 91, 117
Heat, removing (fire fighting), 204
Heyerdahl, Thor, 246
Hogging, 118, 143-46. *See also* Stress
Hose-reel systems (tank cleaning), 167, 171
Hoses, cargo system
  blanking off, 243
  clearing with compressed air, 240
  connections, checking, 78
  draining, 240
  marking with chalk, 80
  securing, proper method of, 240-41
  vapor, 281, 283
  watching, at offshore mooring, 94-95
Hoses, tank cleaning
  bleeder valve, 185
  dimensions of, 167
  draining, 185
  hand-held, 163
  keeping grounded, 183-85
Hydrocarbons, emission standards for, 279
Hydrogenation, 33
Hydrogen sulfide
  dangers of, 188, 278
  described, 27
  pyrophoric oxidation caused by, 278
  "sweetening" products with high con-
    tent of, 33
Hydrometer, 100, 134
Hydrostatic
  curves, 132-33
  pressure, 17, 21. *See also* Mid-deck
    tanker
  tables, 132-33, 139
  values, 130

IG. *See* Inert gas
Ignition temperature, defined, 202
IMO, 177, 248. *See also* Conventions;
    MARPOL
Inert gas. *See also* Vapor control systems
  alarms, 65, 260, 263-64, 267
  cooler/dryer, 272, 276
  constituents of, 186
  deck water seal. *See* Deck water seal
  demister, 264-65
  fans, 260-61, 265
  generators, 257, 270-72, 275-76
  hazardous area, 256, 267
  manual, importance of, 261
  oxygen content of, 186, 257
  precooler, 264
  pressure, adjusting, 260

Inert gas (*cont.*)
    pressure controller, 263, 265
    purging, 256-58
    PV breaker. *See* PV breaker
    recirculating line, 265
    regulating valve (GRV), 264-66
    scrubber. *See* Scrubber, IG
    specialized systems, 270-75
    systems, diagrams of, 72, 120, 186, 256,
        257
    systems, ships requiring, 163, 183, 255,
        260
    tank isolating valves, 270, 274
Insulating oil, 170
Intake, fresh air (IG system), 266
Interface, computer (to ullaging system),
        140-41
Interface, IG (when purging), 257
Interface, oil/water
    detectors, illustrations of, 174, 234
    diagram showing, 233
    locating, 43, 45, 232-34
Interlocks, sootblower, 277
International Maritime Organization, 177,
        248. *See also* Conventions; MAR-
        POL
*ISGOTT,* 287
Isolation valve (vapor manifold), 281, 283

Jet fuel
    commercial, 35
    JP-4, 35, 201

Kerosene
    API gravity, example of, 53
    flammable limits of, 201
*Kong Haakon VII,* explosion aboard, 182,
        184

Lashings, valve handwheel, 79
Lavomatic tank-cleaning machines, 169,
        173, 181
LCB, 132, 139, 142
LCG, 132, 142
LEL, 188, 196. *See also* Flammable limits
Liability, limitation by OPA, 249
Lifeline (used by fire fighters), 221, 224
Lightering, 95
Lightning (cause of explosion), 209
Light ship
    defined, 130
    example of, 138
Line displacements, 97-99, 122

Line drops, 61, 64
Lineup, cargo system (checking), 78
Liquefied natural gas, 13-16
List
    control of, while discharging, 118-19
    natural, 118
    removal of, while loading, 81
Litmus paste, 45
Lloyd's Register of Shipping, 99
LNG carriers
    described, 13-16
    IG systems for, 270-73, 276
Loading arms
    alignment of, 92, 242
    broken, spill caused by, 240-41
    connecting, 59, 61
    draining, 240
Load lines
    described, 125-28
    fresh water allowance, 126, 134
    zones, 126-28, 135-36
Load-on-top
    COW, combining with, 230, 233
    described, 156-58, 174, 229-32
    diagram illustrating, 231
    example of use, 157-58
    history of, 229
Logbook entries, 91-93
Longitudinal center of buoyancy, 132, 139,
        142
Longitudinal center of gravity, 132, 142
Long ton, 6, 42
LOT. *See* Load-on-top
Lower explosive limit, 188, 196. *See also*
        Flammable limits
Lubricating oil, flammability of, 35

*Mactra,* explosion aboard, 182-83
Malacca, Strait of, groundings in, 236
Manifold
    closing block valve to prevent spill, 69
    connecting loading arm to (illustra-
        tions), 59, 103
    connections, blanking off, 240
    crossovers, 64
    described, 62-64
    diagram showing, 149
    pressure gauges, 64
    thermometers, 50, 62
    valves, 69, 71, 102, 281, 283
    vapor control, 281, 283
"Marks," loading to, 99
*Marpessa,* explosion aboard, 182

MARPOL
  annexes to, 245-46
  double-hull requirement, 250
  draft and trim, requirements for, 148
  general requirements of, 245-46
  SBT, requirement for, 245
  tanker, diagram of, 155
Master valves
  cargo system, 61-62
  steam smothering, 214-16
Mast riser bypass valve
  closing in port, 80, 258-59
  diagram showing, 274
  opening to reduce $O_2$ absorption, 261
  operation of, 269-70
  sealed (vapor control), 258-59
Mediterranean ("special area"), 245
Medium-size tanker, defined, 6
*Mega Borg,* explosion and fire on board, 34
Membrane separator, nitrogen, 273-75, 277
Methane, in natural gas, 13
Metric ton, 6, 39, 42
Mexican crude, 278
Mid-deck tanker
  as alternative to double hull, 250
  described, 17-19
  diagram of, 252
Mixed-base crude oil, 26
Molasses, as cargo, 3
Moment
  to change trim one inch, 133-34, 139,
    142
  trimming, 133-34, 142
Mooring lines, tending
  while discharging, 117
  while loading, 89
Moorings, offshore, 79, 94, 96-97, 100
MT1, 133-34, 139, 142
Mucking, 160
Multipoint moorings, 94, 96

NAAQS, 279
Naphtha, flammability of, 35
National Academy of Sciences study, 17
Natural gas, liquefied, 13-16
Natural gasoline, flammability of, 35
Net barrel
  calculating, 51, 55
  common use on tankers, 46
  defined, 42
Nitrogen membrane separator, 273-75, 277
Nitrogen oxides, emission standards for,
  279

Nonreturn valve, IG, 256
Norske Veritas, 99
Nozzle, all-purpose, 211

OBOs
  described, 12-13
  IG systems for, 271-72
Observed volume of cargo, 42, 46-48
Oil Pollution Act of 1990
  double-hull requirement, 238
  *Exxon Valdez* grounding, as justification
    for, 16
  regulations implementing, 252
  summarized, 249-52
Orders
  loading, chief mate's, 83-86
  voyage, 123
Ore, as cargo, 12
Outage, 86
Overfill control system, 285
Oxygen
  absorption from scrubber, 261
  alarm (IG), 263
  amount required for combustion, 199, 203
  analyzer, 263
  content of IG, 263
  content of inerted tanks, 257-58, 260
  as element of fire, 199
  indicator, 119, 188, 191, 263
  recorder (IG), 263
  removing (fire fighting), 204
  required level for tank entry, 190-91,
    261-62
  tank readings, where taken, 288
Ozone, halons as depletors of, 217

*Pacific Glory,* fire on board, 202
Paraffin-base crude oil, 26
Particulates, emission standards for, 279
Persian Gulf ("special area"), 245
Petroleum Tables
  stowage factors, 53-55
  volume correction factors, 49, 51, 53
Pilots, assisting, 237, 239
Pipelines
  flushing, 178
  size of, 58
  system, direct, 58, 60
  underground, 22
  vapor control, 281, 283
Plan
  ballast, 152-54
  loading, 83-86, 135-37

Plastics, disposal at sea, 246
Platforms, drilling, 20, 22-23
"Plimsoll mark," 125
PL/SBT, diagram showing, 155
Pollutants, primary (air quality), 279
Polymerization, 32-33
Portable tank-cleaning machines. *See* Tank-cleaning machines, portable
Positive displacement pumps, 106
Pounding, 149
Precooler, IG, 264
Pressure, cargo system
    manifold gauges, 64
    while discharging, 116
    while loading, 88-89
Pressure drop (vapor control), 287, 289
Pressure, IG
    adjusting, during discharge, 260
    alarms, 260, 263
    automatic "trips," 264
    controller, 263, 265
    indicator/recorder, 263
    in isolated tank, relieving, 270
    monitoring, during discharge, 119
    typical, 263
Pressure, oil well, 22, 24
Pressure, tank-cleaning system, 163-65, 174-75
Pressure, vapor control system
    alarms, 286
    drop, 287, 289
    influenced by loading rate, 287, 289
Pressure, vent system, 75-77. *See also* PV breaker; PV valves
Primary control valve, IG, 266
Priming. *See* Pumps
Product carriers
    clean versus black, 3
    disposal of slops from, 232
    IG systems used on, 270-77
    vapor cross contamination on, 276
Programmable machines. *See* Tank-cleaning machines, fixed
Prohibited zones (dirty ballast), 154, 232, 245
Propeller immersion, when ballasted, 149
Proportioners, foam, 211, 213
Protectively located ballast tanks, 154-55
Pumpman, duties of, 105, 180
Pumproom
    checking, while loading, 90
    described, 64
    diagrams of, 104, 106
    drops, 64, 104

example of explosion in, 207
fighting fire in, 219-20
gassing, 115
isolating while loading, 64, 90
loading through, 90
precautions when entering, 115
preventing fires in, 207-208
rescue, 192-95
sea suctions, checking, 78
valve numbering, 71
vent fans, 219-20
Pumps
    booster, 103, 118
    centrifugal, 107, 108-10, 112
    controls for, 65, 110-11, 113
    deepwell, 64, 110, 114
    drive-shaft seals, 115
    duplex, 106, 109
    eductors, 65, 107, 111-12, 171
    emergency shutdown switches, 117
    flushing, 178
    gear, 107
    loss of suction, 112-13
    oil well, 22, 24
    positive displacement, 106
    priming, 108, 112-13
    reciprocating, 105-107, 109, 112-13
    screw, 107
    self-priming, 108-10
    stripping, 64-65, 105-107, 109, 171-72
    tank-cleaning, 163
Purge pipes, 257, 276. *See also* Purging, IG
Purging, IG
    after COW, 261
    described, 256-58
    diagram of various methods, 259
    ports prohibiting, 260
    after "sour" crude, 278
PV breaker. *See also* PV valves
    as backup to PV valves, 77, 285-86
    diagrams showing operation of, 76, 272
    operation, described, 267-69
    refilling, 269
    settings for, 269, 285-86
PV valves. *See also* PV breaker
    cross-section of, 75
    defective, example of, 288
    diagram showing location of, 274
    high velocity, 258
    on individual tank vent, 273
    pretransfer check, 79
    settings for, 285-86
    typical arrangements of, 273-74

Pyrophoric oxidation, 278

Radar
    monitoring of ships, 235
    ullaging systems, 43, 50-52
Radiation, spread of fire by, 199
Radios, 94, 241
Rates, loading
    calculating, 55-57
    effect on vapor pressure, 287, 289
    form for, 56
    maximum allowed, 287
Reach rods, 58, 62, 87
Reactivity (of petroleum products), 35
Reciprocating pumps, 105-107, 109, 112-13
Reciprocating steam engine, 6, 10
Recirculating line, IG, 265
Red Sea ("special area"), 245
Reforming (refining process), 32
Reid Vapor Pressure, 34
Regulations. *See also* Conventions;
        MARPOL; Oil Pollution Act of 1990
    implementing OPA, 249
    vapor control, 279-80
Relief valves, 69-70. *See also* PV valves
Rescue, tank and pumproom, 192-95
Residuum, 28, 31
Rigs, drilling, 20, 22-23
Rupture disc, 284

Sagging, 143, 146. *See also* Stress
*Salem Maritime* (illustration of fire damage to), 199
Samples
    cargo, 43, 178-80
    dock water, 100, 134
*San Demetrio,* description of fire on board, 197
Satellite, voyage orders sent by, 123
SBT. *See* Segregated ballast tanks
Scale, deadweight, 130-31
Screw pumps, 107
Scrubber, IG
    alarms, 264
    components of, 264
    diagrams of, 187, 265
    high/low water "trips," 264
    $O_2$ absorption from, 261
Scupper plugs, 78
Seal, deck water. *See* Deck water seal
Sea valves
    diagram showing, 149
    importance of checking, 78, 244

improperly set, spill caused by, 242-44
    location of, 156
    opening, proper method, 156
Segregated ballast tanks
    described, 148
    protectively located, 154-55
    required by MARPOL, 245
    ships requiring, 148, 229
Selective arc. *See* Tank-cleaning machines,
    fixed
"Semidry" deck water seal. *See* Deck water
    seal
"Shaker," 21
Shear stress, 138, 142. *See also* Stress
Shipyard
    cleaning tanks prior to, 160
    disposal of slops in, 233
Signals
    displayed while loading, 78
    emergency shutdown, 94, 241
Single-hulled tanker, cross-section of, 176
Single-nozzle machines. *See* Tank-cleaning
    machines, fixed
Single-point moorings, 79, 94, 97, 236, 238
SIP, 279
Slops. *See also* Slop tanks
    accumulating on board, 230-33
    pumping overboard, former practice,
        227-28
    pumping to shore facilities, 159, 232
    stripping of, 171-74, 230-34
Slop tanks. *See also* Slops
    "clean" and "dirty," 174, 232-33
    how used during LOT, 157-58, 231
    multistage, 172-74, 232-33
Sludge, accumulation of, 171. *See also*
    Crude oil washing
Sluice gates, 83
Smoking
    caution regarding, 93
    example of fire caused by, 205-207
Software, computer, 141
SOLAS convention, 248
Sootblowers, interlocks fitted, 277
Soot removal, by scrubber, 264
Sounding rods, precautions when using, 185
Sour crude, 27, 188, 278
"Special areas," (MARPOL), 245
Specifications, cargo, 178-80
Specific gravity. *See also* API gravity
    of cargo, 50, 53
    conversion to API gravity, 50
    of dock water, 134-35

Spill-response contingency plans, 251
Spills
    caused by broken hose, 89, 240
    caused by defective check valve, 69, 102
    caused by overflow of stripping fill tank,
      115
    common causes of, 284
    while discharging, 102
    prevented by mid-deck design, 17, 250,
      252
    prevention, in general, 240-44
    proper action following, 244-45
Spill valve (vapor control), 284
SPMs, 79, 94, 97, 236, 238
Spontaneous combustion, 209-10
Spudding, of oil well, 20
Stability, transverse, 123
Stack gas. *See* Flue gas
Standard volume of cargo, 42, 49-51
State Implementation Plan, 279
Static electricity
    cargoes accumulating, 287
    explosions caused by, 182-84
    generated by COW, 185
STCW convention, 248
Steam-smothering systems, 214-16
"Sternwinders," 10
Stowage factors. *See also* Ullaging
    formula for determining tonnage, 42
    how used, 53-55
    table, extract from, 55
    typical examples of, 42
Strait of Malacca, groundings in, 236
Stratigraphic trap, oil-bearing, 21
Stress
    during ballast passage, 148
    computer updates of, 129
    constituents of, 142-43
    while discharging, 117-118
    forms for calculating, 141-45
    hogging, 118, 143, 146
    while loading, 82
    numerals, 138, 143
    sagging, 143, 146
    shear, 138, 142
Stripping
    crossover to main system, 65
    fill tank, 114-15
    through main line, 65
    pumps. *See* Pumps, stripping
    of slops, 171-74, 230-34
    system, described, 64-65
    while tank cleaning, importance of, 171

    trim, importance during, 114
Submerged sensor ullaging system, 43, 52,
    54
Suction
    bell-mouth, 58, 115
    loss of, 112-13, 172
    valve (pump), 104
Sulphur oxides
    content of inert gas, 186
    emission standards for, 279
    removal by scrubber, 264
SUM-21 ullaging system, 52

T2 tanker
    design and history of, 6-10
    size, compared to VLCC, 9, 183
Tables
    calibration, 42-43, 48
    hydrostatic, 132-33, 139
    Petroleum, 49, 51, 53-55
Tank-cleaning machines, fixed. *See also*
      Crude oil washing
    advantages of, 169-70
    bottom-mounted, 177
    bottom wash, 173
    Butterworth P-60, 164
    gearbox and controls, drawing of, 181
    Gunclean, 166, 168
    Lavomatic, 169, 173, 181
    multistage, 165, 181
    "overlap," 173
    programmable and nonprogrammable,
      175, 177
    selective arc, 173, 181
    single-nozzle, 175
    static charges generated by, 183
    twin-nozzle, 175, 177
    two-stage operation, diagram of, 165
Tank-cleaning machines, portable
    bleeder valve for draining, 185
    Butterworth type "K," 162
    cleaning charts, 170
    drops, height of, 167
    effect on IG system, 275-76
    example of use, 160
    Gamajet II, 172
    hose-reel systems, 167, 171
    hoses, dimensions of, 167
    keeping grounded, 183-85
    operation of, described, 167-69
    precautions when using, 183-85
Tank drops, 61
Tank, fire in, 220-21

Tankscope, 196, 260
Tank valves, 58-60
Tapes. *See also* Ullaging
   "automatic," 47
   floats, 117
   hand, 42-43
   interface detectors, 43, 45-46, 174, 234
   rolling up, 117
Telltale, 60, 91
Temperature
   automatic readout, examples of, 54, 87,
     89
   of fire, 199
   how measured, 43, 45, 50, 87, 89
   IG, automatic "trips," 264
   ignition, defined, 202-203
   standard (cargo), defined, 49
   of tank-cleaning water, 163
   variation in final value, 100
Tension leg platform, 23
Thermal cracking, of crude, 28-31
Thermometers, cargo, 50
Thieving, 43-45
Threshold limit value, 34
Tide, effect on mooring lines, 89
Tipping center, 130
TLP, 23
TLV, 34
Ton
   long, 6, 42
   metric, 6, 39, 42
Tonnage
   automatic readout of, 51, 140-41
   of cargo to load, computing, 138
   computation of, 53-55
   deadweight, 6, 128, 130-31
   displacement, 126, 128, 135-39
   formula for determining, 42
   noncargo, 138
Tons per inch immersion, 130-31
Topping off (of final tank), 90
Topping up generator, IG, 271-72
TPI, 130-31
Traffic lanes, 235
Transverse stability, 123
Trim
   adjusting, after loading, 100-101
   arm, 142
   change in, computing, 133-34
   when cleaning tanks, 148, 172
   computer updates of, 129, 140-41
   corrections, 46-49, 52
   defined, 130

   final, formulas for calculating, 142
   forms for calculating, 141-45
   how affected by LCB/LCG, 132
   MARPOL formula for, 148
   requirements when ballasted, 148-49
   while stripping, 114
Trimming moment, 133-34, 142

ULCCs. *See also* VLCCs
   defined, 6
   described, 10-12
   loading rate, example of, 55
Ullage. *See also* Ullaging
   after closing tanks, checking, 87
   datum, above-deck, 42, 44
   defined, 42
   of full tank, examples, 86, 90
   report form, 39-41
   tape floats, 117
   trim corrections, 46-49
Ullaging. *See also* Ullage
   alarms, 65, 284
   closed systems, 43, 45, 48, 50, 52, 283-84
   datum, 42, 44
   final, 287
   float systems, 43, 47-48, 117
   by hand tape, 42-43
   by independent inspector, 39, 43, 275
   integrated microcomputer systems, 129,
     140-41
   interface detectors, 43, 45-46, 174, 234
   "open," 42
   portable unit, 89
   principles of, 42
   radar systems, 43, 50-52
   by ship's officers, 39
   submerged sensor, 43, 52, 54
   through vapor control valve, 43, 45-46
   when performed, 39
Ultra large crude carriers. *See* ULCCs

Vacuum relief. *See* PV breaker; PV valves
Valves
   angle, 68, 70
   automated, 10, 58, 65, 68, 87
   bleeder (tank cleaning), 185
   butterfly, 68-69
   bypass (IG recirculation), 265
   check, 68-69, 102, 121-22
   "Christmas tree," 24
   crossover, 61, 78, 106
   deck isolating (IG), 256, 267, 274, 281
   drop, 60-61, 103-104

Valves, (cont.)
    "dry" water seal, automatic, 266
    gas regulating, 264-66
    gate, 66-67
    globe, 68
    handwheel lashings, 79
    isolation, vapor manifold, 281, 283
    manifold, 69, 71, 102, 281, 283
    manual operation of, 58-60, 90
    marking, 70-71
    master, 61-62
    mast riser bypass. See Mast riser by-
        pass valve
    nonreturn (IG), 256, 267
    pressure control (IG), 266
    primary control (IG), 266
    PV. See PV valves
    relief, 69-70. See also PV valves
    sea. See Sea valves
    sluice gates, 83
    spill (vapor control system), 284
    steam smothering system, 214-16
    suction, pump, 104
    tank (cargo), 58-60, 79, 87
    tank isolating (IG), 270, 274
    telltale, 60, 91
    vapor control (ullaging), 43, 45-46
Vapor. See also Vapor control systems
    accumulations on deck, 208
    balancing, 120, 156
    boom (LNG), 14
    control valve (ullaging), 43, 45-56
    emissions, as source of pollution, 233-35
    hose, 281, 283
    "lean" mixtures, 203
    manifold, 281, 283
    mixing (contamination), 276
    piping, 281, 283
    "rich" mixtures, 182, 202-203
Vapor control systems. See also Vent
        systems
    alarms, 284, 286
    branch line valves, 281
    checklist, 291-93
    components, 280-83
    diagram of, 82
    DOI addendum for, 289-90
    flange, connecting, 281
    hose, 281-83
    isolation valve (manifold), 281, 283
    loading rates, permissible, 287, 289
    manifold, 281, 283
    overfill control systems, 285
    piping, 281, 283
    pressure drop, 287, 289
    PV protection, 285-86
    regulations, 279-80
    rupture disc, 284
    spill valve, 284
    State Implementation Plan, 279
Vegetable oil, as cargo, 3
Ventilation, tank. See Gas-freeing
Vent systems. See also Vapor control
        systems
    "controlled," 280
    described, 73-77, 280
    example of, 72
    PV protection. See PV breaker; PV
        valves
    typical arrangements, 273-74
Venturi
    deck water seal, 266
    scrubber, 187, 264
Very large crude carriers. See VLCCs
VLCCs. See also ULCCs
    cutaway diagram of, 179
    defined, 6
    described, 10-12
    explosions, 182-84
    groundings, prevention of, 235-37
    IG systems used on, 271-72
    lightering of, 95
    pipeline size, example of, 58
    piping systems, described, 71
    size of, compared to T2, 9, 183
    tank rescue, 192
    wing tank, illustration of, 161
VOCs, 279-80
Void spaces, pretransfer check of, 79
Volatile organic compounds, 279-80
Volume, cargo. See also Ullaging
    computer readout of, 51, 54
    correction factors, 42, 49, 51, 53
    observed, 42, 46-48
    standard, 42, 49-51

Water "cuts," 43-45
Water seal. See Deck water seal
WG (water gauge), 263
Wine, as cargo, 3
Wing tanks
    cross-section of, 176
    of double-hulled tanker (drawing), 18
    loading, 83
    used for removing list, 81
    VLCC, illustration of, 161

Zone allowance, 128, 135-36
Zones
    controlling, 128
    load line, 126-28, 135-36
    prohibited (dirty ballast), 154, 232, 245

# ABOUT THE AUTHOR AND CONTRIBUTORS

G. S. Marton's father and grandfather were merchant marine officers, serving during World War II and in the years immediately following the war. As a consequence, he was exposed to ships and the sea from earliest childhood; his career choice was a logical result of this background.

In 1969 he graduated from the California Maritime Academy, and two days after graduation walked up the gangway of a T2 tanker for his first assignment as a third mate. In the years since that first experience, he has served on all types of merchant ships, including tankers of all types and sizes.

Captain Marton is also a contributor to *U.S. Naval Institute Proceedings, Merchant Marine Officers' Handbook,* and to the journals *Sea* and *Exploring.*

Nicholas Blenkey is editor of *Marine Log* magazine. He is an acknowledged authority on international maritime legislation and regulations.

Mark Huber is a graduate of the State University of New York Maritime College. He also holds a master of science degree in environmental studies from Long Island University. Before accepting his present position as a professor at the United States Merchant Marine Academy, he sailed with Gulf Oil Corporation and Military Sealift Command. He holds an unlimited master's license. Besides his teaching duties, Professor Huber serves as a marine consultant to tanker companies and has served as an expert witness in numerous admiralty cases.

Robert Stewart is a graduate of the United States Merchant Marine Academy at King's Point. During his career, he has served on numerous tankers, freighters, and ocean towing vessels, and he holds an unlimited master's license. At present he is a professor at the California Maritime Academy.

ISBN 0-87033-390-9

53500

9 780870 334320